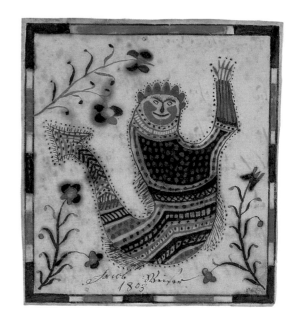

Treasures of American Folk Art

from THE ABBY ALDRICH ROCKEFELLER
FOLK ART CENTER

by Beatrix T. Rumford and Carolyn J. Weekley

Little, Brown and Company · Bulfinch Press
Boston · Toronto · London
in association with The Colonial Williamsburg Foundation

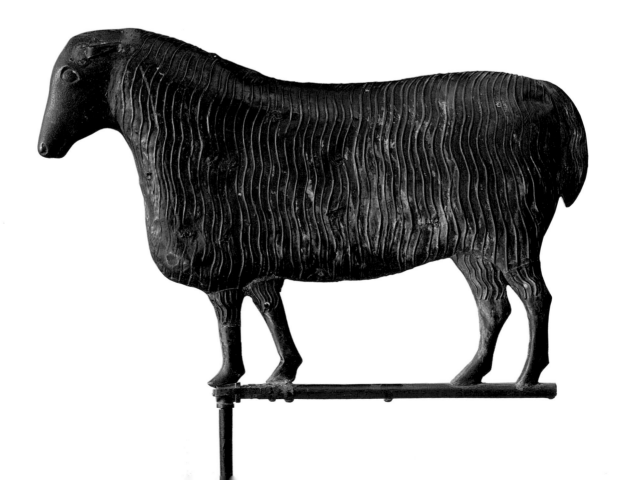

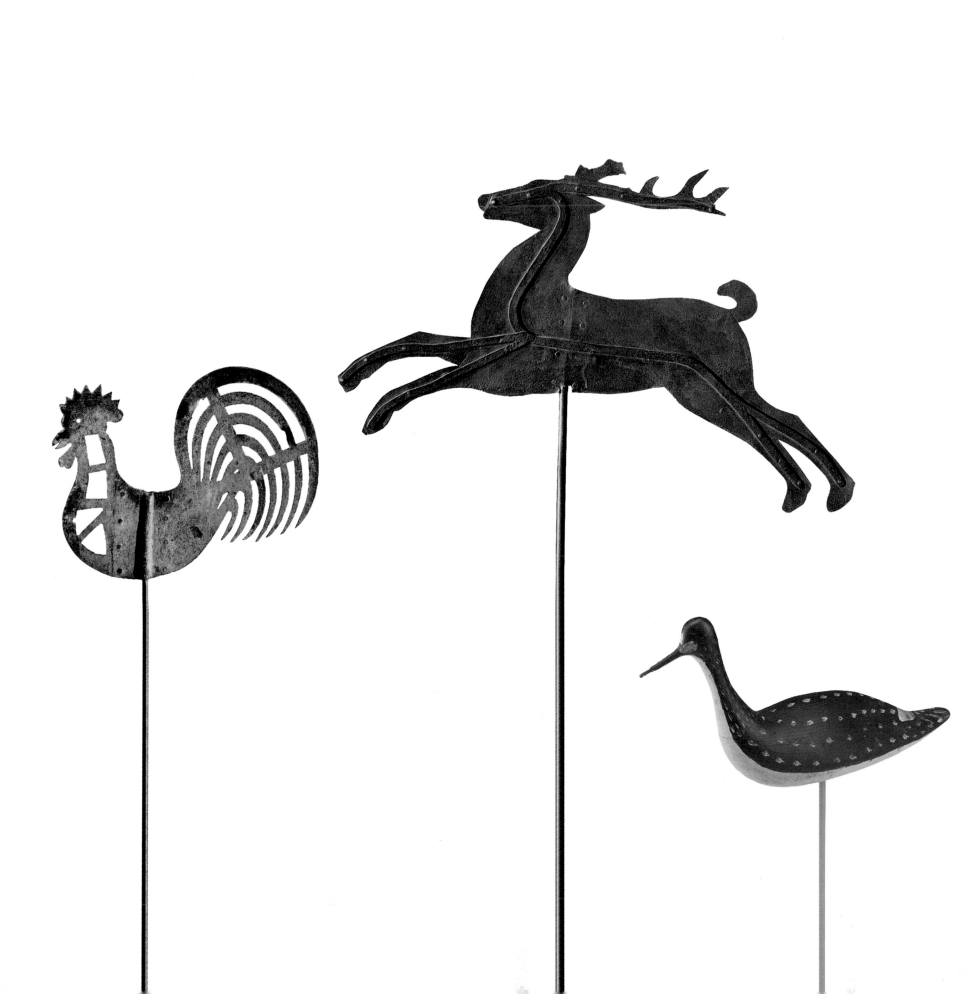

This book was published in connection with an exhibition
organized by the Colonial Williamsburg Foundation
with the Trust for Museum Exhibitions.
The exhibition appeared in 1989–1990 at

Whitney Museum of American Art, New York

Jocelyn Museum, Omaha

North Carolina Museum of Art, Raleigh

Toledo Museum of Art

National Museum of American Art, Washington, D.C.

The Fine Arts Museums of San Francisco

Dallas Museum of Art

Philbrook Art Center, Inc., Tulsa

First edition
Library of Congress Cataloging-in-Publication Data

Abby Aldrich Rockefeller Folk Art Center.
    Treasures of American folk art from the Abby Aldrich Rockefeller
    Folk Art Center / Beatrix T. Rumford, Carolyn J. Weekley. — 1st ed.
      p.   cm.
      1. Folk art — United States.   2. Folk art — Virginia — Williamsburg.
3. Abby Aldrich Rockefeller Folk Art Center.   I. Rumford, Beatrix T.
II. Weekley, Carolyn J.   III. Title.
NK805.A23   1989   709'.73 — dc 19   88-23063   CIP

Cloth ISBN 0-8212-1726-7

Exhibition edition (paperback) ISBN 0-8212-1733-x

Bulfinch Press is an imprint and trademark of Little, Brown and Company (Inc.).
Published simultaneously in Canada by Little, Brown & Company (Canada) Limited.
PRINTED IN THE UNITED STATES OF AMERICA

Contents

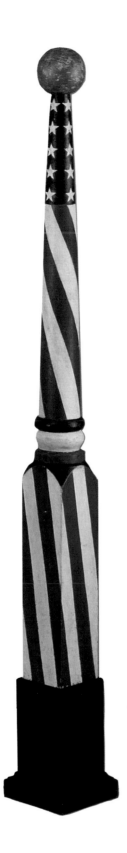

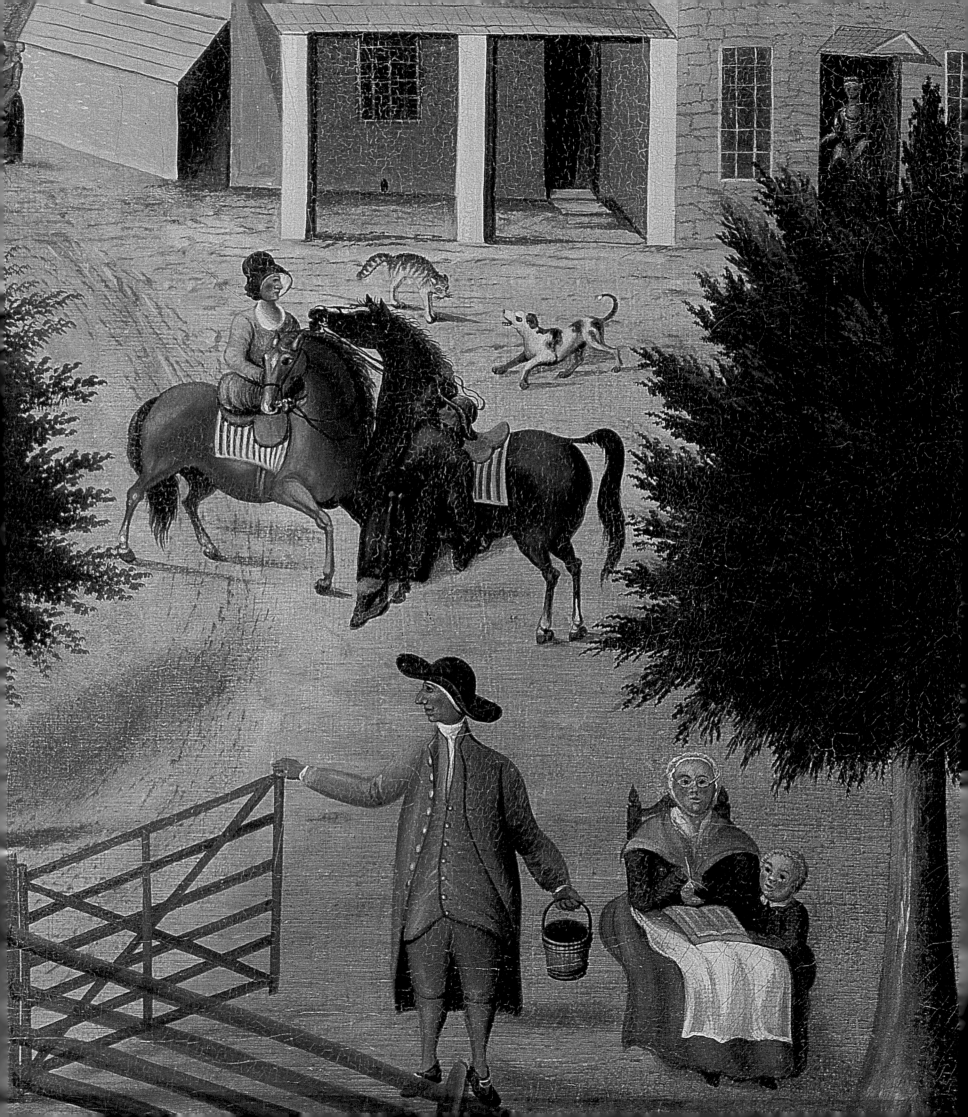

President's Note

Colonial Williamsburg has three principal purposes: to preserve and present the heritage of America's beginnings; to teach the history of early America; and to provide visitors with hospitality, service, and products of quality and value.

Since 1985 we have organized our educational programs around the theme of "Becoming Americans." Our goal is to focus on ordinary citizens as well as on heroes, and to supplement political with social history, by exploring how those who came to the Colonies from Europe and Africa began to adjust to their new surroundings and by determining which of their ways persisted in the New World.

Folk art is one way in which successive generations of average Americans have recorded their impressions of society. As the delightful images in this book and their accompanying text reveal, the material in Colonial Williamsburg's remarkable collection of American folk art, begun by Abby Aldrich Rockefeller, provides visitors with an instructive link between today's world and the past. Most of the objects date from between 1740 and 1865, and thus they reflect shifting perceptions about and attitudes toward family life, mores, and social institutions, as well as the emerging presence of a rapidly growing middle class, a direct result of the American Revolution, in which Williamsburg played a vital part.

For half a century Colonial Williamsburg has led the way in enhancing the understanding and appreciation of all phases and types of American folk art through quality scholarship and interpretation. During the next two years we will reach a still broader audience by circulating to eight major art museums across this country the exceptional examples of folk art discussed and illustrated here.

When the material returns to Williamsburg in 1991, it will be housed in a greatly expanded Folk Art Center building. This enlarged facility will provide permanent exhibition space for 75 percent of the collection, while the remainder— as well as the associated research materials, for which the Abby Aldrich Rockefeller Folk Art Center is equally well known— will be readily accessible to scholars and to the interested public. In the meantime, I take pleasure and pride in sharing with you these Treasures of American Folk Art.

Charles R. Longsworth
President, Colonial Williamsburg Foundation

Celebrating Fifty Years:

THE ABBY ALDRICH ROCKEFELLER

FOLK ART CENTER COLLECTION

Few, if any, of my mother's many interests in art gave her more pleasure
than her collection of American folk art, and none, I think, more clearly demonstrates
her deep pride in the cultural life of the American people.

—Winthrop Rockefeller
Preface, *American Folk Art*, Williamsburg, 1959

In 1989 Colonial Williamsburg celebrates the fiftieth anniversary of its superb folk art collection, which bears the name of its founder, Abby Aldrich Rockefeller. Mrs. John D. Rockefeller, Jr., began acquiring folk art in the late 1920s, at a time when few people acknowledged that the portraits, weather vanes, theorem paintings, and tobacconist figures created by nonacademic or folk artists were anything more than quaint or curious objects, with perhaps some historical interest. Mrs. Rockefeller's interest in folk art was a direct result of her appreciation of contemporary art. A founder and active supporter of the Museum of Modern Art, she knew and patronized many of the artists who exhibited there. She took particular pleasure in discovering and acquiring the work of unrecognized talent.[1]

This appreciation of the innate artistic skills of the untrained painters and carvers of the eighteenth and nineteenth centuries provided a fresh insight into the American past that Mrs. Rockefeller enthu-siastically pursued. Although she rarely wrote or commented publicly about her folk art during those years, one has only to study the 424 pieces comprising her original collection, a number of which are featured in this book,[2] to sense that she shared with the early folk art scholar and collector Holger Cahill an intuitive response to and understanding of what he called "art quality, [a term] not easy to define, though of art in general it is not hard to understand."

Guided and assisted by Edith Gregor Halpert, the owner of the Downtown Gallery in Greenwich Village and the wife of the modernist painter Sam Halpert, by Holger Cahill, and by others, Mrs. Rockefeller devoted nearly ten years to building a wide-ranging collection of distinctive, aesthetically pleasing objects fashioned by craftspeople and tradespeople, amateurs and students, who had little, if any, training in the principles of academic art but were motivated by a desire for artistic expression, whether they were creating for pay, for personal pleasure, or to fulfill a school assignment (see figure 1).

1. For a discussion of Mrs. Rockefeller's years of collecting and other early collectors, see Beatrix T. Rumford, "Uncommon Art of the Common People: A Review of Trends in the Collecting and Exhibiting of American Folk Art," In Ian M. G. Quimby and Scott T. Swank (eds.), *Perspectives on American Folk Art* (New York: W.W. Norton & Company, 1980), pp. 13–53.

2. Objects from Mrs. Rockefeller's original collection are identified by an asterisk following the accession number (e.g., 31.100.1*) in captions throughout this volume.

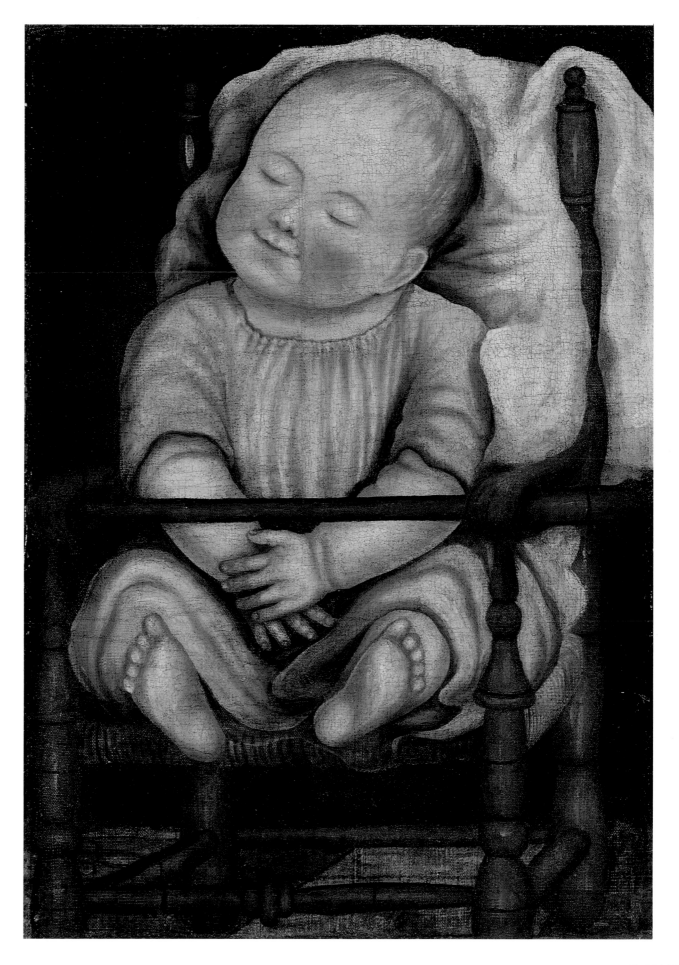

1
Unidentified artist, BABY IN RED
CHAIR, *possibly Pennsylvania, ca.
1810–1830, oil on canvas, 22 × 15
inches (31.100.1).**
*This endearing image of a sleeping
baby by an unidentified artist has
always been a favorite among visitors to the Folk Art Center. Although
the composition appears slightly
cropped, there is no evidence that the
canvas was ever trimmed. The front
of the high chair and the child's feet
seem to press against the picture's
frontal plane. The baby's legs are
convincingly foreshortened, but the
chair is not, providing an interesting
pattern of softly colored forms moving in and out of space.*

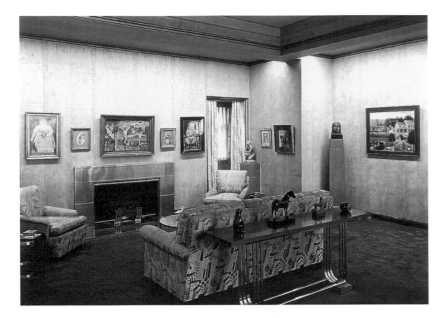

Figure 1

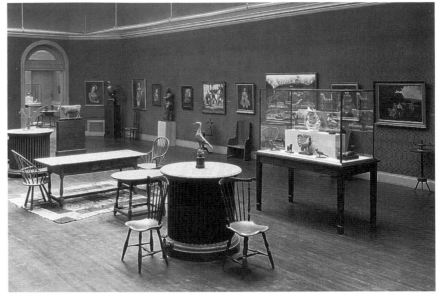

Figure 2

In 1930 and 1931, a selection of Mrs. Rockefeller's paintings and sculptures was exhibited anonymously at the Newark Museum, where Cahill was a staff member. The next year the Museum of Modern Art (MOMA) in New York organized and presented— again anonymously— the first comprehensive showing of her collection, titled "American Folk Art— The Art of the Common Man, 1750–1890" (see figure 2). The general public and the more discerning art critics were delighted both with the exhibition and with Cahill's 225-page catalog for the MOMA show, which traveled to six cities in the continental United States during 1933 and 1934.

These exhibitions were landmark events for the field of American folk art, though they were not the first of their kind. In February 1924 the modern artist Henry Schnackenberg had organized and mounted an exhibit of forty-five examples of folk art for the Whitney Studio Club in New York City. A few months later an exhibition of locally owned pictures, including a striking group of likenesses now recognized as the work of Ammi Phillips, was held in Kent, Connecticut. But the MOMA show was a larger effort, and one that brought wide-

spread national attention to American folk art for the first time. Even today, Cahill's introduction to the 1932 catalog continues to be regarded by scholars as one of the most succinct and pertinent statements ever put forward about American folk art and its creators.

Few people who visited the 1930 and 1931 Newark Museum shows or the 1932–1934 traveling MOMA exhibit realized that the unidentified lender/collector was Mrs. Rockefeller. But it was not long before her name became associated with the collection. Perhaps the popularity of the 1930s exhibits, with the enormous interest they engendered among the viewing public and the critical success they enjoyed, prompted her to consider, as early as 1932, where the collection might be permanently displayed and appreciated.

In 1934 Mrs. Rockefeller confirmed her plans to loan a principal part (more than 250 objects) of her folk art collection to Colonial Williamsburg, where it would be exhibited in the restored Ludwell-Paradise House on the Duke of Gloucester Street. Holger Cahill supervised the packing of the pieces in New York that November and, along with Edith

Figure 1
Photograph taken about 1931, showing some of Mrs. Rockefeller's folk art collection, including BABY IN RED CHAIR (plate 1) and THE RESIDENCE OF DAVID TWINING 1787 (plate 62), installed in one of several galleries designed by Donald Deskey on the top floor of the Rockefeller residence on West Fifty-fourth Street in New York City.

Figure 2
View of the 1932 "Art of the Common Man" exhibition, as installed at the Rhode Island School of Design.

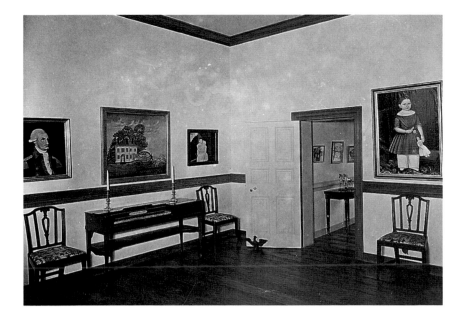

Figure 3

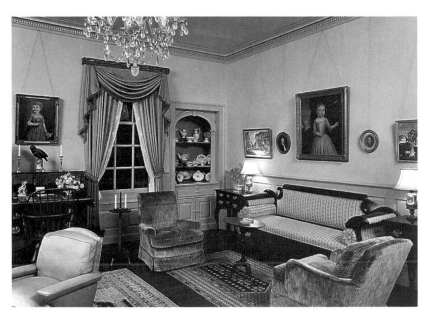

Figure 4

Figure 3
Interior of the Ludwell-Paradise House in Williamsburg, about 1937, with Mrs. Rockefeller's folk art on view.

Figure 4
View of the Morning Room at Bassett Hall, featuring a number of Mrs. Rockefeller's folk art paintings.

Halpert, continued to work with Mrs. Rockefeller throughout the next months, recommending objects suitable for the installation in Williamsburg (see figure 3). Mrs. Rockefeller was still actively collecting at this time, and she took particular interest in the selection process, sometimes substituting newly acquired, better-quality examples for art objects already slated for the Williamsburg loan.

The Ludwell-Paradise House exhibits opened in March 1935. Numerous notes, as well as correspondence, sketches of floor plans with objects positioned thereon, and various photographs in the AARFAC archival files, document the exhibits and record how different displays were achieved. Mrs. Rockefeller continued to refine the collection and to add examples to the initial installation throughout the mid-1930s; in 1939 she presented this portion of her folk art collection to Colonial Williamsburg. At the same time, Mrs. Rockefeller gave fifty-four pieces of folk art to the Museum of Modern Art, which later shared the gift with the Metropolitan Museum of Art. Through the cooperation of these two museums and her son David, a number of these works, including the delightful portrait *Baby in Red Chair* (plate 1), were reunited with the Williamsburg collection in 1956.

Even after Mrs. Rockefeller placed the best of her collection on view in Williamsburg, her enthusiasm for folk art remained undiminished, and she continued to collect with a keen eye for strong design, bold color, and fine workmanship. Conscious of the need for a better representation of Southern folk art in the collection, in 1934 she sent Holger Cahill on a four-month trip through Virginia, the Carolinas, and Georgia. His most significant find was a remarkable watercolor documenting blacks performing a dance, which he discovered in Orangeburg, South Carolina, and which was subsequently titled *The Old Plantation* (plate 68). During the late 1930s Mrs. Rockefeller purchased a wide variety of folk art objects—chiefly chalkware, weather vanes, portraits of children, theorems, and memorials—for Bassett Hall, the Rockefellers' Williamsburg home (see figure 4). She ceased actively collecting folk art in 1942, and thereafter no significant additions were made either to the exhibits at the Ludwell-Paradise House or to the furnishings at Bassett Hall.

The folk art exhibits at the Ludwell-Paradise House remained open to the public until January 1, 1956, well after Mrs. Rockefeller's death in 1948.

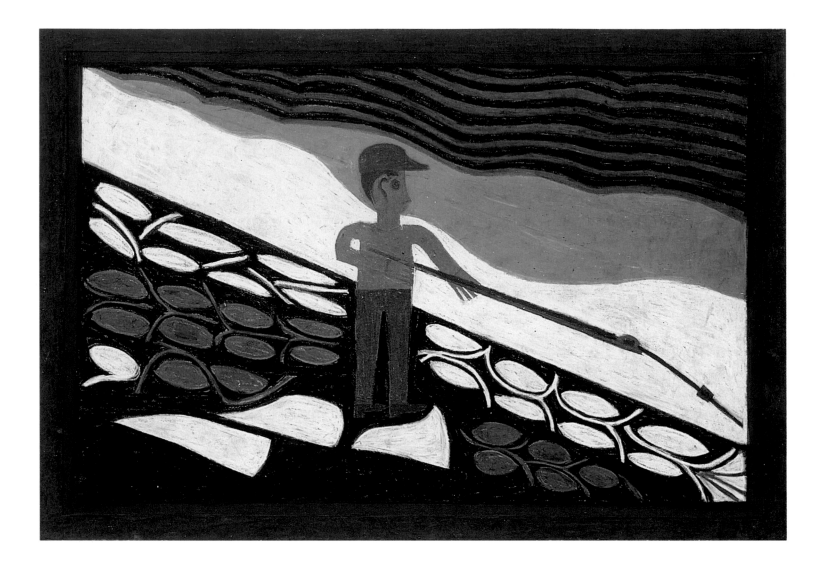

2

Eddie Arning, MAN FISHING FROM ROCKY COAST, *Austin, Texas, April 2–9, 1970, oil, pastel, and pencil on laid green paper, 22 × 32 inches, gift of Dr. and Mrs. Alexander Sackton (84.201.5).*

Print sources have been identified for a number of folk art pictures dating from the nineteenth century, and this practice of borrowing ideas was evidently commonplace in the period. The makers possessed varying degrees of innate artistic capability and ingenuity; some amateurs produced copies that were aesthetic failures, while others made real improvements over their printed sources. Yet none of the originality observed in this early copywork, such as THE QUILTING PARTY *(plate 84), compares with or prepares the viewer for the work of Eddie Arning (active 1964–1973), who transformed magazine illustrations into imaginative, powerfully abstract pictures. Arning had earlier produced pictures based on his memories of childhood farm life, but about 1965 he began to leaf through the periodicals made available to the residents of the various institutions in which he lived.* MAN FISHING FROM ROCKY COAST, *one of several works by Arning owned by the Folk Art Center, was based on a color photograph that appeared in the February 1970 issue* of Field & Stream. *Eddie's symptoms of mental illness, diagnosed as schizophrenia, began to appear when he was in his midtwenties; it was during his stay in the Austin State Hospital that he began to draw with crayons and later craypas, giving us the wonderfully colorful pictures he is known for today. His artistic career was brief, spanning only nine years; he stopped drawing late in 1973, when he was living with his widowed sister, after being released from the nursing home where he had been a patient for several years.*

In March 1954 *Antiques* magazine carried an announcement "of great interest to students and collectors of American painting": the Abby Aldrich Rockefeller Museum of American Folk Art would soon be housed in a new building "designed expressly as an appropriate background" for the collection and located adjacent to Williamsburg's Historic Area. The actual announcement by Williamsburg officials had occurred some weeks earlier, at the 1954 Antiques Forum, when it was made known that the new museum would be built with and maintained through funds provided by John D. Rockefeller, Jr. (figure 5).

Just as Mrs. Rockefeller had been a pioneer in her interest in and formation of a collection of folk art, Mr. Rockefeller, through his generous support, enabled Colonial Williamsburg to establish this country's first folk art museum and thus ensured the subject's future as a viable aspect of American art. That it should be a museum and thereby nurture and encourage activities traditionally associated with such institutions was important to those concerned with the project. All realized that the collection must, of necessity, continue to grow and be refined by the addition of superior examples of folk art that would enhance the original nucleus of 424 pieces. With this realization came the immediate establishment of an endowment fund provided by Mr. Rockefeller, whereby the folk art museum was able to acquire more than one hundred items during its first year of operation. Many of these acquisitions were of exceptional quality and were purchased from the private collections of Mrs. Halpert, Holger Cahill, Mrs. John Law Robertson, and J. Stuart Halladay and Herrel G. Thomas.

The enrichment and expansion of what was already an excellent collection of American folk art was a studied and methodical exercise in 1957–1958, and it remains so today for the museum's curatorial staff. Acquisition always has been related closely to another important aspect of the museum's mission, one that was identified by Nina Fletcher Little in

her work on the first catalogue of the collection, published in 1957.[3] She reiterated this a year later in a letter to the museum's staff, observing that "intelligent planning can assure the collection a unique function in its own field, and I think this function might tend gradually toward the establishment of a research center and clearing house for folk art information. . . ." Today the Abby Aldrich Rockefeller Folk Art Center not only enjoys a reputation for housing and displaying this country's premier collection of American folk art but also serves as a leading center for research on the subject.

The exciting, formative years outlined here were the carefully designed foundation upon which later directors and staff members have continued to build the collection, all the while adding to the literature on folk art and artists working in America from the Colonial period to today. Major exhibitions by the Center— those that have contributed new knowledge and scholarship to the folk art field — have included Mary C. Black's "Erastus Salisbury Field, 1805–1900" (1963) and "Merchants and Planters of the Upper Hudson Valley, 1700–1750" (1967), mounted by Peter A. G. Brown, the Center's then-director, working with then-curator Mary Black. With Nina Fletcher Little, Brown also was responsible for "Land and Seascape as Observed by the Folk Artist," a large installation of folk art loaned by Little and her husband, Bertram K. Little, in 1969. The first extensive exhibition of Pennsylvania almshouse paintings had been organized the year before by Thomas N. Armstrong, the present director of the Whitney Museum, who was then serving under Brown as curator.

In 1972 Graham Hood, Colonial Williamsburg's chief curator, and Beatrix T. Rumford, then the associate director, collaborated with Christine Schloss

3. See Nina Fletcher Little, *The Abby Aldrich Rockefeller Folk Art Collection* (Williamsburg: Colonial Williamsburg, Inc., 1957). Mrs. Little also served as a consultant to Colonial Williamsburg, reviewing architectural designs for the interior spaces of the 1957 building.

in organizing a loan show and catalogue featuring portraits by the unidentified artist who is still known as the Beardsley Limner. More recently, under the leadership of Rumford and Carolyn J. Weekley, the Center's staff cooperated with the Maryland Historical Society in organizing the first major exhibition and catalogue devoted to the work and life of Joshua Johnson.

Other noteworthy exhibitions organized by the Center during the 1970s and 1980s featured decorated Virginia folk furniture, paintings by Asahel Powers, Queena Stovall, and Zedekiah Belknap, Virginia fraktur, Shenandoah Valley pottery, the fraktur of Henry Young, John Conrad Gilbert, and Friedrich Krebs, and the work of the twentieth-century artists Karol Kozlowski and Eddie Arning (see plate 2).

The Folk Art Center's holdings now number more than 2,600 objects. The fivefold increase in the collection, attained through many fine gifts and purchases, traditionally has been guided by a serious concern for aesthetic quality and for regional and chronological representation. Among the collection's outstanding features are its large number of paintings by Edward Hicks, Joseph H. Hidley, Ammi Phillips, and the Prior-Hamblin group, as well as numerous carved works by Wilhelm Schimmel, the sketchbooks of Lewis Miller, outstanding examples of woven coverlets, and a wide variety of folk art forms, including many examples of signed works in all media, dating from the eighteenth, nineteenth, and twentieth centuries. A number of these pieces are discussed in this book, among them the handsome portraits by Ammi Phillips of the Russell Dorr family (plates 8, 9, and 26); the

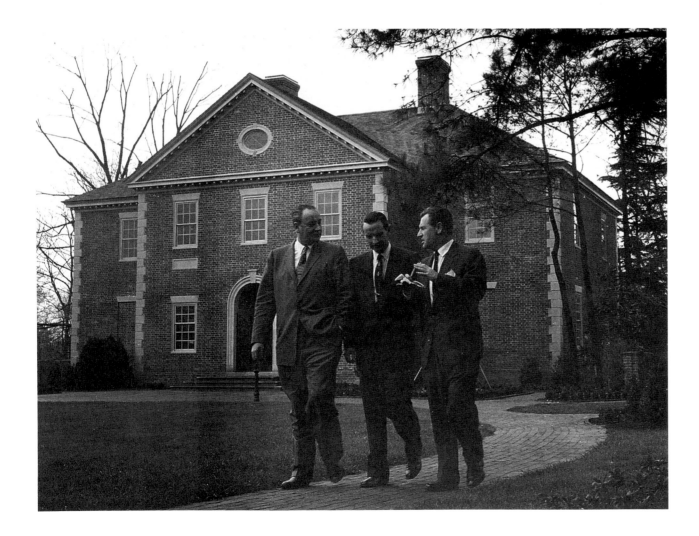

Figure 5
Winthrop, Laurance, and Nelson Rockefeller standing outside the Abby Aldrich Rockefeller Folk Art Collection at the time of its opening in spring 1957.

lively watercolor sketches by Lewis Miller (plates 145 through 150) that rank among the museum's most important drawings; self-portraits by American folk artists, including a large oil-on-canvas example by Jonathan Adams Bartlett (plate 5); and the rare and delightful early portrait of Deborah Glen (plate 15), acquired by Colonial Williamsburg in 1964 as part of an impressive collection of early furnishings that descended in the Glen-Sanders family of Scotia, in upstate New York. Also included here are several works acquired in 1957, the year the museum building opened to the public, such as the colorful *Fruit in Wicker Basket* (plate 158), one of the 347 items that were collected by J. Stuart Halladay and Herrel G. Thomas and purchased with funds provided by John D. Rockefeller, Jr.

Today the Center's accessions and activities continue to focus, as they did a half century ago, on enhancing visitors' understanding and appreciation of all phases and types of American folk art through a varied and ongoing program of special exhibitions and publications. Potential additions to the collection, whether by gift or by purchase, are reviewed by Colonial Williamsburg's curatorial staff and its president, Charles R. Longsworth. Since Mrs. Rockefeller collected the work of unschooled artists with vastly different social and professional backgrounds, the museum continues to subscribe to a broad definition of folk or popular art, and the collection has no cutoff date. In selecting the objects for this volume, the authors have strived to present an inclusive and varied representation of the finest examples in the permanent collection. This has not been an easy task, but few projects have been so enjoyable.

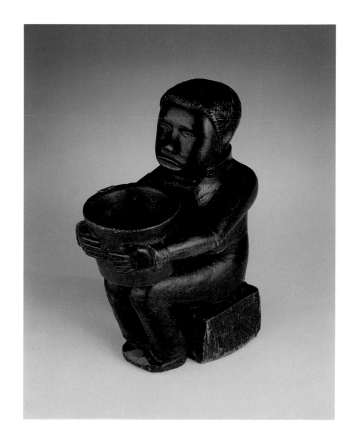

3
Unidentified maker, CHILD WITH BUCKET, *probably New York State, ca. 1860, carved wood, 8 × 3 × 5¼ inches (61.701.2).*
This wonderfully expressive carving of a black child ranks among the most powerful pieces of folk sculpture in the Center's collection. The unidentified maker may have been influenced by a dim memory of traditional African figures; whatever the inspiration, in shaping a small block of pine, the artist has successfully abstracted the human form, sensitively emphasizing the head and hands as the most salient features.

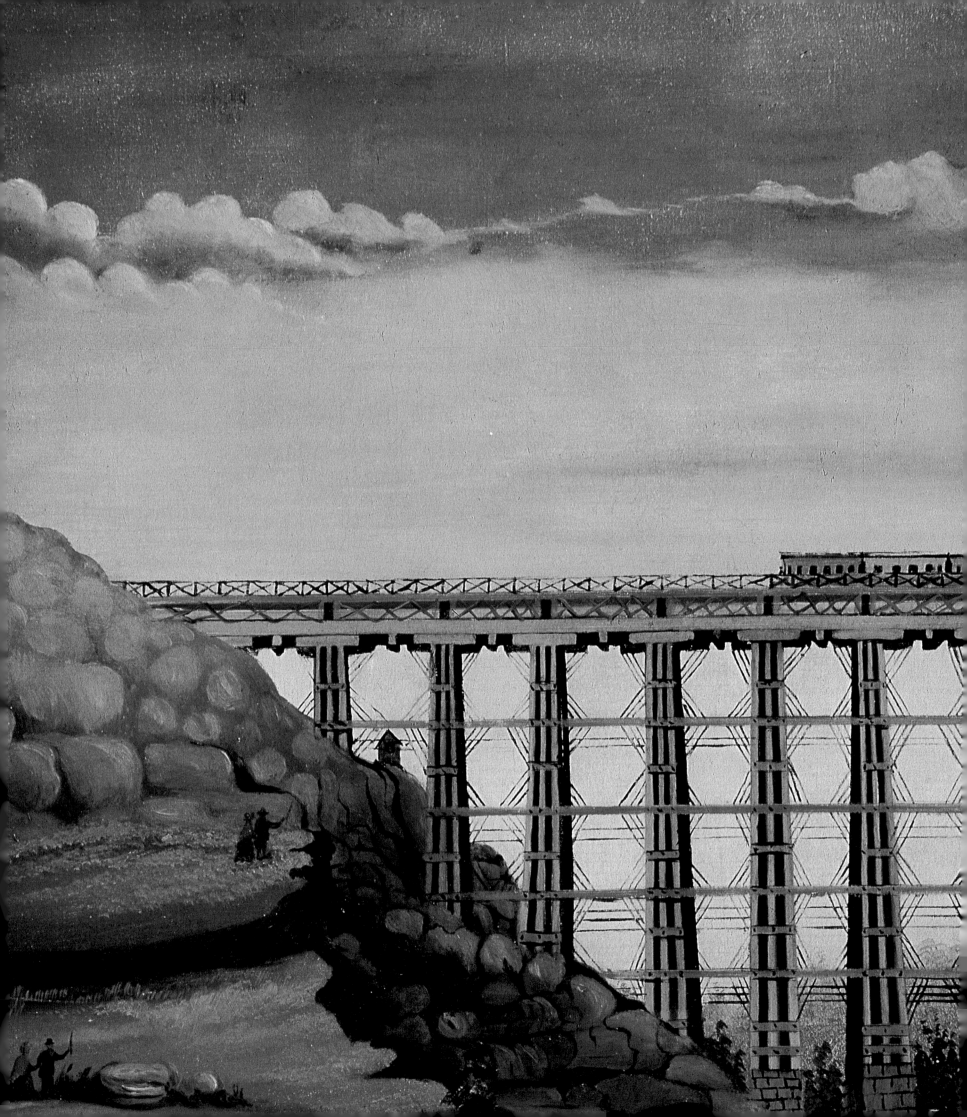

Treasures of American Folk Art

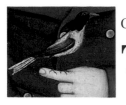

CHAPTER ONE
The Folks

Art of the kind discussed and illustrated in this book is tied either directly or indirectly to the ideas, experiences, needs, and traditions of a large segment of the American population— those ordinary people whom we call the folks. In the eighteenth and nineteenth centuries this included the men, women, and children who sat for artists such as Ammi Phillips and Asa Ames and who commissioned and used household objects similar to those illustrated in the following pages, or, in fact, produced them themselves. In terms of social standing, wealth, and background, these folk counted in their number doctors, merchants, farmers, tradespeople, and craftspeople— that is, individuals with modest to upper-middle-class incomes and tastes.[1] Most of these artists were neither especially poor nor extremely rich but simply the average citizens of America— "the common man."[2]

As both a producer and consumer of goods, the common man, like his elitist counterpart, traditionally owned, used, or created objects that reflected both particular and general social and cultural preferences. Handmade portraiture was a favored art format until the 1860s, when the accuracy, immediacy, and inexpensiveness of the photograph diminished the demand for portraits by semiskilled painters and carvers. Many Americans, then as now, wanted to have pictures of themselves and of their loved ones. Mortality rates were high in the eighteenth and nineteenth centuries, and a tightly structured family unit was more vital to social mobility and economic survival than it is today. Hence, family portraits fulfilled several needs, functioning as visual genealogical records, as reflections of taste and status, as embellishments for the home, and as sentimental remembrances.

Although the efforts of America's folk portraitists may appear unsophisticated to modern eyes, the demand for their work grew steadily as an increasingly affluent and status-conscious middle class emerged in the decades after the American Revolution. Burgeoning industrialization, improved road and canal systems, westward expansion and development, and all the other factors that contributed to the common man's prosperity also resulted in a new sense of individual and national identity.

The concept of self— encompassing both one's self-worth and the way one was perceived by society or by the community— was extraordinarily important to our middle-class American ancestors. Nowhere is this better observed than in their surviving portraits. Jonathan Adams Bartlett (1817–1902) left a rare and important self-portrait (plate 5) that provides a glimpse into the folk artist's attitudes about himself and his vocation, just as it documents the tools of his trade. Bartlett's pride in his personal and artistic achievements is clearly evident in his pose and in the prominent display of his brushes, palette, palette knife, grinding slab, and muller. He wears a

1. Twentieth-century folk artists tend to have somewhat similar backgrounds and artistic motivations, though at least in some cases their products are fashioned specifically for art collectors and dealers, not only for themselves, their families, and their acquaintances.

2. This phrase is taken from Holger Cahill, *American Folk Art: The Art of the Common Man in America, 1750–1900* (New York: Museum of Modern Art, 1932).

4
Attributed to John Brewster, Jr., BOY WITH FINCH, *New England or New York State, ca. 1800, oil on canvas, 39 × 24 inches (39.100.5).*

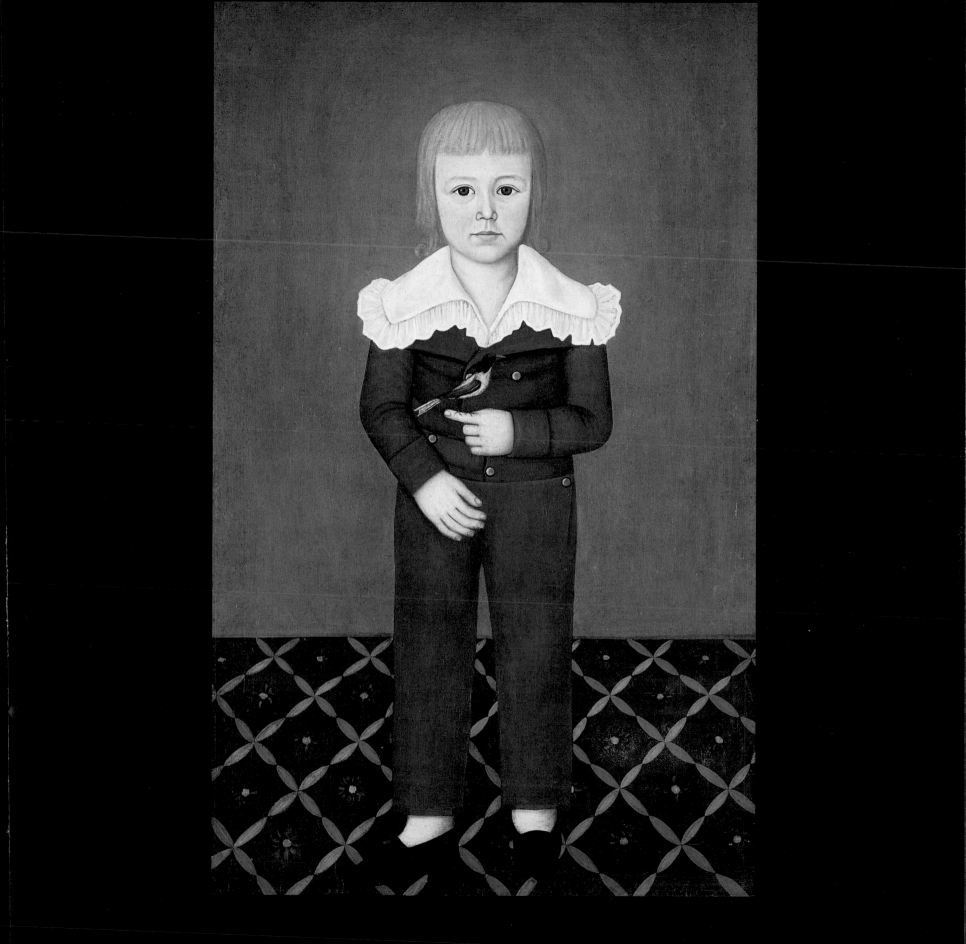

stickpin that contains a small likeness of his wife, Harriet (see figure 6), which suggests that Bartlett also did miniature portraits.

According to family tradition, Bartlett considered himself an accomplished painter, even though, like his customers and a number of other artists now classified as folk, he could not derive sufficient income from a single occupation to support his family — a wife and eight children, not an unusually large family for the 1840s. Several other paintings by him are known, but he was not so prolific a portraitist as many of his contemporaries. Bartlett was also a farmer and a house carpenter by trade, and he seems to have tried his hand at a number of other activities, including playing music, cabinetmaking, ornamental painting, photography, and teaching.

The enterprising ways and industrious aspirations of Mr. Calvin Hall (plate 7) typify the spirit of many middle-class Americans during the early years of the nineteenth century. Calvin Hall served with a New York state regiment during the American Revolution. In 1804 he built a house in Cheshire, Massachusetts, where he and John D. Leeland kept a tavern, visible in the distant background of Mr. Hall's portrait. In 1808 they built a store adjacent to the tavern and four years later incorporated a glass factory. By 1816 Calvin Hall and his wife (plate 6) had moved to Deerfield, New York (now North Utica), where they established, on their own, a new glass factory.

At the present time there are no data on the elusive and skilled New England artist who painted the Halls' likenesses. He signed himself "J. Brown" on these and three other portraits of Massachusetts subjects, all painted between 1803 and 1808. While Brown's surviving portraits vary in size, format, and complexity of composition, they are literal depictions that always project the personalities of the sitters. The portraits of the Halls are among Brown's best works, and the hard-edged technique he used for rendering their facial features results in star-

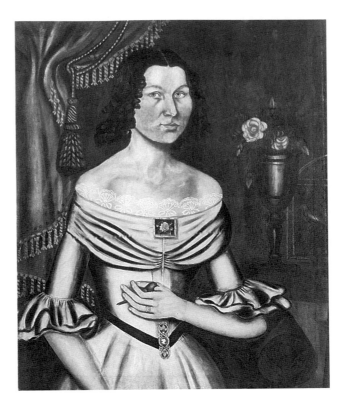

Figure 6
Jonathan Adams Bartlett, HARRIET A. GLINES *(the artist's wife, 1818–1893), probably South Rumford, Maine, probably 1841, oil on canvas, 31⅞ × 27 inches (76.100.3).*

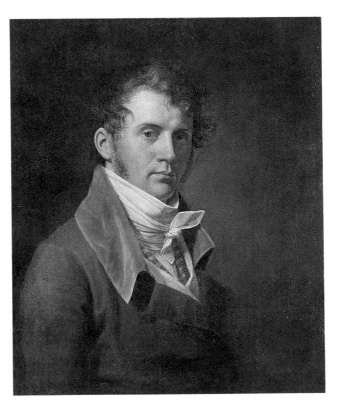

Figure 7
John Vanderlyn, SELF-PORTRAIT, *New York State, ca. 1815, oil on canvas, 25¼ × 20⅞ inches. Courtesy of the Metropolitan Museum of Art.*

5
Jonathan Adams Bartlett, SELF-PORTRAIT, *probably South Rumford, Maine, probably 1841, oil on canvas, 33 × 27 inches (76.100.2).*

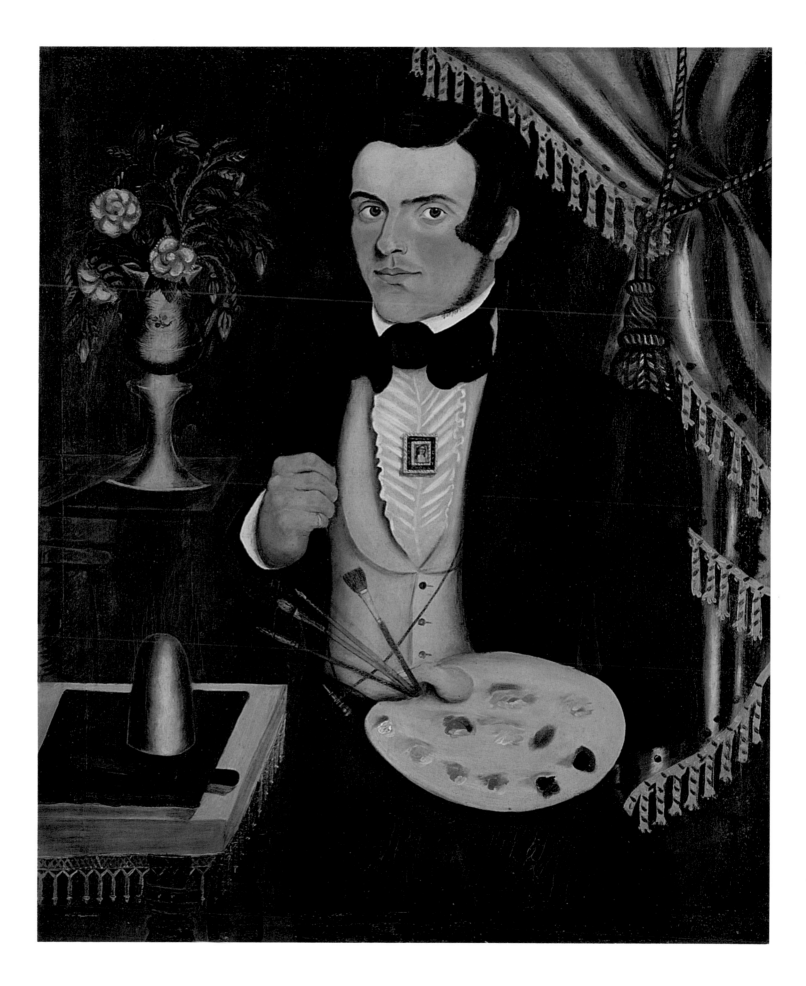

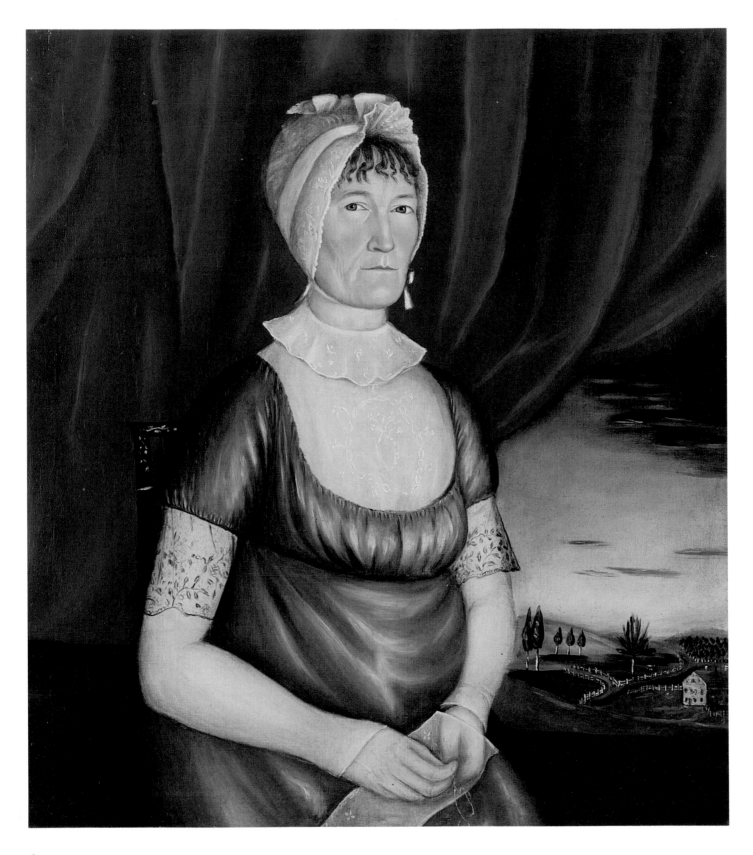

6
J. Brown, MRS. CALVIN HALL,
probably Cheshire, Massachusetts,
January 1808, oil on fine linen, 34½
× 30½ inches (57.100.2).

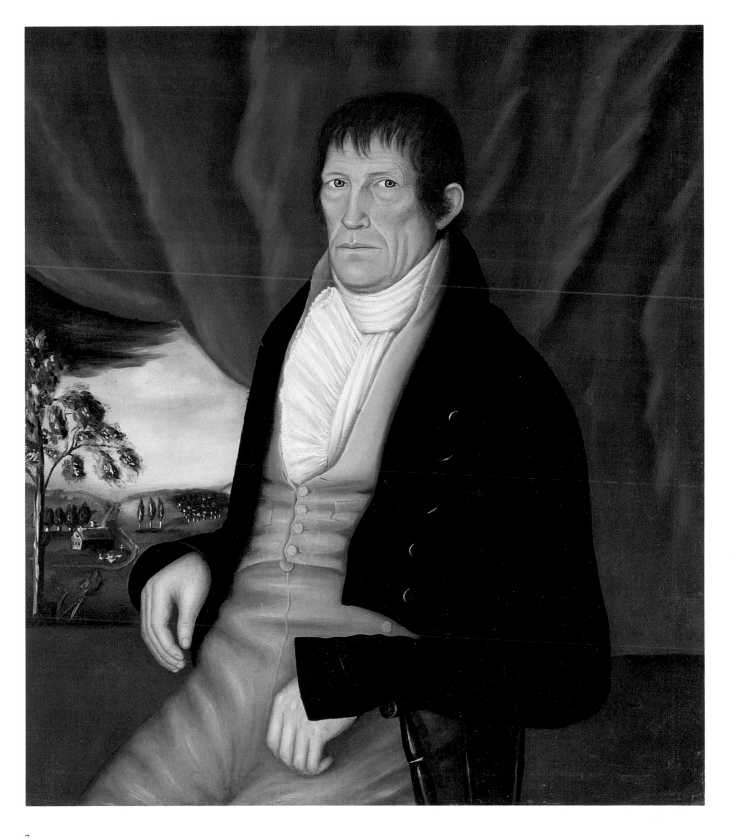

7
J. Brown, CALVIN HALL, *probably Cheshire, Massachusetts, January 1808, oil on fine linen, 34 × 30 inches (57.100.1).*

tlingly realistic characterizations. Both Halls look shrewd and perhaps a little mistrustful of life yet keen to succeed in their small-business ventures.

Portraits like those of Mr. and Mrs. Calvin Hall serve as collective expressions of a culture's values, despite the individualistic treatment of faces, costumes, or props and the idiosyncratic styles of the artists who created them. A group of folk portraits from a given region and dating from approximately the same time often reveals significant information about local tastes in clothes and furnishings. This can be especially true when there is a sizable number of works by one artist, as is the case with Ammi Phillips (1788–1865), who ranks among the most active folk painters of his day. Undoubtedly it was Phillips's ability to successfully and quickly complete numerous commissions that prompted John Vanderlyn's much-quoted remarks on his work. Vanderlyn (figure 7), an American academic painter trained abroad, noted in a letter written to his nephew in 1825 that

Were I to begin life again, I should not hesitate to follow this plan, that is to paint portraits cheap and slight, for the mass of folks can't judge of the merits of a well finished picture, I am more and more persuaded of this. Indeed, moving about through the country as Phillips did and probably still does, must be an agreeable way of passing ones [sic] time. I saw four of his works at Jacobus Hardenburgh's the other day painted a year or two ago, which seemed to satisfy them.[3]

Vanderlyn's "cheap" was presumably a reference to the low prices Phillips and artists like him charged for quickly painted portraits, while "slight" was probably descriptive of Phillips's style, which was devoid of the many academic techniques practiced by artists of Vanderlyn's skill and training. This style underwent a series of striking changes between 1811, when Phillips launched his career in

3. Barbara and Lawrence Holdridge, *Ammi Phillips: Portrait Painter 1788–1865* (New York: Clarkson N. Potter, 1969), 14.

Connecticut, and 1862, the year of his last known commissions, but we can imagine what Vanderlyn might have said about the dreamlike portrayals of Dr. Russell Dorr, his wife, and their children (plates 8, 9, and 26), all created in upstate New York in 1814–1815. These are extraordinarily artful images, principally due to their pleasing combination of softly rounded forms, their pastel coloration, and their unusually pale backgrounds.

The Dorr portraits are powerful abstractions, and for their time they were highly unorthodox renderings. The painter's unrealistic handling of anatomy and perspective, typical of a young, untutored artist, contributes to the abstract appearance of his works. Despite these qualities, which we value today as innovative and aesthetically pleasing, there is considerable realism in the Dorr likenesses, as can be seen in the nicely detailed costumes, the hairstyles, the furniture, and the small accessories shown in the pictures. The Dorrs were moderately well-off and owned unpretentious but stylish furnishings such as the painted "fancy" chairs seen in the portraits. Dr. Dorr was a respected physician in Chatham Center, and a portion of his library, presumably consisting of medical books, is shown with him. All of the ten Dorr children were well educated. It is also known that Dr. Dorr had a personal interest in painting, and this, as well as the common urge to commemorate the family, may have prompted him to commission Phillips.

Ammi Phillips's lifelong career as a portraitist was spent in western Connecticut and Massachusetts and in the neighboring counties of upstate New York. His remarkable series of eight portraits of the Russell Dorr family dates from his so-called "Border Period" of about 1812–1819. By about 1820 Phillips's closer observance and more skillful depiction of the effects and appearance of light and shadow gave his work a new realism that is evident in his portrait of William Harder (plate 12). The "Kent Period" portraits of about 1829–1838, when many of the painter's commissions were from resi-

Detail of plate 6

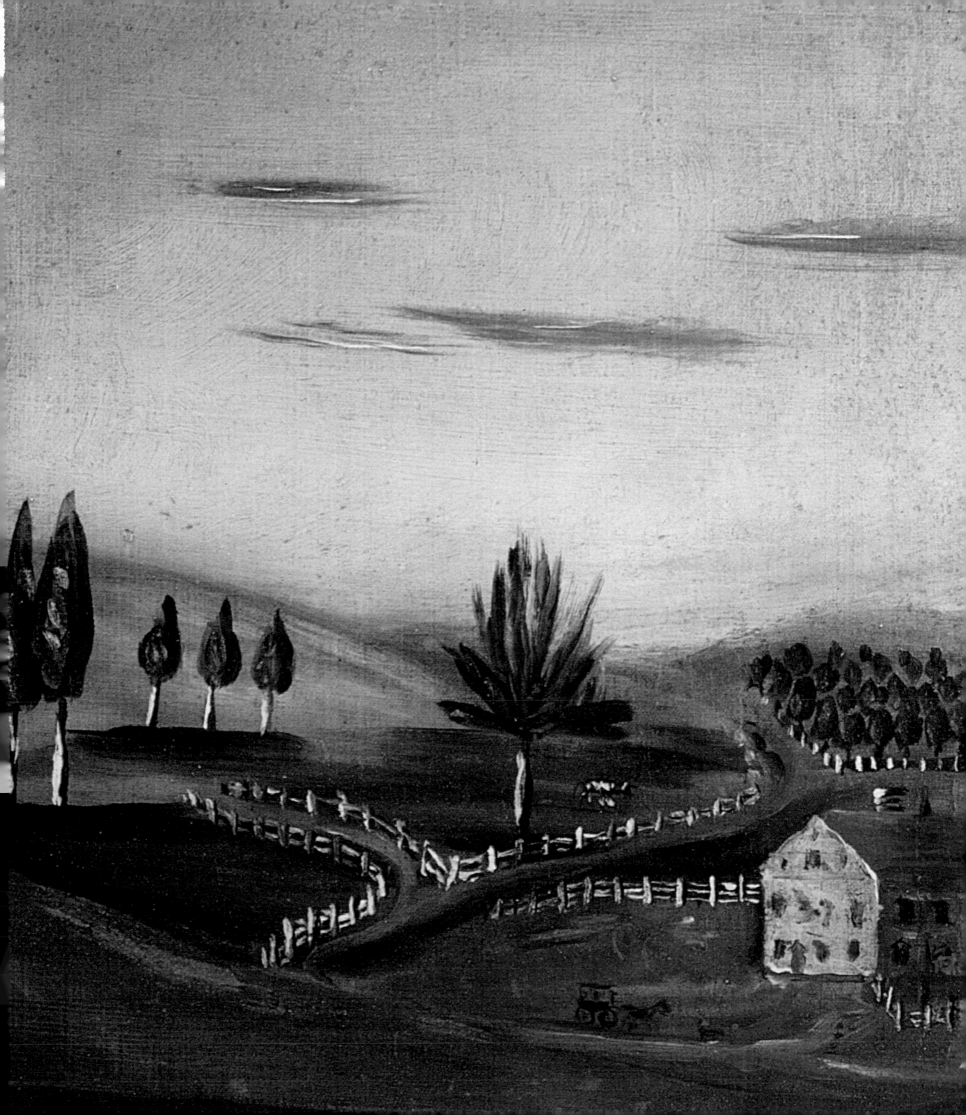

dents of Kent, Connecticut, show that Phillips had by that time developed a striking, highly stylized formula for turning out portraits that probably speeded production. *Young Physician* (plate 10) is typical of his new, abbreviated technique. The black jacket appears flat and was painted rapidly and with only minimal highlights to suggest detail and to separate the figure from the very dark background. Women in portraits of this period frequently lean forward, while men are often shown with one hand draped across the crest rail of a stenciled chair. Phillips's style became less dramatic and more straightforward after 1840, as exemplified by *Lady on Red Sofa* (plate 11). Large areas of the canvas are quickly defined with fluid brushstrokes— the result of many years of experience— while the treatment of the features is crisp, precise, and individualized.

It is not known whether Ammi Phillips ever received instruction from a trained artist; like most folk painters, he apparently began his career by experimenting with original solutions to the technical problems he confronted, and then he continued to develop by modifying and absorbing academic influences without compromising his distinctive personal style. The length of his career and the large body of his work clearly testify to Phillips's ongoing ability to please his clientele.

Rufus Hathaway (1770–1822) was a medical doctor, like Russell Dorr, but he was also a portrait painter. Only about a dozen of his works survive, but today he ranks among America's most acclaimed folk artists, a position that may seem ironic in light of his small production and his only parttime pursuit of painting. The visual appeal of his paintings and the details known about his life and his small-town patronage offer an important and revealing commentary on concepts fundamental to folk art and to its popular appreciation.

Hathaway was born in Freetown, Rhode Island, in 1770, and his family seems to have moved to sev-

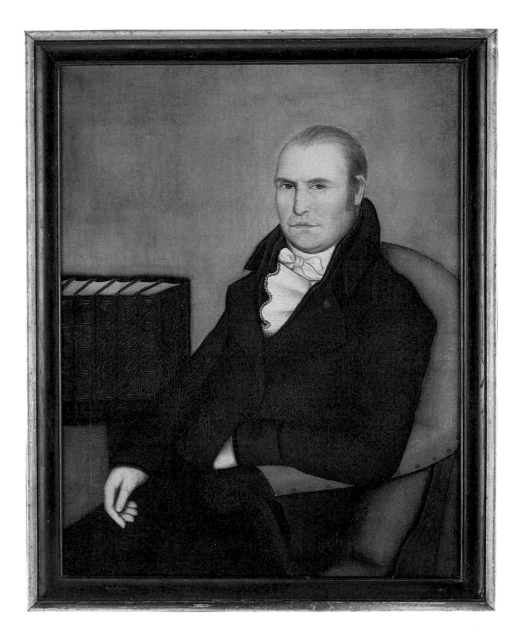

8
Attributed to Ammi Phillips, DR. RUSSELL DORR, *Chatham Center, Columbia County, New York, probably 1814–1815, oil on canvas, 38 × 29⅞ inches (58.100.16).*

9
Attributed to Ammi Phillips, ROBERT LOTTRIDGE DORR, *Chatham Center, Columbia County, New York, probably 1814–1815, oil on canvas, 22¼ × 18 inches (58.100.8).*

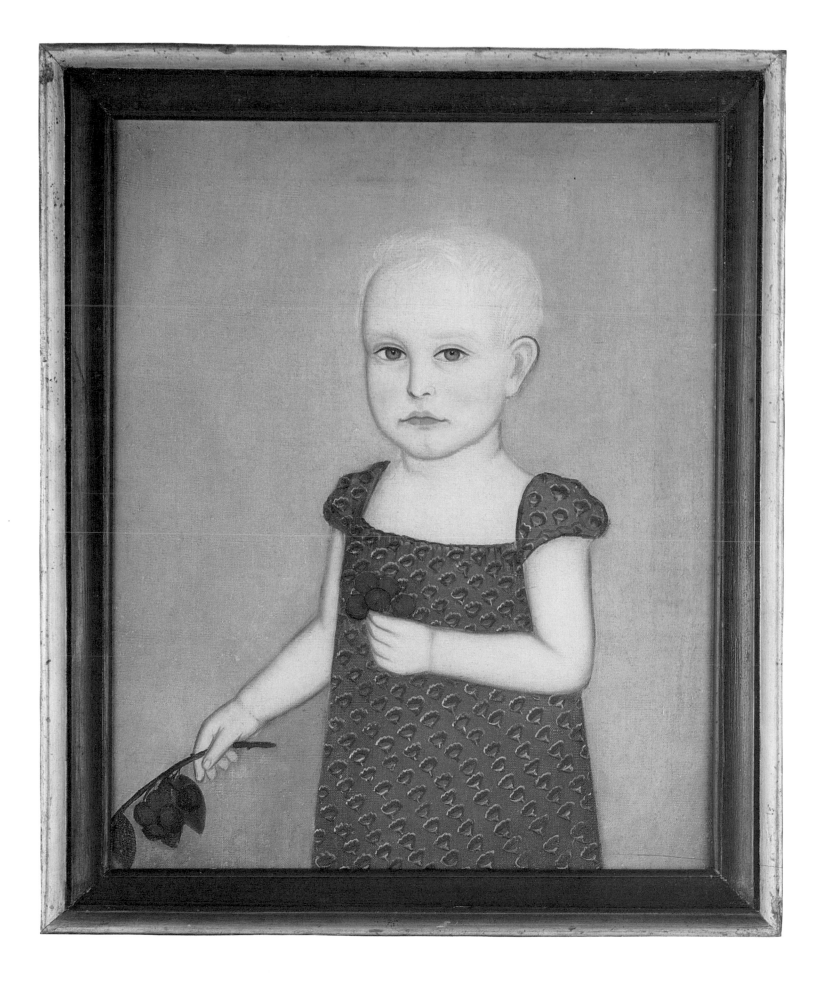

eral other Rhode Island towns in the following years. He evidently left his parents' home well before his father died in 1816, probably in pursuit of portrait commissions. Presumably he traveled to Duxbury, Massachusetts, during this time, because he married Judith Winsor, one of his sitters, there in 1795. According to family tradition, the young artist-husband was urged to pursue a more socially acceptable and lucrative profession by his in-laws, and so he decided to study medicine. He was a practicing physician in Duxbury until his death in 1822.

The Westons, whose portraits are shown in plates 13 and 14, were well-known, prosperous residents of Duxbury whom Hathaway undoubtedly saw socially as well as professionally. Their portraits are impressive, and they illustrate the full range of characteristics associated with this artist's work. The figures are drawn in confined spaces, and the compositions are unusually vertical in format. Hathaway used strong contrasts of light and dark tones and a crisp delineation of individual elements to suggest three-dimensionality. These are conservative pictures, yet they evoke the strength of character and the self-reliance of moderately wealthy townspeople living in New England during the nationalistic and prosperous period that followed the Revolution. Jerusha's stylish hat, with its elongated crown, was probably a recent acquisition; the hat boasts a feather that Hathaway painted with broad, repeated brushstrokes, a treatment he also used for hair.

Hathaway's late-eighteenth-century likenesses reveal some of the characteristics observed in earlier American portraits, including stiff poses and very formal, restrained attitudes. One could argue that Hathaway's peculiar way of seeing and drawing the human form was responsible for what some might describe as the woodenness of his figures. Recent research has revealed that such postures were in fact reflective of real life: rules for proper deportment and the constraints of period dress, especially

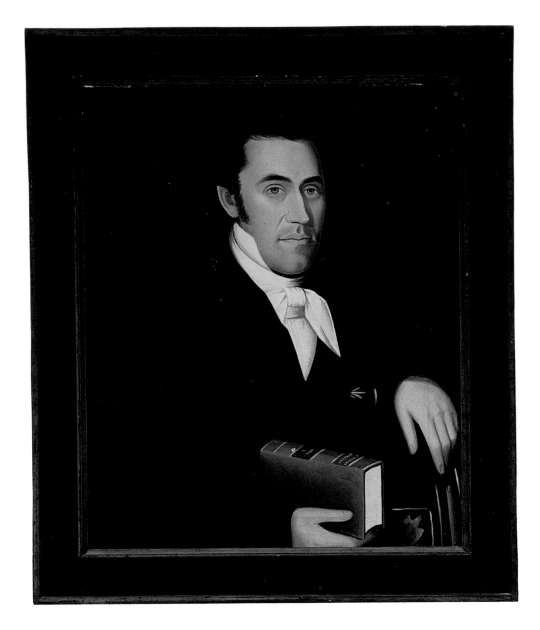

10
Attributed to Ammi Phillips, YOUNG PHYSICIAN, *probably Dutchess County, New York, ca. 1830, oil on canvas, 31 × 25 inches (58.100.42).*

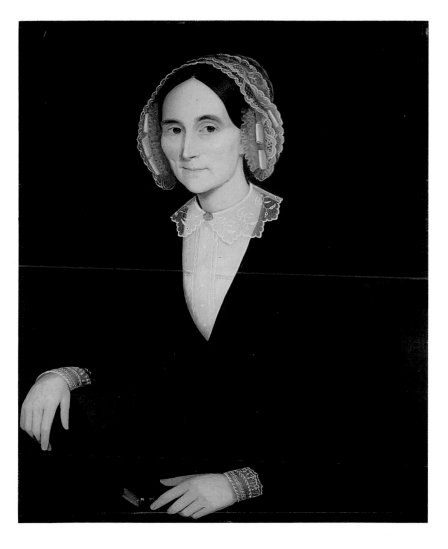

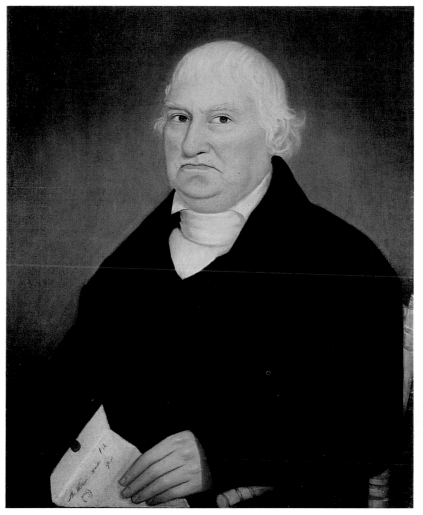

11
Attributed to Ammi Phillips, LADY
ON RED SOFA, *New York–*
Massachusetts–Connecticut border
area, ca. 1850, oil on canvas, 33¾
× 27½ inches (48.100.2). *

12
Attributed to Ammi Phillips,
WILLIAM HARDER, *Ghent, New*
York, probably 1820–1825, oil on
canvas, 30⁹/₁₆ × 24¾ inches
(58.100.28).

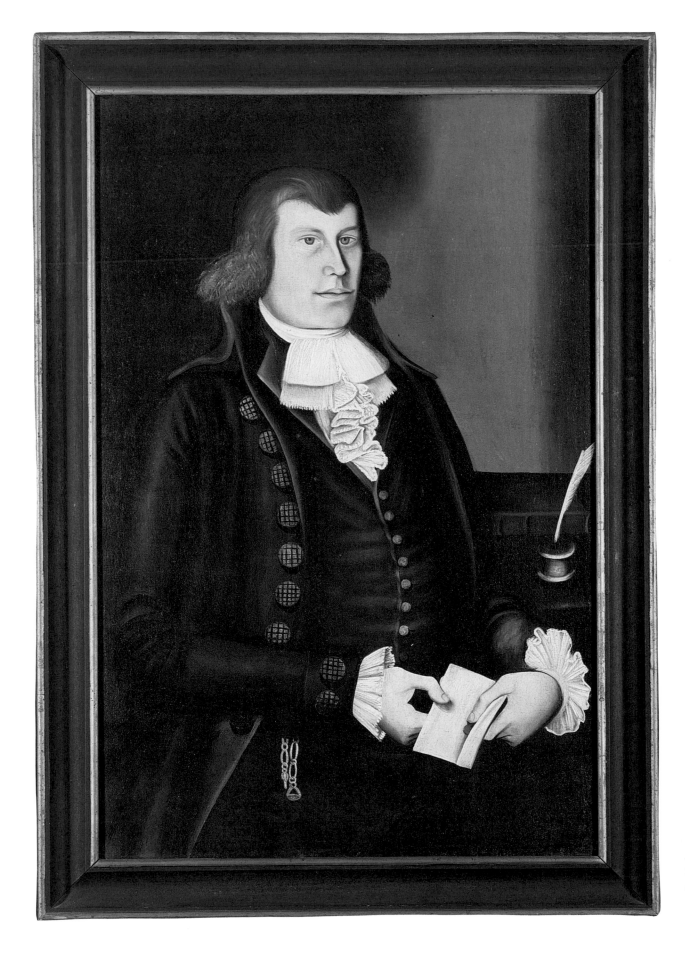

13
Attributed to Rufus Hathaway,
EZRA WESTON, JR., *probably
Duxbury, Massachusetts, probably
1793, oil on canvas, 37³/₄ × 25
inches (72.100.7).*

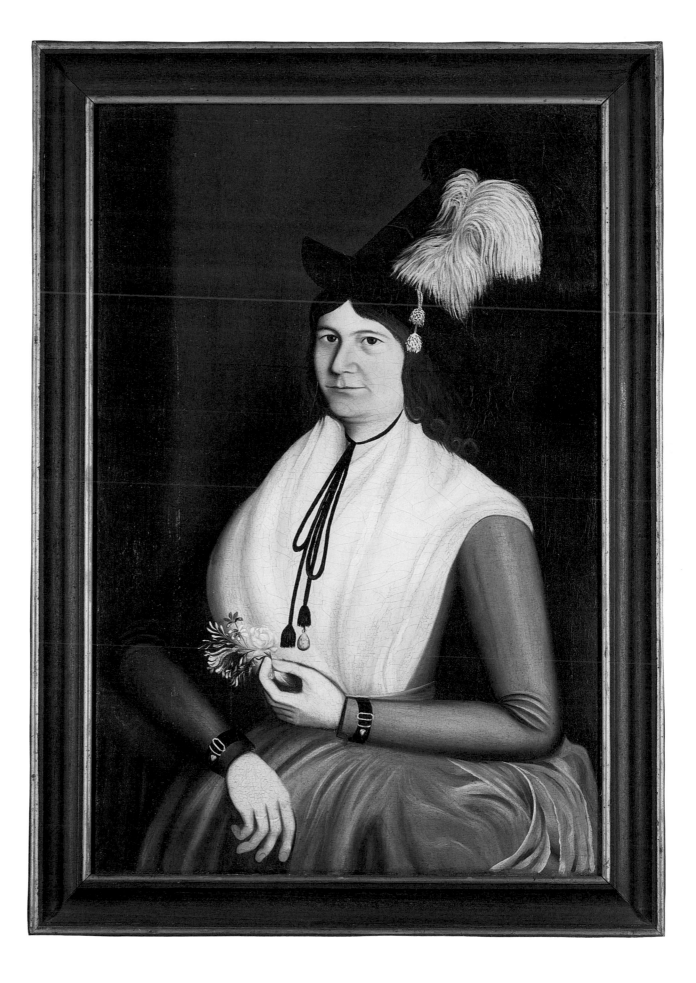

14
Attributed to Rufus Hathaway,
MRS. EZRA WESTON, JR.
(JERUSHA BRADFORD), *probably*
Duxbury, Massachusetts, probably
1793, oil on canvas, 38¼ × 25⅛
inches (73.100.7).

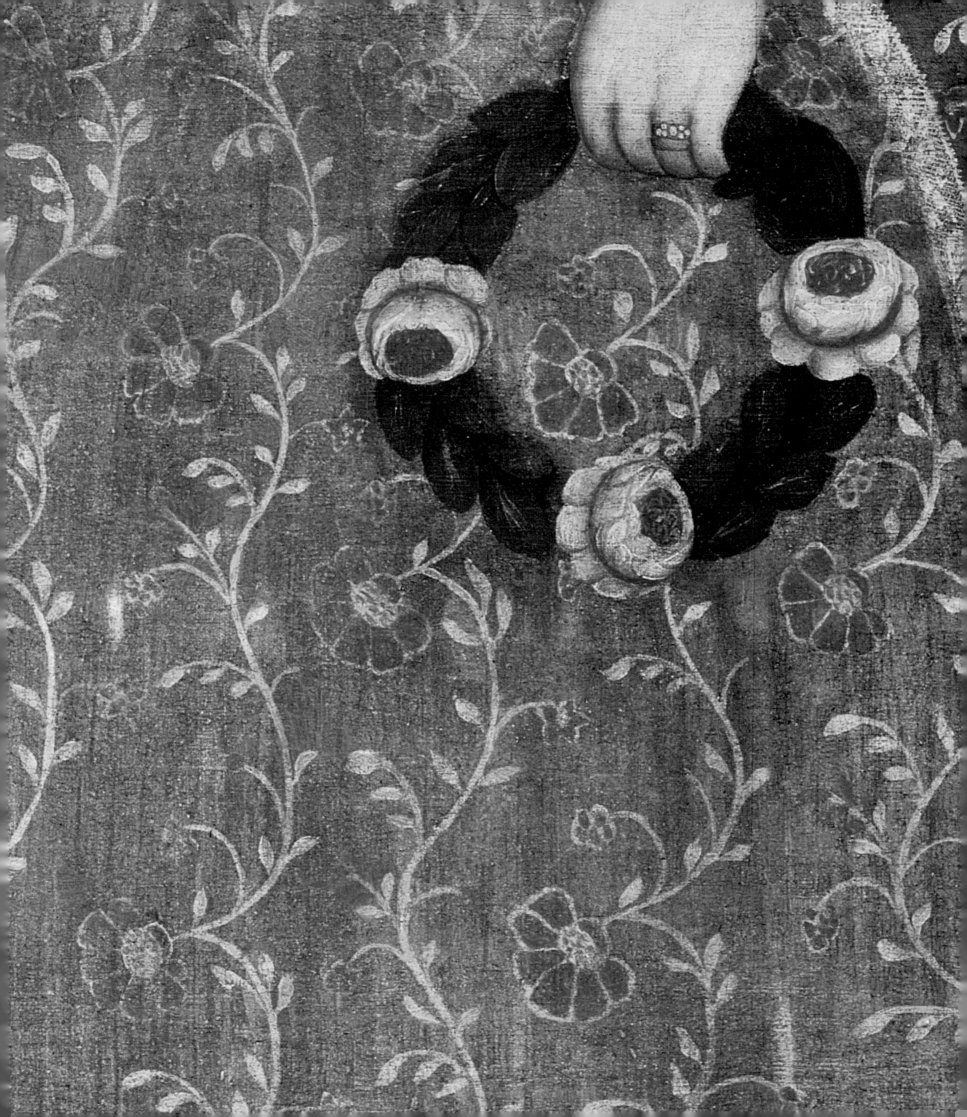

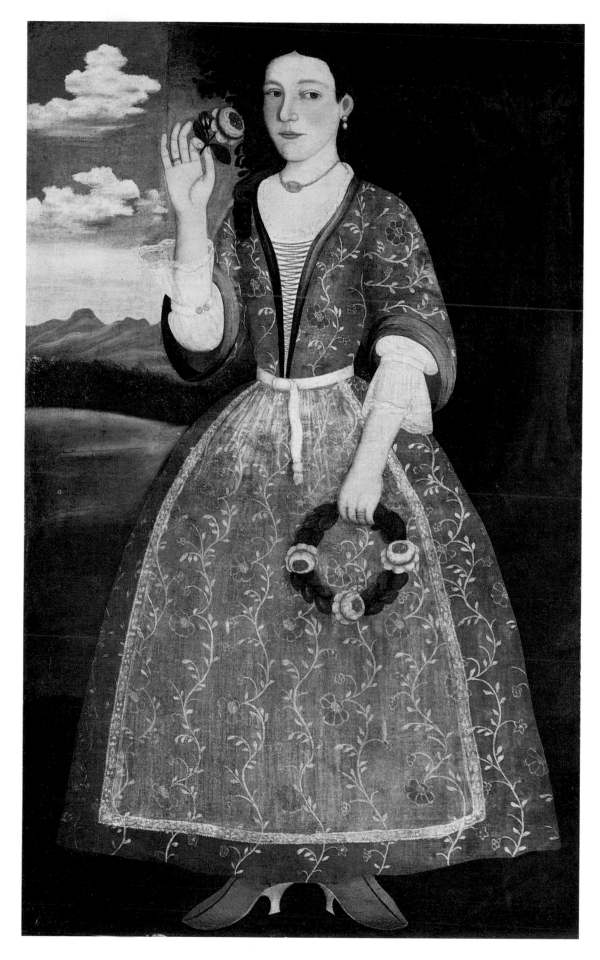

< *Detail of plate 15*

15
Unidentified artist, DEBORAH
GLEN, *Albany area, New York, ca.
1739, oil on canvas, 57½ × 35⅞
inches (64.100.1).*

that falleth to me and he divided unto them his

into a far country and there wasted his

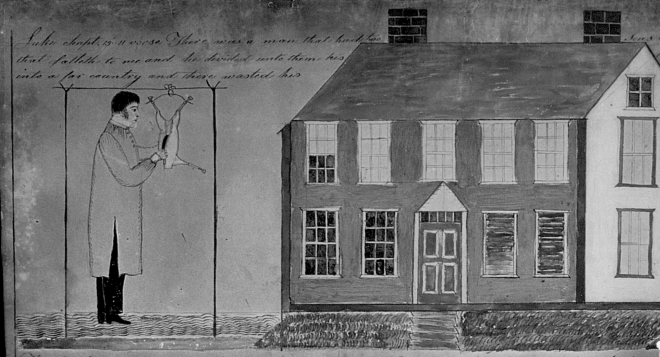

Famine in that land and he began to be in want 15th And he went and joined himself to a

have filled his belly with the husks the swine did eat and no man gave unto unto him 11th the

enough and to spare and I perish with hunger 18th I will arise and go unto my Father and will

worthy to be called thy son make me as one of thy hired servants 19th And he arose and came to his

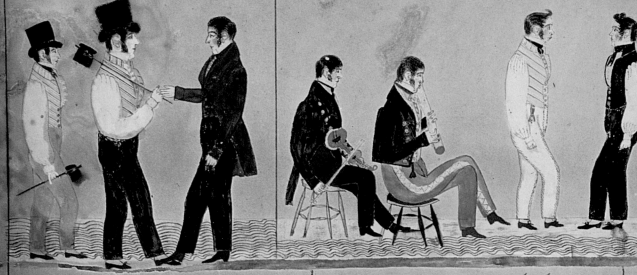

and fell on his neck and kissed him 21st And the | on him and put a ring on his hand and

son said unto him Father I have sinned against | shoes on his feet 23 and bring hither the fatted

heaven and in thy sight and am no more worthy | calf and kill it and let us eat and make

to be called thy son 22d But the Father said to | merry 25th For this my son was dead and is

his servant bring forth the best robe an put it | alive again he was lost and is found and

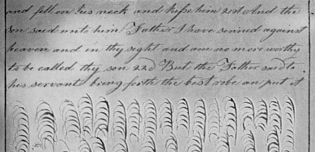

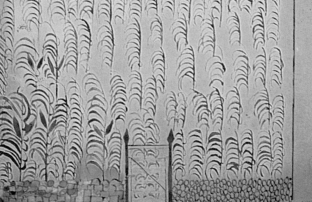

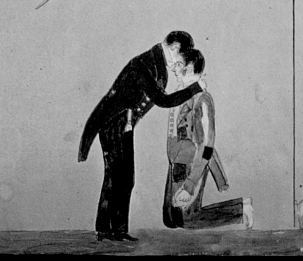

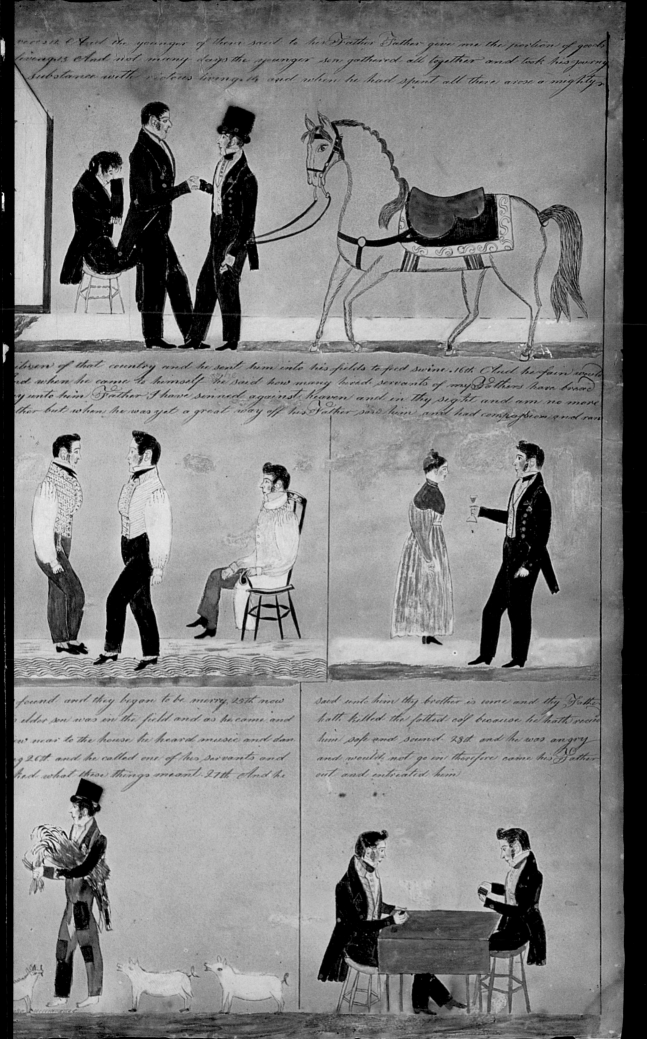

Ruby Devol Finch, THE PRODIGAL SON, *Westport, Massachusetts, ca. 1830–1843, watercolor on paper, 18¾ × 22 inches (36.301.1).**

interesting and diverse material was executed in a variety of formats, by artists of differing levels of expertise. The jewel-like profile image of Rebecca Freese (plate 18), of Cairo Forge, New York, painted about 1835–1840, is one of the most sensitive specimens of this type of art in the Williamsburg collection, possessing a degree of refinement and subtlety lacking in most folk portraits of this size. Unfortunately, we know nothing about the sitter except her name and where she lived, and we know even less about the artist. During Rebecca Freese's lifetime, Cairo Forge was a small rural community like many others dotting the eastern United States. The lack of frills, jewelry, and other personalizing finery in Miss Freese's attire suggests that she was a person of modest means.

An entirely different impression is given by *Lady in Blue* (plate 23) and by Miss Huston's portrait (plate 19), both also done in this small format. The latter boasts an elaborate frame that is believed to be original to the picture. The subject may have been the granddaughter of John Huston, the founder of the Bank of Union Town, in Pennsylvania, though this association has not been verified. A similar portrait by the same hand is documented for a nearby community. Miss Huston is posed somewhat awkwardly in her green-painted Windsor chair, and the abundance of ribbons, bows, flowers, sashes, and laces reveals that she wore her prettiest finery to have her picture "taken" by the artist. Only a few other small portraits recorded by the Center staff show such a profusion of costume trimmings.

The subject of *Lady in Blue*, attributed to Ruth Whittier Shute (1803–1882) and Dr. Samuel Addison Shute (1803–1836), is also rather elegantly dressed. She may have been from Peterborough, New Hampshire, or a nearby town. The Shutes, who were married on October 16, 1827, and then lived in Weare, New Hampshire, traveled throughout New England and upper New York State in search of portrait commissions. Presumably their joint artistic endeavors began with their marriage,

because no paintings or drawings by either that are known conclusively to predate their union have been found. Samuel was a physician and is thought to have practiced medicine along with painting portraits.

Several simpler forms of portrait art are illustrated by the small watercolor-and-pencil likeness of John Abbe (plate 21), Lucius Barnes's profile drawing of his grandmother (plate 20), and the cut silhouettes in plates 22 and 24. Abbe wears a costume typical of the 1825–1830 period, which the unidentified artist has treated in a rather hard-edged and abstract manner. The price scale for portraiture was based entirely on the amount of time the artist spent on a portrait, and the effect of economic considerations on the "look" of the end product is nowhere better illustrated than in small-scale portraits such as Abbe's. Not only were these paintings less expensive than larger oil portraits, they were also portable and could readily be placed atop a mantelpiece, bureau, or table in the privacy of one's bedroom, to serve as an intimate remembrance of a friend or loved one.

Martha Atkins Barnes, the subject of plate 20, lived all of her ninety-five years in Middletown, Connecticut. She died in 1834, presumably the same year in which this portrait and at least seven others were created by her fifteen-year-old grandson Lucius Barnes (1819–1836), possibly to illustrate copies of her memoir, which was written and locally published by the pastor of the Middletown Baptist Church. Lucius, the son of Martha Barnes's tenth and youngest child, was crippled early in his short life and died at the age of seventeen. His eight recorded profile likenesses of his grandmother show her either walking with a cane— sometimes while smoking a clay pipe— or seated in a chair, reading the Bible.

Aged 25 (plate 22) is among the most stylized of American silhouettes in its treatment of its subject's costume, which was executed with watercolor and

18
Unidentified artist, MISS REBECCA FREESE OF CAIRO FORGE, NEW YORK, *probably New York State, ca. 1835–1840, watercolor and ink on laid paper, 6³/₈ × 5 inches (58.300.6).*

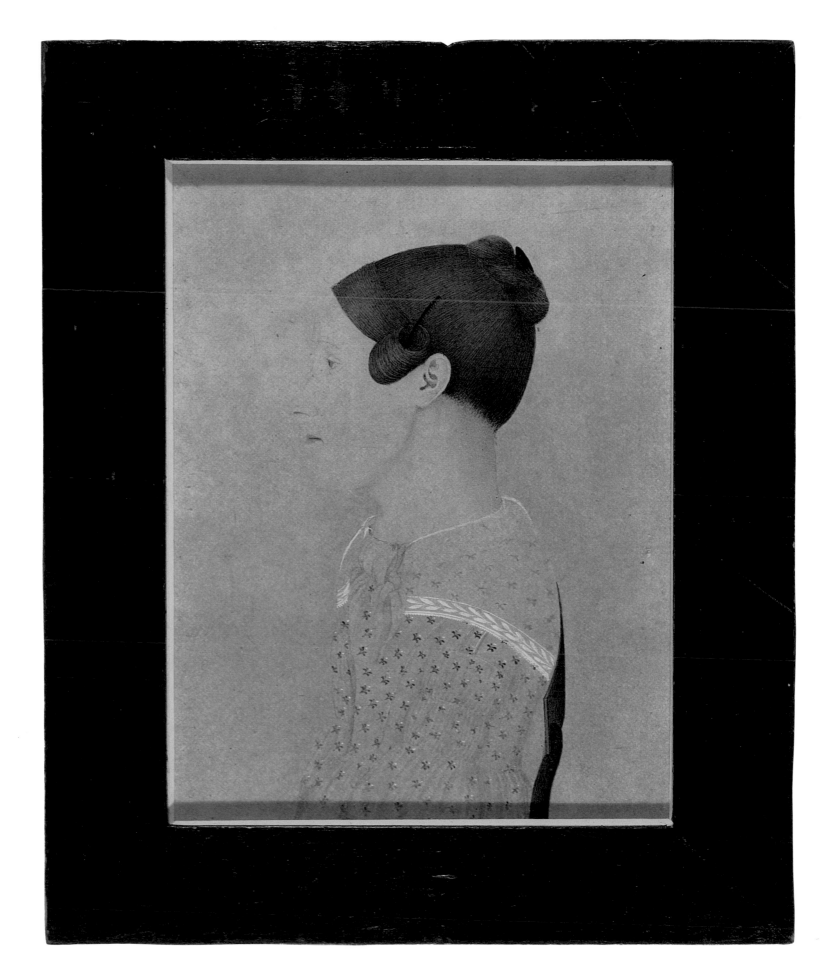

and the compositional complexity of children's portraits make them very appealing. The painting of an unidentified little girl with her doll (plate 29) by John Bradley (active 1831–1847) is an exceptional example of the form. Here stands a small future mother, embracing her doll with one hand and clutching the strings of the doll's cap in the other. Perhaps the sitter removed the cap so the doll could nap in the miniature cradle on the left; then she may have sat quietly on the nearby Empire-style stool while her doll rested. Any viewer who played with dolls as a child can identify with the sturdy youngster and understand immediately the emotions portrayed on Bradley's canvas.

While the Bradley portrait illustrates one child's affection for her doll, it also provides a rare and colorful record of the furnishings of an average, middle-class nineteenth-century American household, and of children's dress at the time. The little girl's costume is nicely detailed; she wears blue shoes that match her dress, and a coral necklace; the doll's dress is almost identical, only in pink. The colorful patterned carpet is drawn in perspective so that the convergence of its stripes will lead the viewer's eye to the child.

The doll shown with three-year-old Emma Clark (plate 28) in a small watercolor portrait executed in 1829 by an unidentified artist is endowed with almost human attributes, and looks more like a miniature adult than a porcelain-headed toy. This contributes to the somewhat surreal quality of the composition. The diminutive figure of Emma, with her large, pale head, is isolated against a boldly patterned floor that recedes into seemingly infinite darkness. Several other notable children's portraits included here are *Boy Holding Dog*, attributed to Noah North (plate 34), *Child Holding Rattle*, attributed to Erastus Salisbury Field (plate 30), and two portraits by John Brewster, Jr. (plates 4 and 33).

The beguiling portrait of a child with a rattle by Erastus Salisbury Field (1805–1900) is one of a

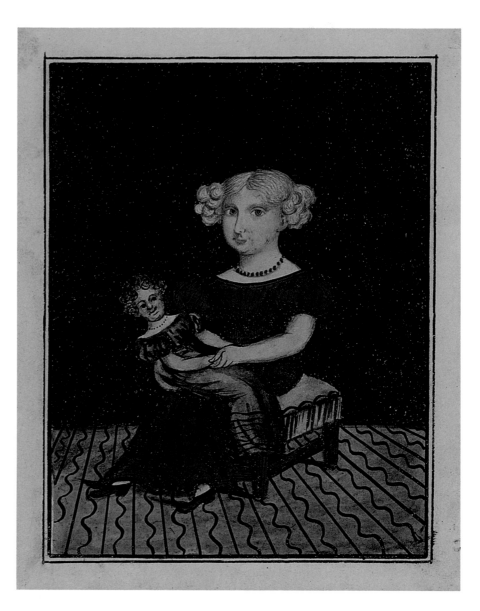

28
Unidentified artist, EMMA CLARK, *New England, possibly Massachusetts, 1829, watercolor, pencil, and ink on wove paper, 5⁹/₁₆ × 4⁷/₁₆ inches (58.300.5).*

29
J. Bradley, GIRL WITH DOLL, *probably New York City or immediate area, 1836, oil on canvas, 34¼ × 28¼ inches (57.100.4).*

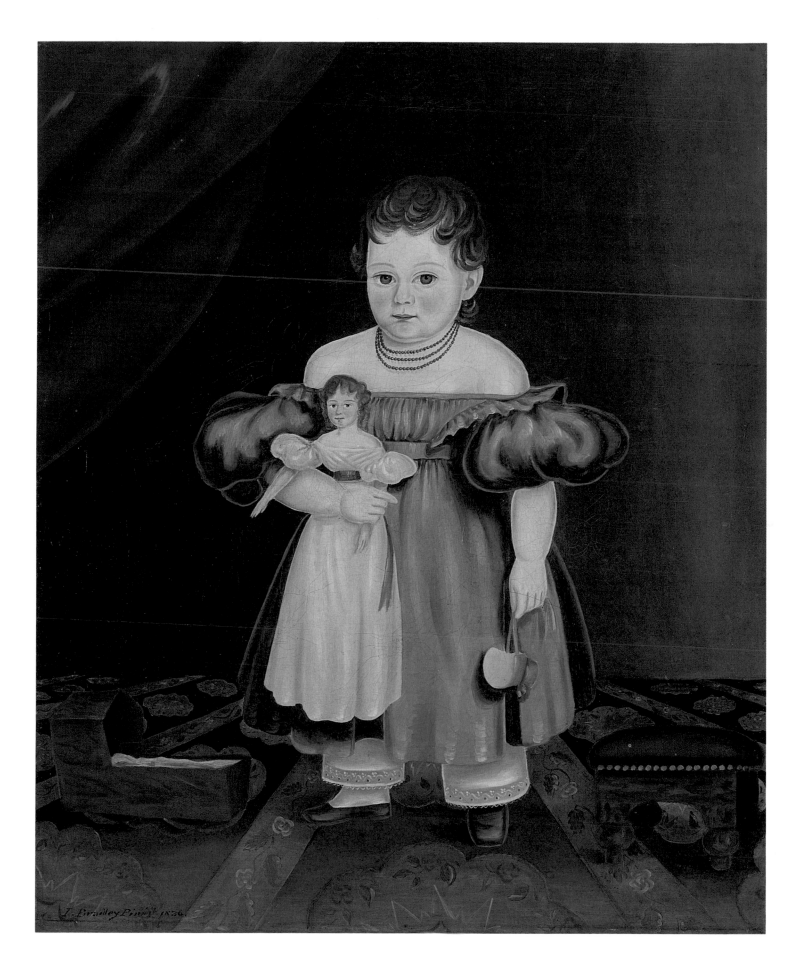

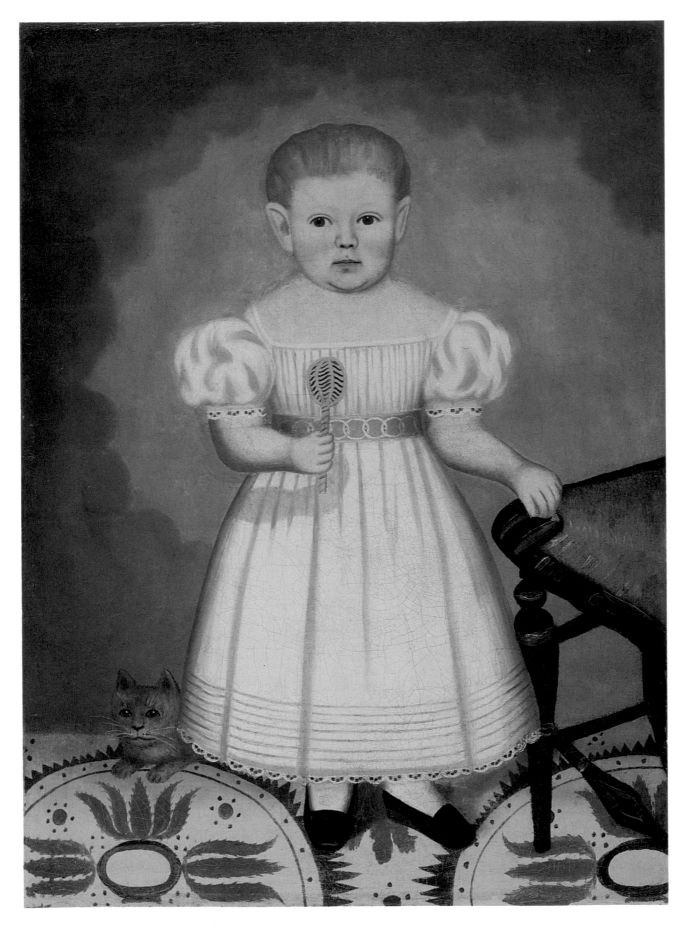

30
Attributed to Erastus Salisbury
Field, CHILD HOLDING RATTLE,
probably Lee, Massachusetts, ca.
1838, oil on canvas, 34¼ × 25½
*inches (31.100.4).**

Detail of plate 30 >

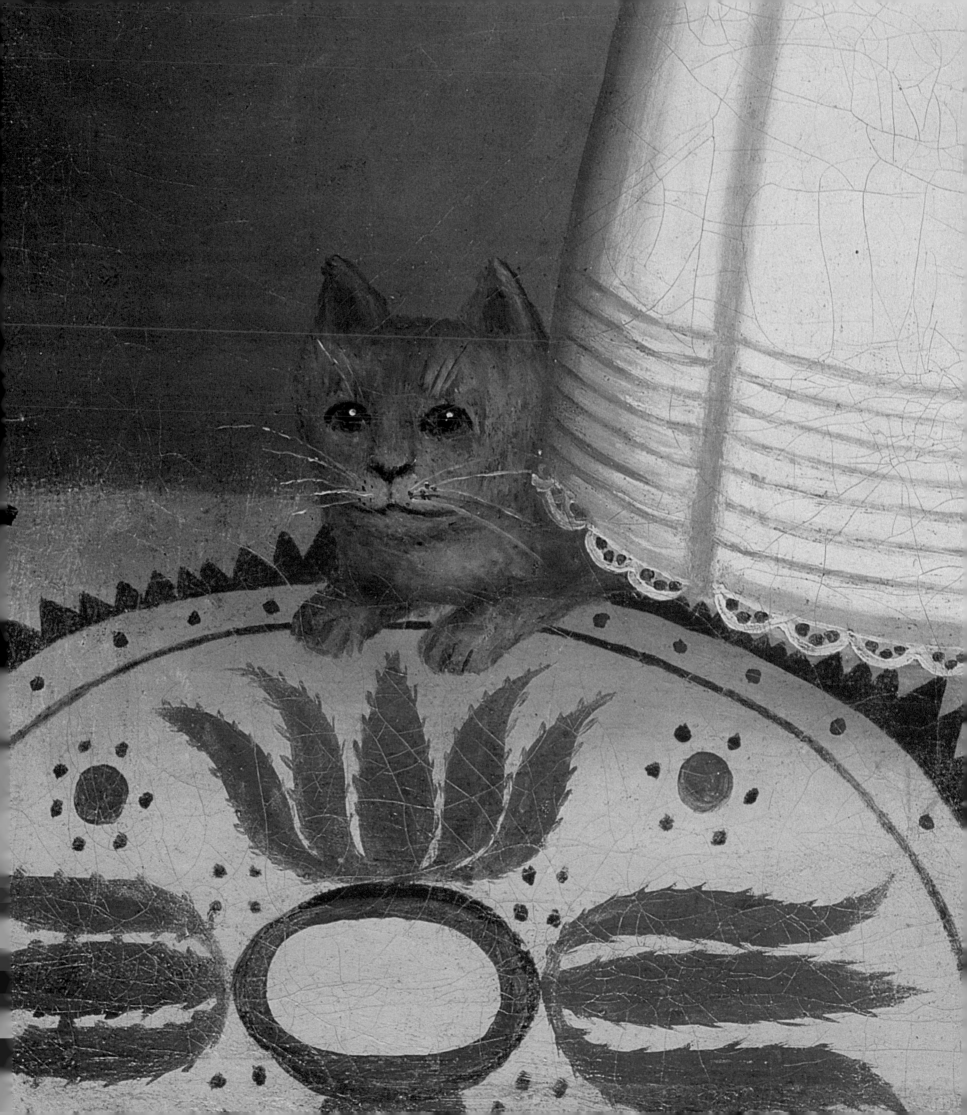

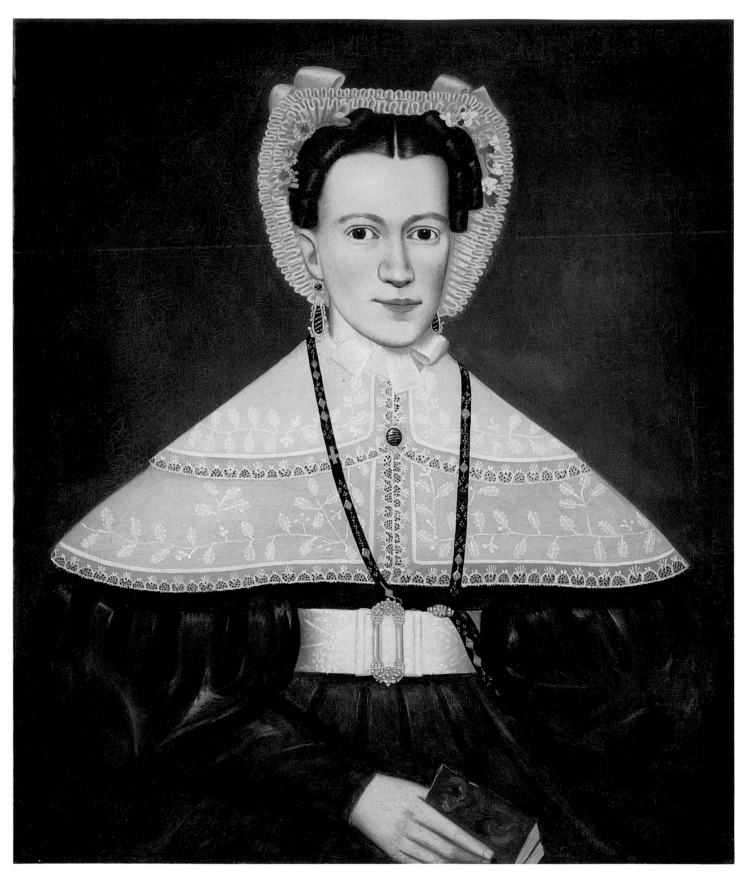

31
Attributed to Erastus Salisbury Field, MRS. PEARCE, *possibly Hadley, Massachusetts,*
*ca. 1835, oil on canvas, 30 × 26 inches (39.100.8).**

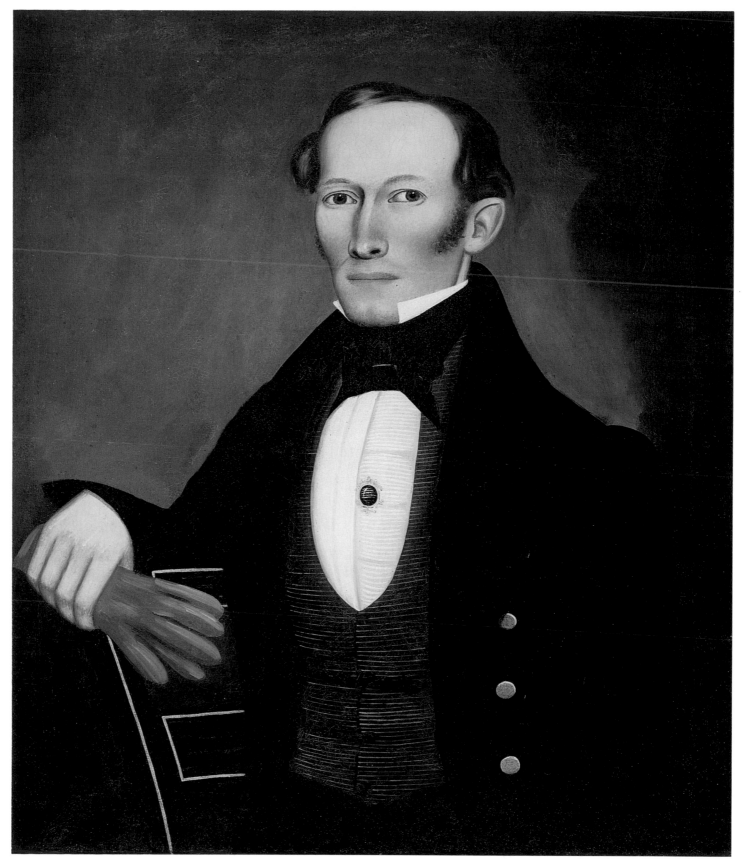

Attributed to Erastus Salisbury Field, MR. PEARCE, *possibly Hadley, Massachusetts,*
ca. 1835, oil on canvas, 30 × 26 inches (39.100.7).*

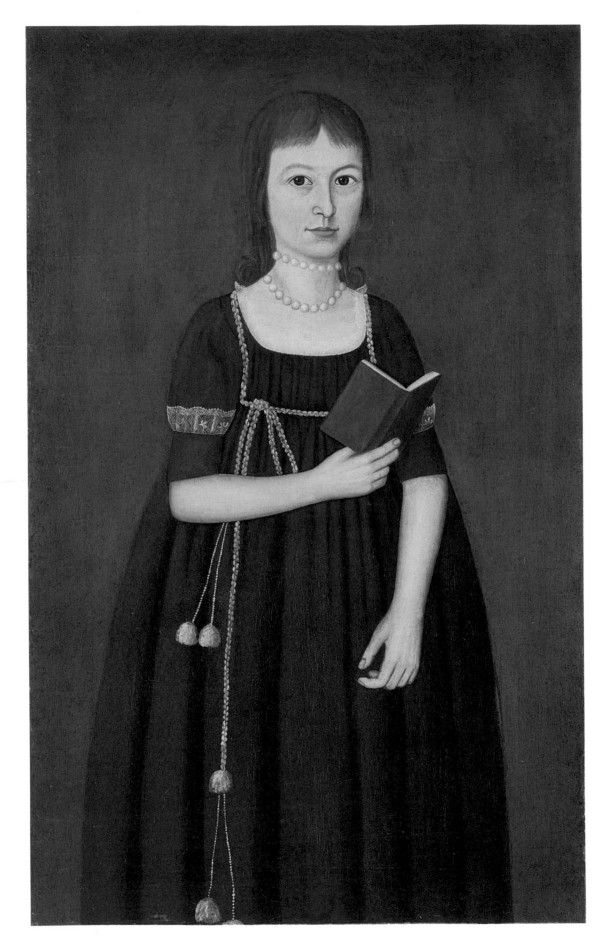

33
Attributed to John Brewster, Jr.,
GIRL IN GREEN, *New England or
New York State, ca. 1800, oil on
canvas, 39 × 24 inches (39.100.6).**

pair owned by the Center, and it ranks among Field's best work. The sex of the child is unknown, since little girls and boys wore similar costumes and hairstyles during the 1830s. The rattle was probably of the cheap woven straw sort, then popular in this country and often imported from Europe. Although only a portion of the chair on the right is shown, the details are sufficient to indicate that it was of the inexpensive painted Hitchcock variety, available throughout the United States after 1825 and often seen in folk portraits. The boldly figured and stylized floor covering was probably a carpet, though stenciled floors or floor cloths in designs imitating carpets were also used during these years. The size of the chair, the carpet pattern, and the friendly gray cat quietly crouched by the sitter's side convey to us the child's small size and something of the tranquillity of the household.

Erastus Salisbury Field lived most of his long life in the area around Leverett and Sunderland, Massachusetts. When he was nineteen he spent three months in the studio of Samuel F. B. Morse in New York City. This was Field's only formal exposure to the world of academic painting. After he returned to Leverett, he became an itinerant professional painter and traveled the Connecticut River valley painting portraits.

To meet the demands of patrons eager for his services, by 1838 Field had evolved an efficient shorthand technique that enabled him to complete a half-length portrait in a day, for a price of four dollars. The portraits of Mr. and Mrs. Pearce (plates 31 and 32) are typical of these. Among the stylistic mannerisms most often observed in his quickly painted likenesses are stiff frontal poses, square and shortened hands, pointed ears, stippled flesh tones, patterned highlights or cloudlike effects behind his subjects, and the use of black dots to delineate the form and texture of lace.

The daguerreotype, invented in 1839, became increasingly popular in the United States throughout the 1850s, and from this time on Field found it convenient to base his portraits on photographs of his subjects rather than to paint from life. His dreary group portrait of the Smith family (figure 8) illustrates the unfortunate result of this practice. As he aged and the demand for painted likenesses dwindled, Field turned to biblical and historical subjects, often deriving his compositions from prints. On Field's death in 1900, a Greenfield, Massachusetts, newspaper printed the following obituary:

Although Mr. Field was an all-around painter of the old school, his work which has been most highly appreciated is that of portrait painting; his likenesses of people of past generations are as nearly correct as can well be made in oil, and give to posterity faithful ideas of the personal appearance of their ancestors.

The sensitive portraits of an unidentified boy (plate 4) and his sister (plate 33) by John Brewster, Jr. (1776–1854), predate Field's best pictures by some thirty years and were painted at a time when eighteenth-century restraints, both in life-styles and in portrait art, were gradually being supplanted by more informal activities and compositions. Brewster's work compares favorably in some ways with the early portraits of Ammi Phillips. There is a stark directness in both artists' work, an uncluttered clarity that forces us to meet their sitters' gazes head-on. Part of this can be credited to the painters' adeptness at providing detail, but it is also due to the light or muted backgrounds they used, which contrast with the skin tones and the other colors used for costumes and furnishings.

Brewster is particularly interesting in this regard. He was born a deaf-mute in 1766 in Hampton, Connecticut, one of seven children of a respected doctor, John Brewster, and his first wife, Mary Durkee Brewster. He learned to read and write, and his talent for painting was nurtured under the tutelage of the Reverend Joseph Steward (1753–1822), a local minister and portraitist. Brewster began painting portraits of his family and neighbors

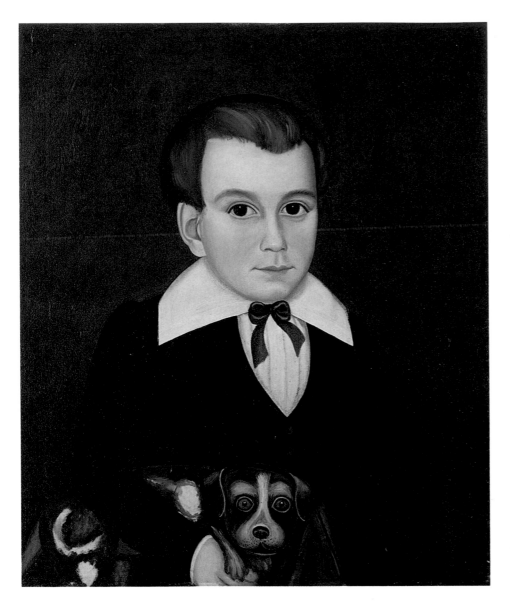

*34
Attributed to Noah North,* BOY
HOLDING DOG, *probably New
York State, ca. 1835, oil on yellow
poplar panel, 20¾ × 17½ inches
(41.100.1).**

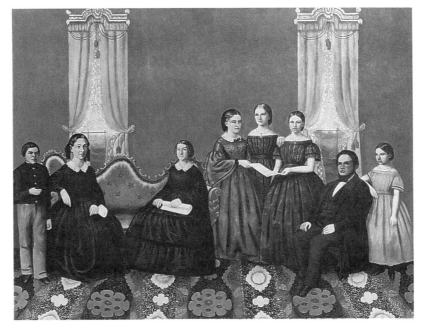

*Figure 8
Attributed to Erastus Salisbury
Field,* THE SMITH FAMILY,
*probably North Amherst,
Massachusetts, ca. 1865, oil on
canvas, 36 × 47 inches (71.100.6).*

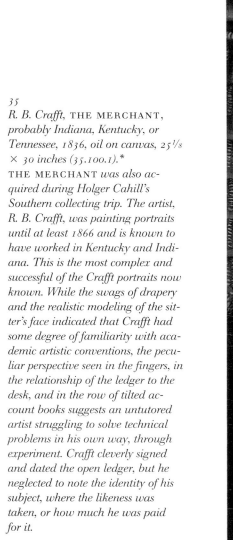

35
R. B. Crafft, THE MERCHANT, *probably Indiana, Kentucky, or Tennessee, 1836, oil on canvas, 25 ⅛ × 30 inches (35.100.1).**

THE MERCHANT *was also acquired during Holger Cahill's Southern collecting trip. The artist, R. B. Crafft, was painting portraits until at least 1866 and is known to have worked in Kentucky and Indiana. This is the most complex and successful of the Crafft portraits now known. While the swags of drapery and the realistic modeling of the sitter's face indicated that Crafft had some degree of familiarity with academic artistic conventions, the peculiar perspective seen in the fingers, in the relationship of the ledger to the desk, and in the row of tilted account books suggests an untutored artist struggling to solve technical problems in his own way, through experiment. Crafft cleverly signed and dated the open ledger, but he neglected to note the identity of his subject, where the likeness was taken, or how much he was paid for it.*

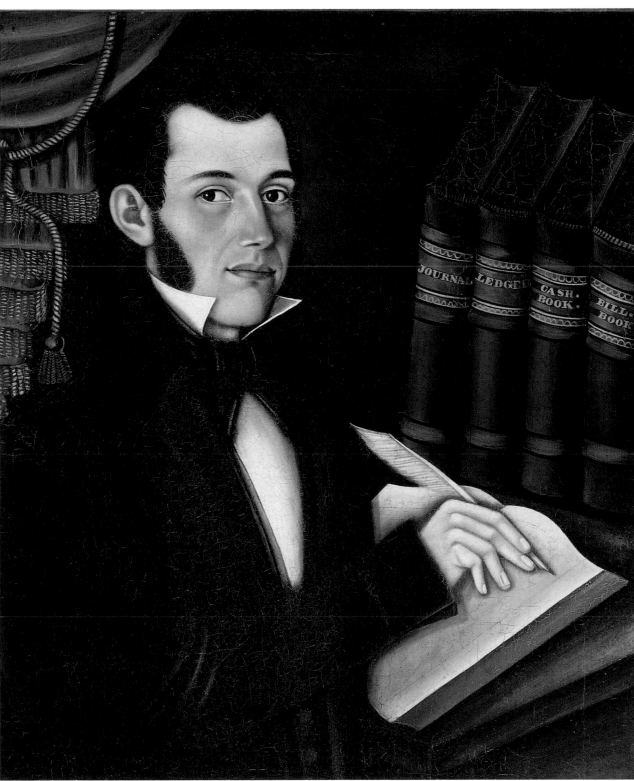

in the 1790s; by 1796 he was in Maine, probably living with his brother's family while taking likenesses in the area. He managed to support himself entirely by producing portraits and miniatures as he traveled about Maine, Massachusetts, Connecticut, and eastern New York. His characterizations of the local people from town and country in these areas have long been recognized as some of the strongest, and often the most serene, likenesses painted in New England.

The flat likeness executed in paint, pencil, or other media, suitable for framing and hanging on the wall or for more private use or display in the homes of average Americans, was the chief form of portraiture prior to 1850, though there were carvers who produced three-dimensional portraits. Asa Ames (1824–1851) was one of these. His bust of a woman (plate 36), probably carved in the vicinity of Buffalo, New York, about 1847–1851, is among the rare examples of early American portrait sculpture in the folk tradition. The woman's facial features, hairstyle, and clothing are nicely detailed in Ames's crisp, sure style. Ames is also known to have carved likenesses of children. Of the dozen or so works now attributed to him, seven depict young children and infants. An "A. Ames," presumably the artist, appeared in the 1850 federal census for the town of Evans, in Erie County, New York, with his occupation listed as "sculpturing."

Probably few average-income American families had this kind of portraiture in their homes, though other types of carved or sculpted works were common, both for exterior and for interior use. Woodcarvers rarely were itinerant, since the material and tools of their trade were less portable than those of the painter and profilist.

There are not many documented comments by those Americans who commissioned and owned folk portraits to help us understand how they reacted to or regarded these likenesses. Few Americans shared John Vanderlyn's learned art background and exposure to European painting, or the intellectual pretensions that nurtured his aesthetic education; they were less concerned than he, perhaps, with the ennobling and heroic ideals championed by academic artists and by the connoisseurs who patronized them. The fact that so much of surviving early American portraiture falls outside the academic mainstream— either verging on being or actually qualifying as folk, or nonacademic, painting— indicates that these pictures were fully acceptable to the society for which they were created.

The twentieth-century enthusiasm for folk portraits reflects both a revival of interest in the lives and culture of ordinary people and an awareness and acceptance of contemporary aesthetics. Many of the qualities that we admire in portraits such as *Boy Holding Dog* (plate 34) by Noah North (1809–1880)— distortion, abstraction, and multipoint perspective— simply represent intuitive solutions to the technical problems the artist confronted in rendering anatomy, light, and space. Today artists, art critics, and scholars, as well as much of the general public, often find the end results more aesthetically pleasing than the conventional work produced by second- and lesser-rank academic portrait painters of the same years.

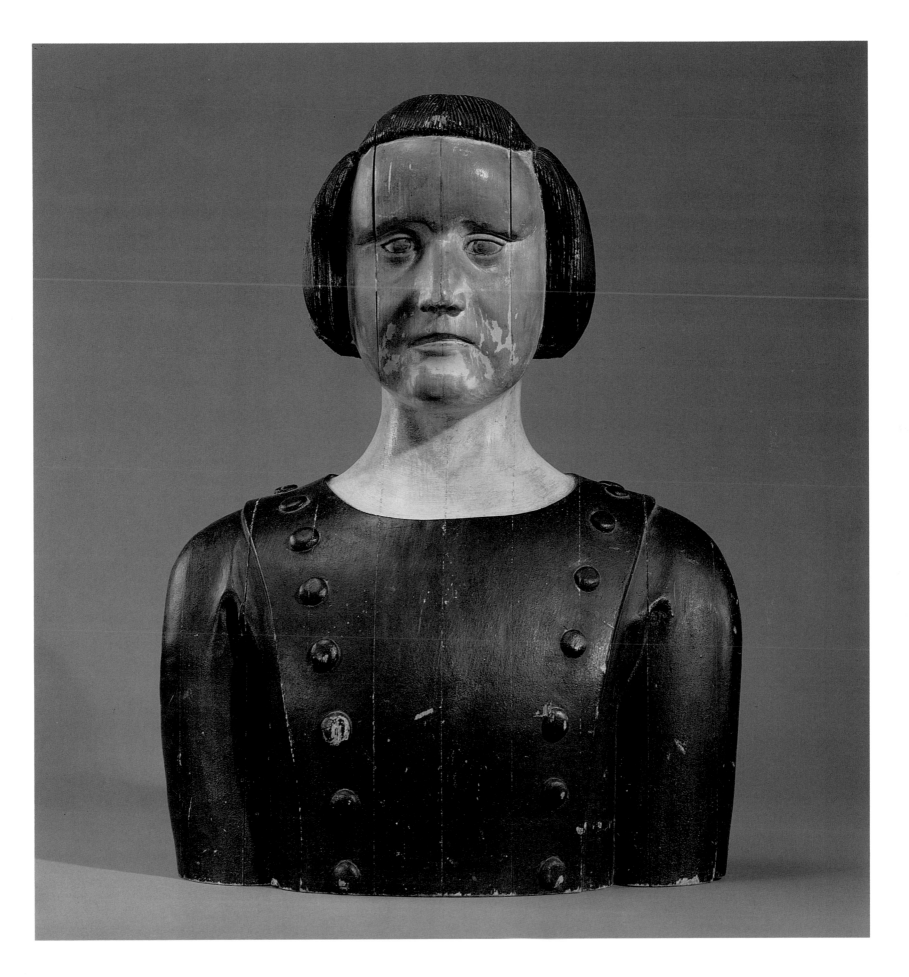

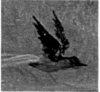

CHAPTER TWO

Down by the Shore

In America no sophisticated traditions of landscape and seascape painting emerged until the second half of the nineteenth century, though a few pictures in these genres were produced by artisan-painters as early as the seventeenth century. In purpose and appearance, however, these pictures could never be confused with the mainstream paintings of the mid– and later nineteenth century, magnificent atmospheric views reflecting the transience of man in the face of the majestic grandeur and uncontrollable forces of nature. Academic artists trained in European as well as in American ateliers, including Thomas Doughty, Asher B. Durand, Thomas Cole, and Frederick Edwin Church, achieved success and popularity with dramatic scenes of the Adirondack mountains, Niagara Falls, and the West. These painters shared a deep and reverent respect for nature that was guided and nurtured as much by their training and their observations as by literary works of the day.

The common man respected nature and knew its power, though his artistic interpretations usually celebrated its beauty in periods of tranquillity. The quiet, almost surreal paintings of Steve Harley (1863–1947) form an interesting counterpoint to the academic pictures of the early nineteenth century because they reflect the folk artist's emphasis on nature's serene aspects. Few folk painters would have been able to articulate in words Durand's belief that through nature man could communicate with the spiritual world, but Harley conveys the idea in his paintings. The concept behind Harley's three known pictures, including his jewel-like rendering of Wallowa Lake (plate 38), seems to paral-

lel the more sophisticated artistic philosophy of painters such as Durand, though in a different way. In Harley's scenes there is no human protagonist and no hint of civilization; he shows nature viewed from a distance, rather than as a force that overwhelms man, who, when he *is* present, is a small, inconsequential part of the whole. Harley sets us apart from the view and simply asks that we stand back and admire it; our experience is principally visual rather than emotional.

Steve Harley is one of those perplexing folk painters whose personal life is well documented but whose years of artistic development are represented by only three oil paintings, two small pencil sketches, and a very few references. He was born in Fremont, Ohio, but was raised on a farm his family owned in Scottville, Michigan. Harley later inherited the farm, but he took little interest in it. He hired a caretaker for the place and devoted his time to wandering in Michigan forests. He was an avid hunter and trail rider. He learned taxidermy and eventually preserved animals for himself and his friends; he also sold a few of these trophies. Sometime during the late 1880s or 1890s Harley took a correspondence course in drawing and drafting. Nothing else is known about his training.

Early in the 1920s he left the farm and went to Washington State to visit his brother. Over the course of several years he traveled throughout Washington, Oregon, and northern California and took a trip to Alaska. During 1927–1928, following his return from Alaska to Washington, Harley painted the triad of landscapes that includes

37
Unidentified maker, SANDHILL CRANE, *probably western Texas, 1880–1900, carved and painted wood with glass eyes, 20 × 21 × 4 inches (84.702.1).*

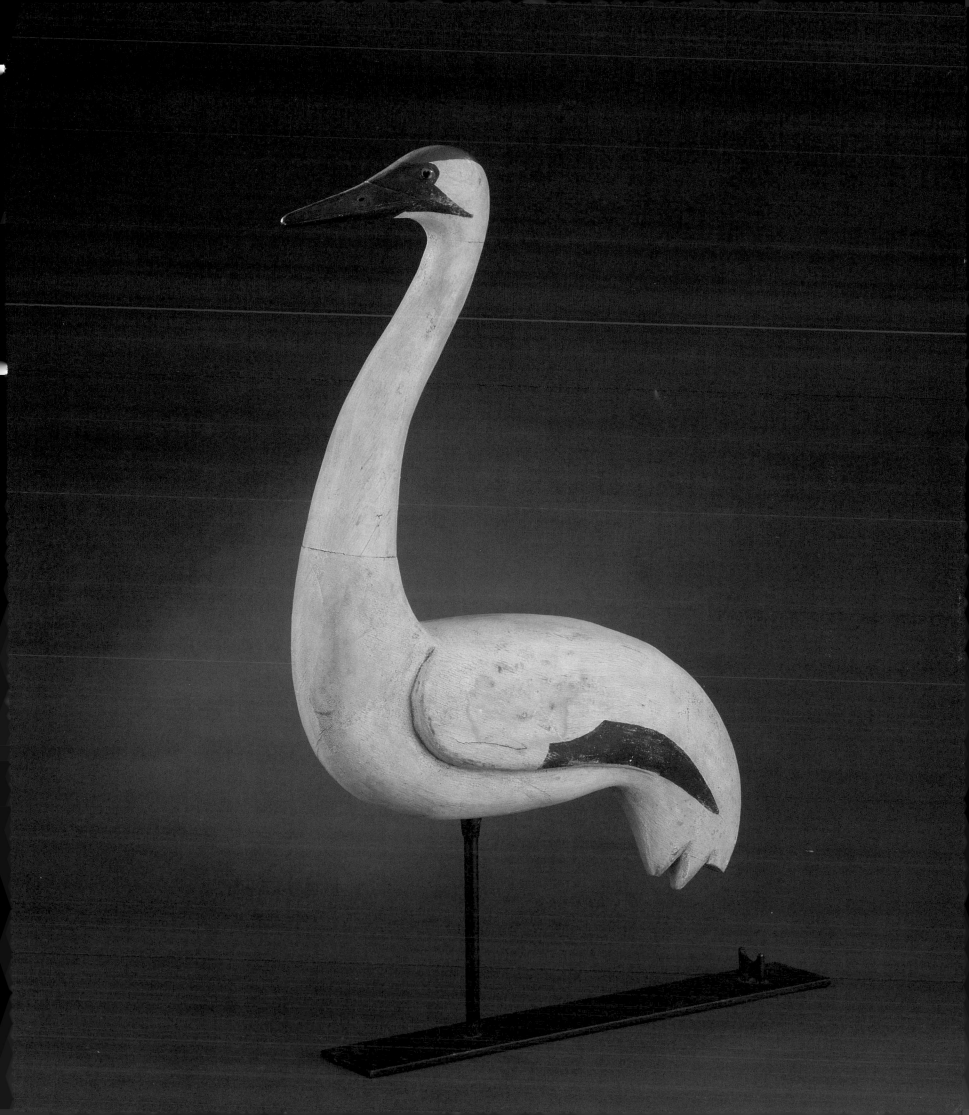

Wallowa Lake, which is the most dramatic of the three in terms of coloration and composition.

Harley's paintings tend to have a strong central focal point— in this case, the eagle gliding over the lake. The picture is minutely detailed, and from the brushwork it is apparent that the artist developed the complex areas slowly and over a long period of time. Such passages as the small trees in early fall foliage and the wild grasses growing in the foreground are good examples of Harley's meticulously realistic manner.

Folk art landscapes such as Harley's, created well after the era of the Hudson River School of painters, are the exception rather than the rule, since most folk art views were created as visual documentations of towns, homes, and other structures (see chapter 3). Works that combined land and water views, however, enjoyed a widespread popularity fostered by the public's love of the picturesque as well as by its firsthand experience. This is illustrated by *Outing on the Hudson* (plate 40), a small painting showing fashionably attired adults and children enjoying a leisurely excursion along the banks of what is thought to be the Hudson River. The town visible across the river may represent Catskill, New York. Rich in detail, the painting records a variety of sailboats and steam-powered craft. The ladies' elaborate Victorian dresses, with their impractical trailing skirts, suggest that the painting dates from about 1875. The poses are reminiscent of those seen in illustrations in popular nineteenth-century periodicals, and the picture itself, either in its entirety or in part, may have been inspired by a printed source.

Several views in the Center collection seem to be associated with the Hudson River, though in most cases there is no supporting documentation. The title *Palisades along the Hudson* was assigned to the painting shown in plate 39 prior to its acquisition by the Center in 1960, and it may or may not be geographically accurate. A nearly identical view signed by the artist Horace Bundy bears the same title. There are more than one hundred other very similar compositions known from the last half of the nineteenth century, however, all with different designations. All were copied from engravings based on one or both versions of Jasper Francis Cropsey's celebrated *American Harvesting Scene.*

Interestingly, many of these copies have either New York or New England histories, indicating that highly regarded artists associated with the Hudson River School of academic painters, such as Cropsey, were widely known and appreciated by the general public, probably through printed reproductions circulated by the American Art Union or published in such magazines as *Harper's Weekly* or *Peterson's.* A few of the copies, including this example, may have been conceived as school exercises, as the several versions signed by women suggest; in their art classes older girls who had mastered the fundamental skills were encouraged to paint scenic views, but the compositions were almost always based on printed sources rather than executed on location.

The fine brushwork in *Palisades along the Hudson* and its lively coloration make it one of the most appealing of the river views created by folk artists in the northeastern United States. The rich yellow and ocher hay-making vignette unites the picture and draws attention to the softer colors of the river and its banks in the distance.

Because *Palisades along the Hudson* was copied, it captures some of the ideas fostered by academic artists working during the same years, but it also retains the literal, linear quality that typifies most folk painting. Folk painters were usually astute observers, and their pictorial renderings tend to be highly descriptive. The fact that material objects often are depicted in distorted perspective, appear out of proportion, or seem too brightly colored to be faithful and realistic likenesses does not contradict this general observation but simply reflects these artists' level (or lack) of formal training.

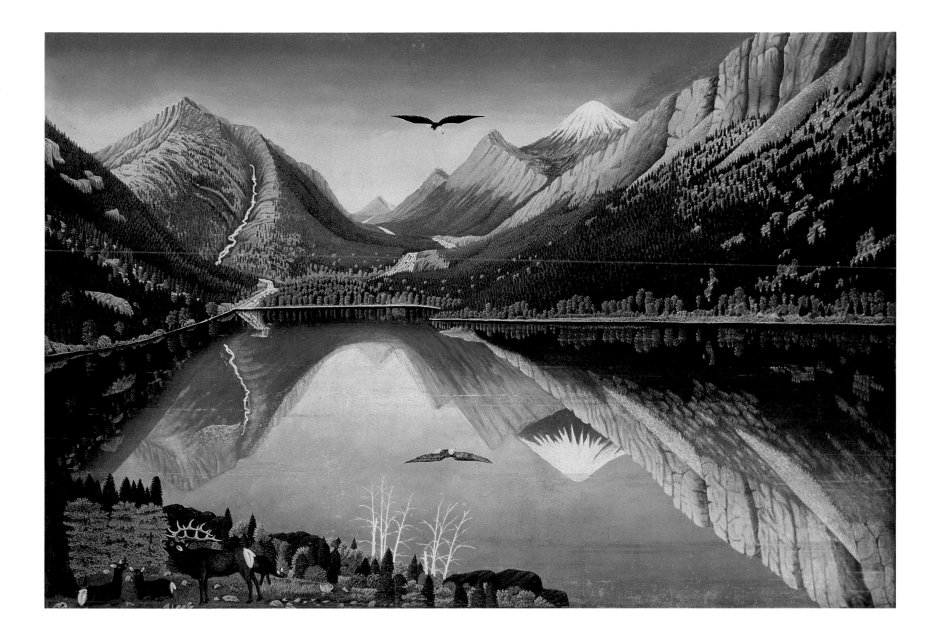

38
Steve W. Harley, WALLOWA LAKE,
Oregon, 1927–1928, oil on canvas,
24³/₄ × 36¹/₄ inches (57.102.4).

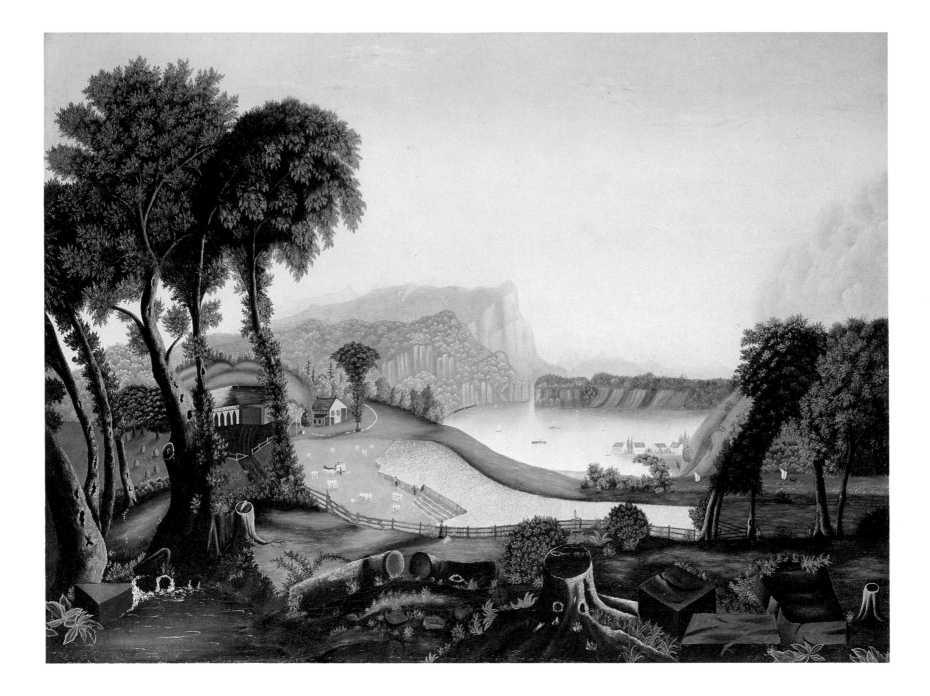

Seascapes by folk artists are similar in intent to folk art views of towns and buildings, in that many were depictions of familiar seaport towns, of naval engagements, or of ships of various types— these last commissioned by the ships' owners or captains. There are actually more pictures related to the sea and to the waterways of early America than there are landscape views. The reason for this greater popularity was partly that a large percentage of the population lived in coastal areas, and the sea and

navigable rivers were central to their livelihood. The artists who created these pictures and other objects associated with the sea were often sailors, ship's painters or carvers, or landsmen whose families were involved with the maritime trades. Most of these artists, regardless of the type of works they produced, were keen observers.

The narrative pictures (see plate 41) of John Orne Johnson Frost (1852–1928) are important exam-

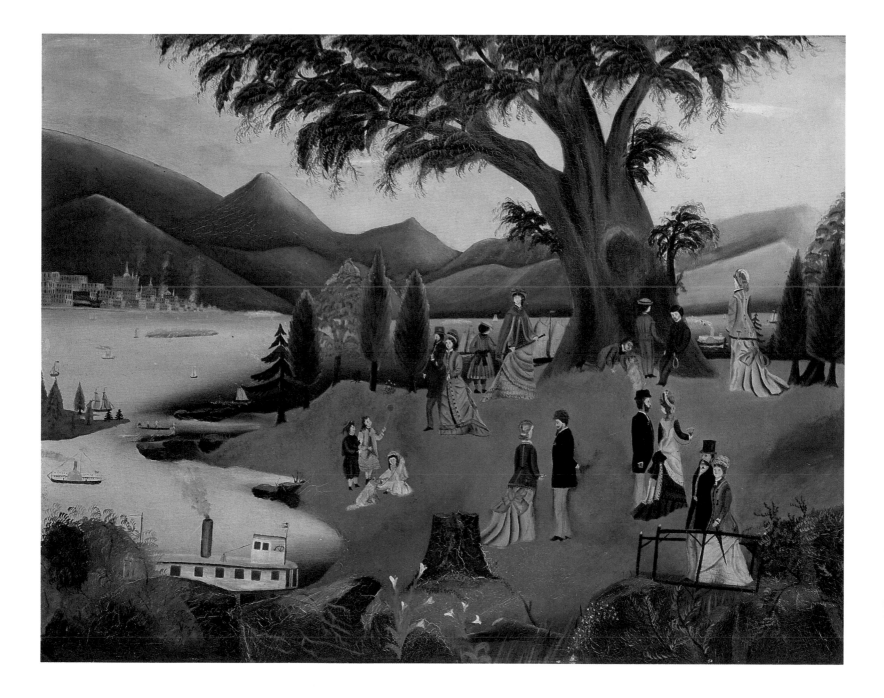

ples of the continuation of this tradition into the twentieth century. Frost was born and grew up in Marblehead, Massachusetts, the son of Mehitable Frost and Amos Dennis Tucker Frost, both descendants of early settlers in the area. He quit school in 1868 and decided to go to sea on one of the fishing vessels that provided a living for many of the townsfolk. He made two trips, in the late summer of 1868 and in the spring of 1869, but following the second venture he acceded to the requests of his bride,

Amy Lillibridge, and did not continue as a fisherman. Together the couple ran a seafood restaurant in Marblehead. Though brief, Frost's time on the North Atlantic left an indelible impression on him, one that he eventually recalled in his paintings. He became intensely interested in Marblehead's history, particularly those aspects tied to the sea, and this fascination is clearly reflected in his paintings. Frost did not begin painting until after his wife's death in 1919. He eventually opened a curious little

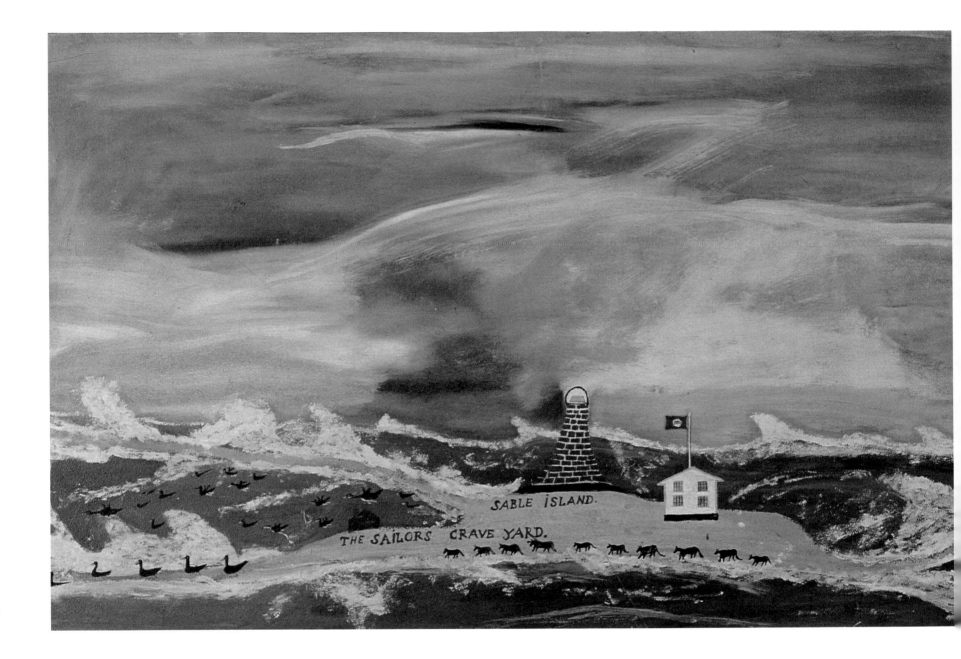

gallery where he exhibited a few chronological pan-oramas of early Marblehead as well as some other historical artifacts.

Sable Island is a landmark for fishermen, located off the Grand Banks near Nova Scotia. Frost's ama-teurish but strong narrative style and his innate pic-torial sense imbue his picture of the island with emotion and energy, perhaps reminiscent of the artist's own feelings in 1868 when, as a young boy, he made his first voyage to the area. The seas are

heavy, the ship runs hard before the wind, and all the fishermen wear oilskins. In most of Frost's ocean scenes the waves form strong diagonals, and the treatment of the sky indicates the wind's motion through irregular streaks and swirls of blue, white, and gray.

The sailors' nickname for Sable Island provides an ominous note: "The Sailors Graveyard" is painted on the sand beneath the island's proper name. The title and the wind-whipped seas are vivid pictorial

41
Attributed to John Orne Johnson Frost, SABLE ISLAND: THE SAILORS GRAVE YARD, *Marblehead, Massachusetts, 1922–1928, water-based paint and pencil on wallboard, 22⁹/₁₆ × 67⁹/₁₆ inches (69.101.1).*

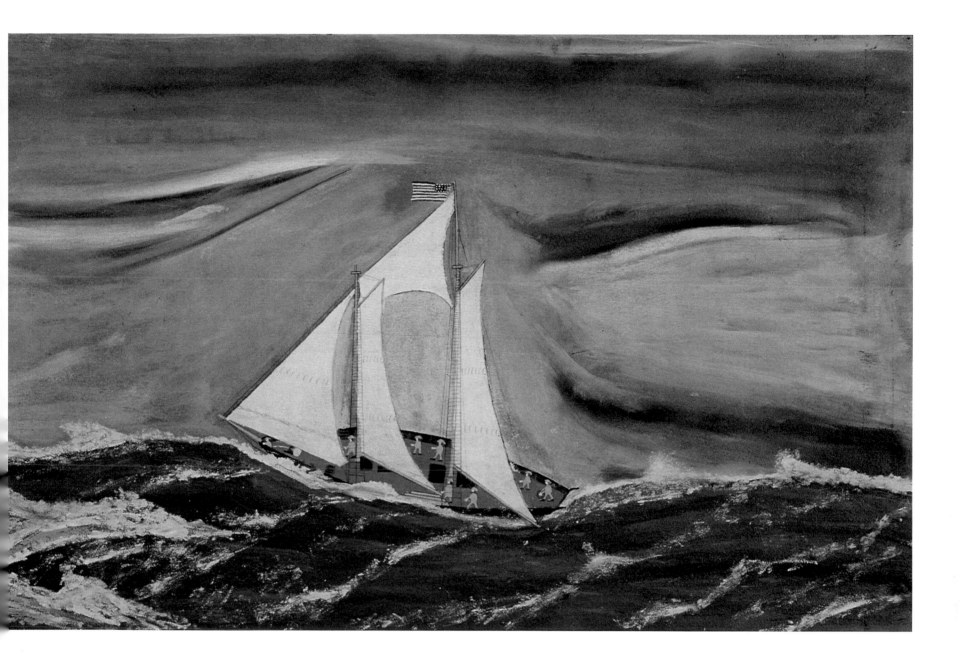

reminders of the difficulties and dangers encountered by fishermen off the Grand Banks in the 1860s as well as today.

The earlier *Constitution and Java*, by Richard Dummer Jewett, Jr. (1792–1814), is typical of the descriptive purpose of many folk art seascapes. The inscription beneath the lower margin of this picture reads: "Painted at Bridgetown Prison island of Barbados April 19, 1813 by an American prisoner." Jewett, a native of Ipswich, Massachusetts, was cap-

tured with his shipmates by a British frigate and transferred to the brig at Bridgetown in January 1813. While in prison he painted his view of the *Constitution* next to her shattered prize, the British frigate *Java*, after their engagement on December 29, 1812, about a month before Jewett's capture. Although it is unlikely that Jewett witnessed the actual event, news of the battle doubtless reached the Bridgetown prison through other imprisoned American seamen.

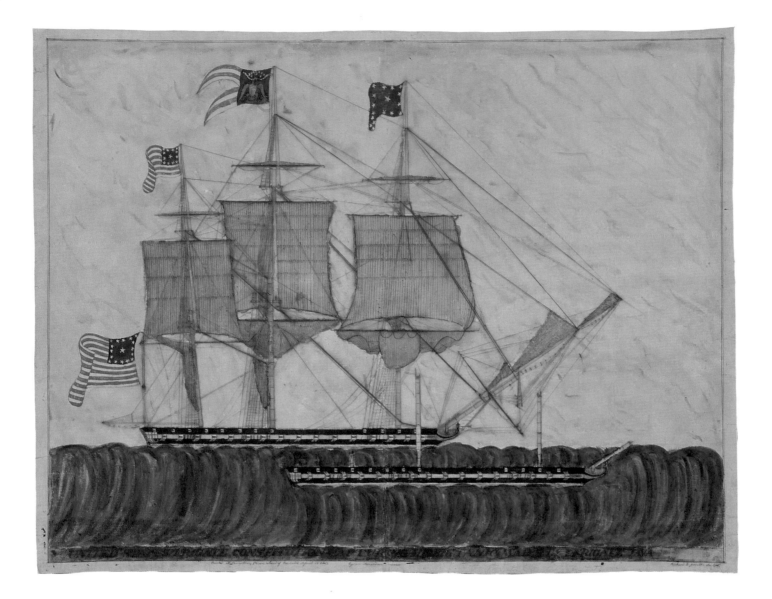

Jewett depicted the *Java* as the lifeless skeleton of a ship, dismasted, with its rigging shot away; in contrast, the *Constitution* rides the crest of the sea, unscathed and triumphant, its sails reefed. American pride could hardly be more dramatically or more clearly expressed. Jewett was eventually released from prison and traveled home in late November 1813. He soon returned to sea and was lost on a voyage to France in 1814.

Ships' portraits figured prominently in marine pictures by American folk painters. Some painters,

such as James Bard (1815–1897) and his twin brother, John (1815–1856), specialized in these works. The Bards were native New Yorkers who collaborated on their first boat painting at the age of twelve. By their midtwenties the brothers had achieved sufficient recognition to be able to live on the proceeds from their pictures, most of which were commissioned by the owners, captains, or promoters of Hudson River steamboats. The brothers' partnership was apparently dissolved in the winter of 1849, but James continued painting on his own for some years.

42
Richard Dummer Jewett, Jr.,
CONSTITUTION AND JAVA,
Bridgetown, Barbados, 1813,
watercolor and ink on laid paper,
18¹/₁₆ × 23⁹/₁₆ inches (57.311.1).

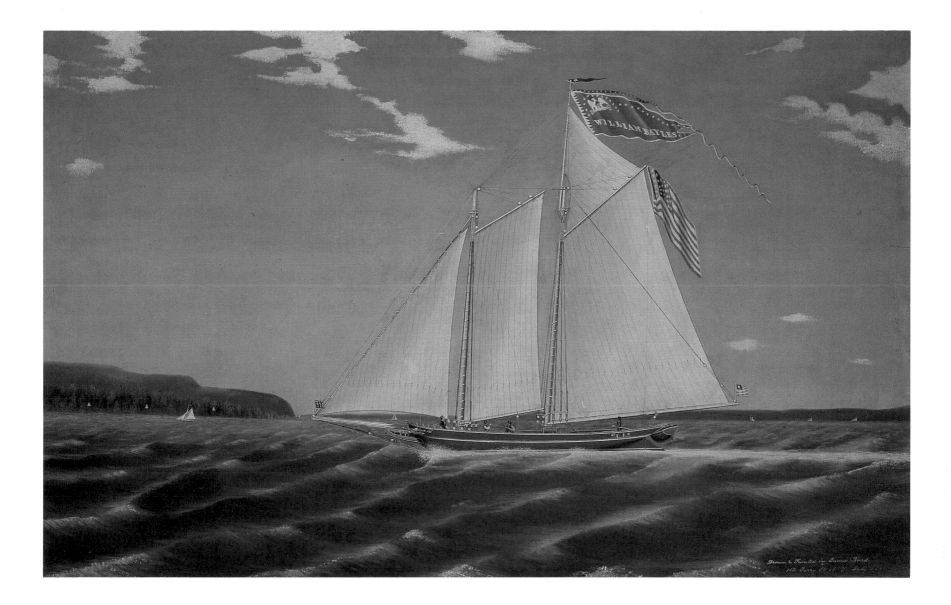

43
James Bard, THE SCHOONER
WILLIAM BAYLES, *New York City,
1854, oil on canvas with penciled
details, 32³/₄ × 52 inches (63.111.2).*

James Bard made a name for himself as a meticulous and accurate recorder of small sailing craft and especially of steamboats. His friend Samuel Ward Stanton, a historian and fellow artist, stated that Bard would record the dimensions of the boats he painted from bow to stern, leaving no parts unmeasured, and would then return to his studio for the actual painting. Thus his pictures (such as that of the schooner *William Bayles*, plate 43) are highly accurate in their details. If Stanton is to be believed, James Bard created about four thousand portraits of steamboats in his lifetime, as well as numerous images of schooners and other sailing vessels.

The *William Bayles* was built at Nyack, New York, in 1853 under the direction of John B. Voriz, and was first owned and mastered by Daniel O. Archer of New York City. One unsubstantiated source alludes to the vessel's having been used to haul stone from a Tarrytown quarry to New York City. This may be true, but the *Bayles* probably served a variety of other purposes as well during her enrollment at the port of New York, for schooners and sloops commonly hauled both passengers and assorted goods up and down the Hudson River during the nineteenth century. The fifteen extant enrollment documents for the *Bayles* indicate numerous changes in owners, masters, and home ports during her nineteen years afloat. After New York she saw service in Connecticut, New Hampshire, and Massachusetts, whence she was reported "lost at sea" on May 31, 1874.

The schooner's vivid green hull makes a striking contrast with the blue-gray water and the warm, peach-colored sky at the horizon. Bard created three portraits of the *William Bayles*— two in 1854 and one in 1860— but to date the names of the commissioners of these paintings remain unknown. The 1854 version shown in plate 43 bears the sailmaker's name on the mainsails.

An earlier ship's picture (plate 45) that has long been a great favorite of folk art enthusiasts boasts a decorative paper border glued to the outer edges of the canvas face. This provides an interesting and unusual framing device for the painting, which seems never to have had a wooden frame. The ship appears to be a type of frigate used in the first navy of the new American republic, but the simplification of the artist's rendering makes identification difficult. A lively sense of motion is conveyed by the foamy waves, the billowing sails, and the streaming flags.

Life aboard ship, whether for a seaman earning a livelihood by fishing or whaling or for a merchant or naval sailor, could involve not only moments of adventure and brushes with death but also many lonely hours, allowing ample time for reflection on the comforts of home and on absent loved ones. Watermen who harvested the sea did most of their work in the daylight hours; their evenings were marked by inactivity. Some whiled away their idle hours by creating decorative or useful tokens for themselves, their family members, or their sweethearts, such as the mermaid made of whalebone in plate 44 or the whale's teeth with their intricately engraved and inked designs in plate 47.

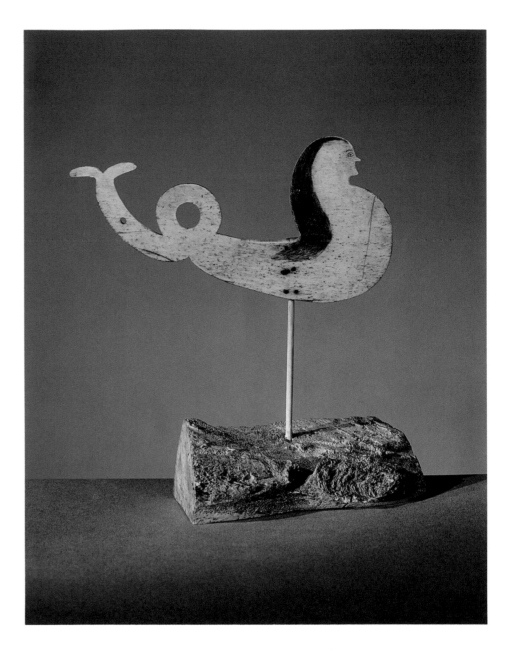

44
Unidentified maker, MERMAID, *United States, 1825–1850, ink on carved whalebone with iron, 9 × 8 × 3 inches (57.908.1).*

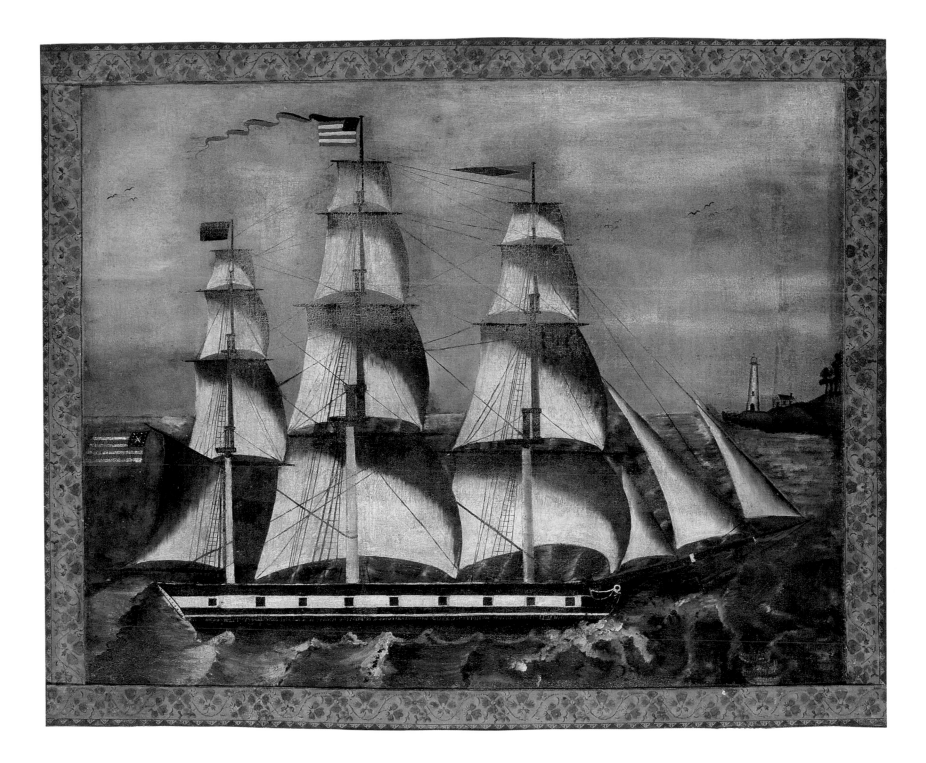

45
Unidentified artist, SHIP WITH
PAPER BORDER, *United States,
1805–1825, oil on canvas with
block-printed paper border, 36¹/₂ ×
45 inches (58.111.3).*

Not surprisingly, the narrative and symbolic details on such pieces varied widely among makers. Patriotic devices and designs associated with sea lore and life at sea were among the most common motifs. Mermaids and mermen, whose alluring beauty is emblematic of the appeal of the unknown, have a long tradition in American folk art made both by seamen and by others, including fraktur artists of German extraction (see plate 46). Other examples of the mythical temptress and her cohort appear on tombstones, on textiles, and in a variety of drawings.

The two teeth (plate 47) from the lower jaw of a sperm whale were probably acquired by the unidentified maker from his ship's catch, or bartered for with other goods or labor, to create a bit of scrimshaw— the term for the small carvings and engravings on whalebone, ivory, and wood made by sailors in their spare time. These examples feature images of Justice and Liberty; the former, shown blindfolded, holds her scales aloft, while her companion bears a Liberty cap on a pole.

Many objects of this type were made during the late eighteenth and the nineteenth centuries. Most of the surviving examples date from after 1825, when American mercantile interests, and shipyards along the East Coast, expanded to compete in world trade. The scrimshaw illustrated here had a purely decorative function, but many pieces were fashioned as kitchen utensils, yarn winders, corset busks, and other devices for personal use and for household chores.

Americans have been intricately involved with the sea, its tributaries, and their resources since the first years of settlement and colonization. Industries of all sorts emerged and grew to support shipping and commercial fishing, both of which continue to be an important component of coastal economies. The harvesting of fish and shellfish was but one of the early enterprises that developed along the East Coast. Other natural sources of food, such as water-

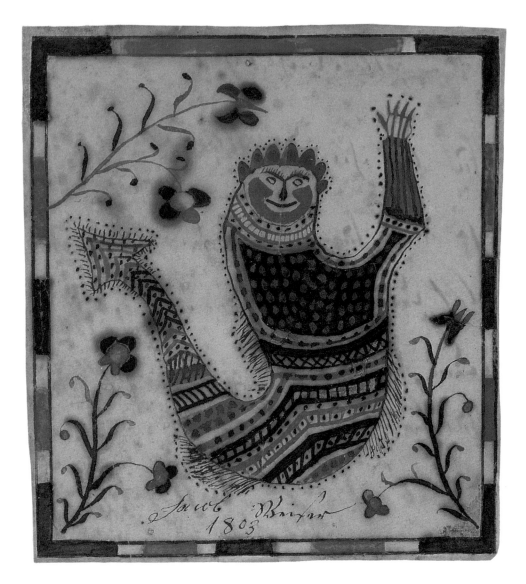

46
Attributed to Jacob Weiser,
MERMAN, *Pennsylvania, 1803,*
watercolor and ink on laid paper,
5⅝ × 5 inches (57.305.10).

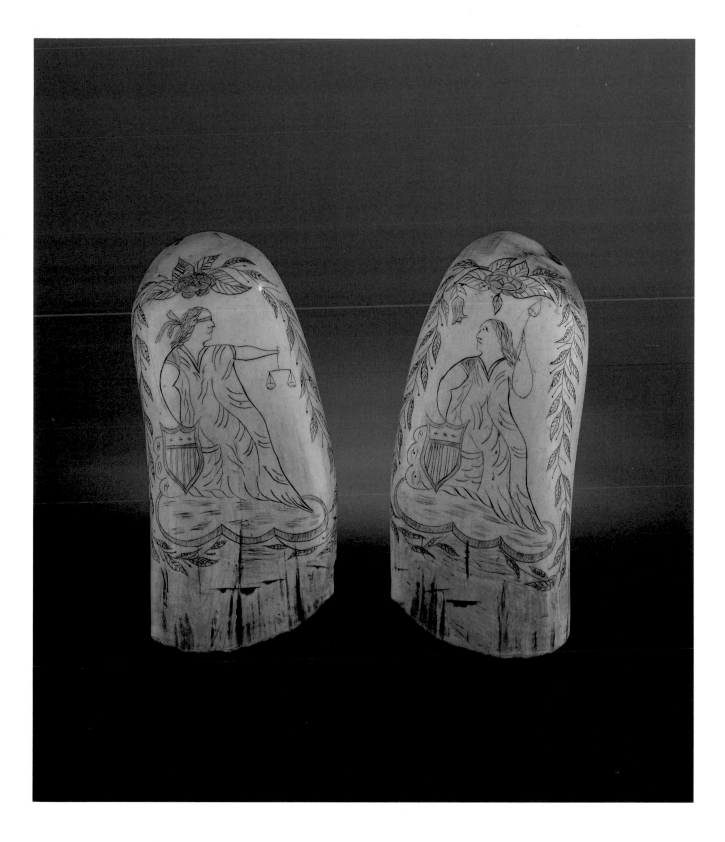

47
Unidentified maker, WHALE'S
TEETH, *United States, probably
1850–1875, 5$\frac{1}{2}$ × 5$\frac{1}{2}$ × 2 inches
(66.908.1, 1 and 2).*

fowl, had been exploited since well before Europeans settled along the bays, rivers, and estuaries that mark the coast from Florida northward, as well as inland.

The American Indians were probably the first to hunt waterfowl in a systematic way by using bird lures to attract flocks to their hunting areas. The 1924 excavations at Lovelock Cave in Nevada revealed a basket containing a dozen bird decoys made of tule grass, some with the actual dried heads of waterfowl attached to their grass bodies. These archaeological specimens are believed to be at least a thousand years old, and perhaps older. As early as the seventeenth century a European traveling in the vicinity of Lake Champlain gave an eye-

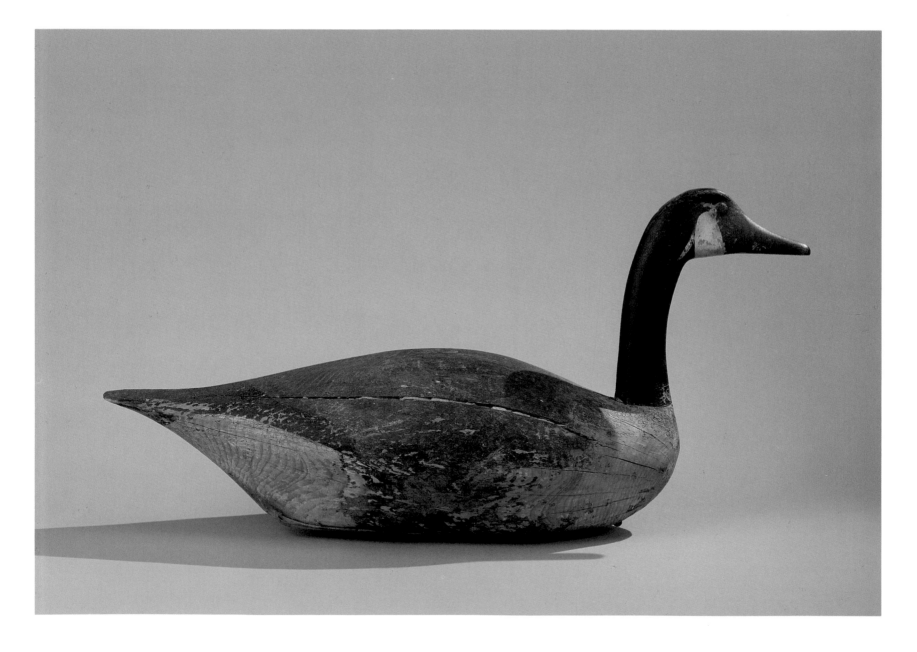

49
Unidentified maker, DRAKE AND
HEN MERGANSERS, *North
America, carved and painted pine
with leather and nails; drake, 5⁷⁄₈ ×
19¹⁄₄ × 6¹⁄₂ inches; hen, 5¹⁄₄ × 18 ×
5⁷⁄₈ inches; bequest of Edward S.
George (78.702.1 and 78.202.2).*

witness account of local Indians creating decoys by mounting stuffed skins of waterfowl on poles stuck up along marshes.

It is difficult to know precisely when European settlers adapted the Indian methods for luring birds. Most scholars believe that this was a gradual development and that the earliest forms were probably

stick-ups set out along the shoreline, probably in the style of Indian prototypes. By the late eighteenth century there are references to wooden decoys being used with floating rafts and other vessels at some distance from the water's edge.

There are surviving wooden decoys that date from the first decade of the nineteenth century, but most

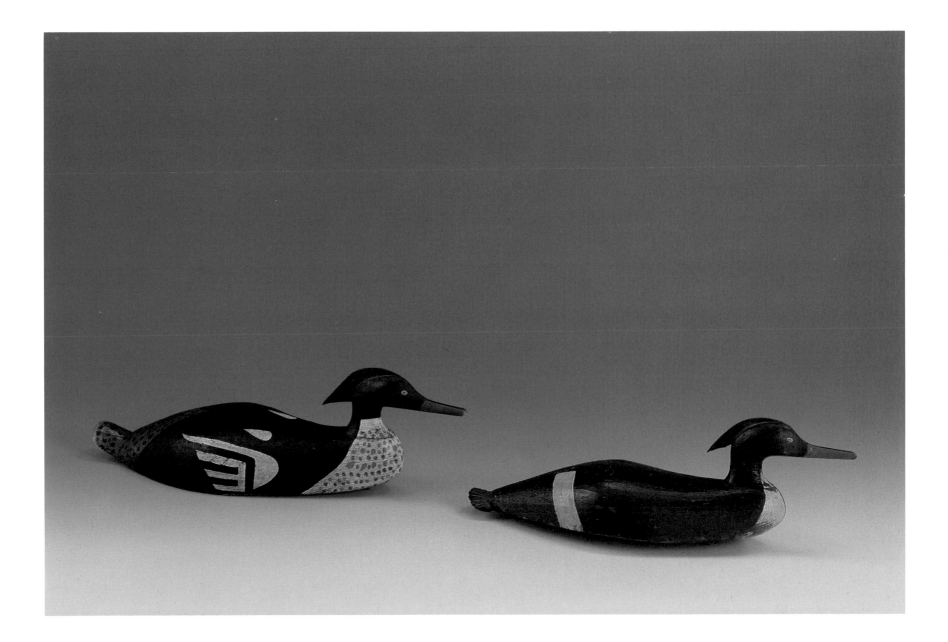

of the decoys collected today were carved in the late nineteenth and early twentieth centuries, when there was an established and reliable demand for game birds. The markets for edible wildfowl (shorebirds, ducks, and geese) and for flocks sought purely for their plumage (herons, cranes, gulls, and swans) emerged in the mid–nineteenth century in Atlantic coastal cities such as New York, Baltimore, and Philadelphia, and later in some interior cities. The introduction of a more efficient and dependable breech-loading shotgun also aided commercial hunters, who slaughtered vast numbers of wild birds, in contrast to sportsmen, who took relatively few. Regional styles of decoys developed out of the requirements of different waters and the varying talents of the carvers and painters. Production of certain types of decoys declined in some areas after the passage of the 1918 Migratory Wild Fowl Act, a preservation measure that declared illegal the sale of the birds, thus outlawing market gunning. Shorebirds were declared off-limits in 1924, when species began to dwindle dangerously.

The mergansers in plate 49 date from the market-gunning period and illustrate the traditional means of decorating decoys— with carving and painting. Both are sleek in profile, and the painted surfaces capture the spirit of the bird's plumage rather than slavishly copying it. Few early makers worried about conveying highly realistic detail, and few could devote the hours required for preparing such surfaces. Although the quality of abstraction is highly valued in bird carvings, the original makers viewed this stylization simply as an expedient means of production. Of primary importance was the general shape, the proportion, the coloration, and the overall effect of the decoy as a convincing lure. The mergansers illustrated represent classic expressions of these basic requirements.

Their maker has not yet been identified, as is often the case with early decoys. Most of the rural makers of bird lures were not particularly concerned with authorship. Some stamped their names for advertis-

ing purposes on the base of the birds or on the weights that were affixed to many decoys to keep them upright in the water; a name or initial, however, often indicates the owner or the gunning club rather than the carver. Professional carvers— those who produced thousands of birds for a living — were the exception rather than the rule, and these men usually did mark their wares, but most decoys were made for personal use by market hunters who had an intimate knowledge of waterfowl, their seasonal plumage, and their migratory patterns.

Edward James Phillips (1901–1964) was such a maker. Born in Dorchester County, Maryland, he began waterfowling in the area of nearby Tar Bay as a youngster. He started making decoys in 1920 and quickly earned a wide reputation for quality craftsmanship both in woodworking and in the painting of his birds. The striking abstract design of his Canada goose (plate 48) demonstrates his keen aptitude for capturing the salient features of an elusive, vital creature while simultaneously transforming its representation into a personal aesthetic statement. Like most carvers, Phillips fashioned a wide variety of species, including canvasbacks, redheads, black ducks, pintails, and widgeons, all for his own use.

John Vickers (1901–1974) was another of the decoy carvers who worked in Maryland, and his whistling swan (plate 52) dates from between 1930 and 1935, when hunting for sport prevailed. Vickers lived in the small town of Cambridge, near the Chesapeake Bay, one of the greatest wintering spots for waterfowl along the Atlantic flyway. Vickers's decoys are unusually bold in form and are often made out of Atlantic white cedar.

Joseph Sieger (ca. 1871–1959) was another decoy maker celebrated in his own time for a particular style of canvasback decoy. He was born and raised on the shores of Lake Poygan, Wisconsin, an area noted for canvasback hunting at the turn of the

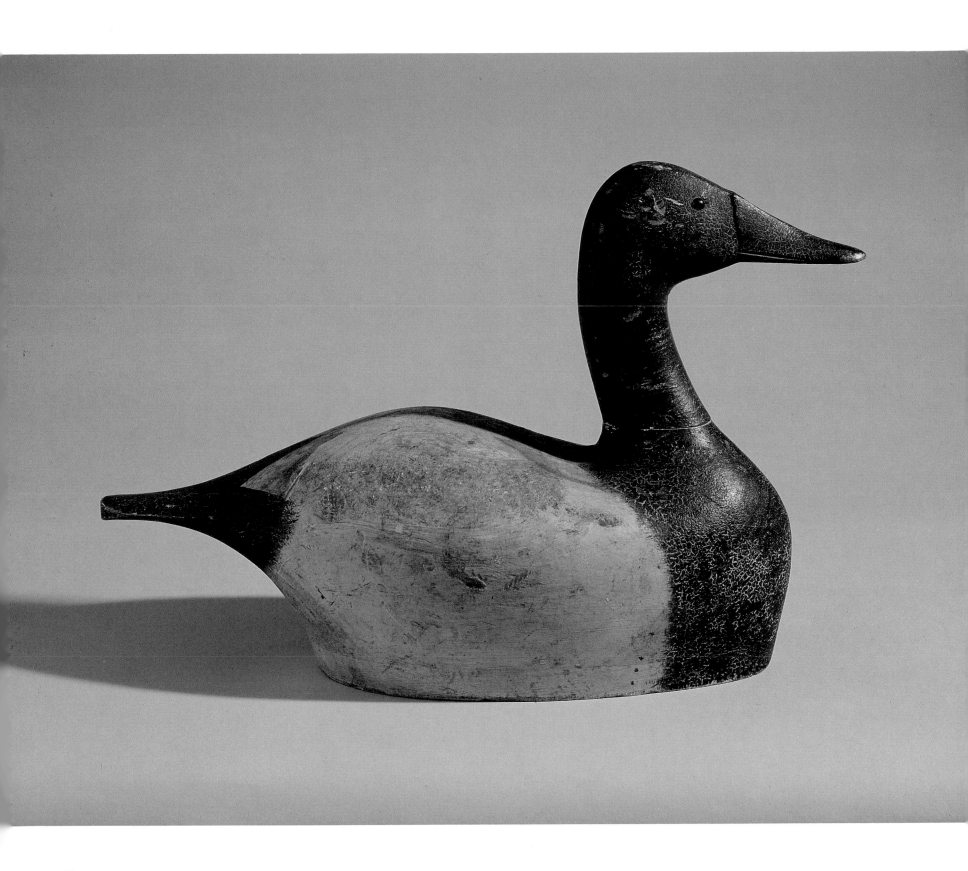

50
Joseph Sieger, CANVASBACK, *Lake Poygan area, Wisconsin, ca. 1925, carved and painted wood with glass eyes, 10 × 15½ × 6¼ inches (77.702.1).*

nineteenth century, when Sieger made the decoy shown in plate 50. Sieger was a wildfowl hunter and a proficient carver, fashioning his birds in much the same manner as August Moak, a contemporary of Sieger's from Tustin, Wisconsin. Sieger's canvasbacks usually have long necks and high heads, giving them an overall profile more typical of geese. This example's alert attitude, combined with the graceful, swelling form of his body, makes his silhouette an especially striking one.

Large water birds were plentiful along the Eastern Seaboard throughout the first three decades of the nineteenth century, after which their numbers began slowly to decline, principally as a result of unregulated hunting and an expanding market for them. By 1900 the populations of the larger birds were drastically reduced. Hunters began to turn to smaller fowl for both income and sport; shorebirds were particularly favored. Even the tiny sandpiper was eagerly sought; referred to as peeps, these little birds were usually cooked up in a stew called peep pie.

The hunting of shorebirds had been begun as early as 1850 (see plate 51) and continued to be a thriving business until market gunning was outlawed. The hunting of these small birds and larger waterfowl for sport did not become common until the 1920s; when it did, there was a revival of interest in and a renewed need for decoys, though most factory producers had gone out of business. A resurgence in decoy carving followed soon thereafter.

The yellowlegs decoy shown in plate 51b was made by an unidentified carver about 1900, just as the shorebird market was peaking. Holes were drilled in the bottom of these small decoys to receive a stick so the figures could be set out in the marshy feeding areas preferred by their living counterparts. This simply carved, graceful example still bears traces of its original paint. Both this and the yellowlegs by George Boyd (plate 51a) are carved full-bodied rather than cut from boards in the flat,

silhouette-type construction often seen in small-bird decoys. The latter were the earliest types used; they were easily portable and seemed to work just as effectively as the full-bodied variety.

The yellowlegs by George Boyd (1873–1941) was probably made in Seabrook, New Hampshire, also about 1900. Boyd's work is unusually fine in terms of both the carving and the quickly applied, stippled paint, which gives the effect of variegated plumage. This style of painting was used by a number of makers, though Boyd's method of outlining the wings with stippling just below their lower edges is a particular characteristic of his work. The nicely rounded shape of the head, with the eye placed slightly higher than normal on either side, is also typical of most of the birds attributed to him. Boyd made decoys of several different species of shorebirds, which he sold at Iver Johnson's store in Boston.

One of the most delicate and appealing of the decoys in the Center collection is the black-necked stilt shown in plate 51c. The elongated form of the body and the minimal, though refined, painted plumage, as well as the subtle colors of the paint, are all successfully combined in this exceptional bird. The bill was fashioned of a nail wrapped with cord and then either painted or varnished (or both), a method used by a number of New York and New England makers.

One of the rarest types of decoys surviving in America is the sandhill crane, associated with the Mississippi flyway. These magnificent birds were hunted primarily for their plumage, and only over a brief period of time. Less than half a dozen of these decoys, which were placed in fields and marshy areas along the flyway route, are known today. The example in plate 37, by an unidentified maker, was probably made in western Texas between 1880 and 1900. It is skillfully carved and painted and is in extraordinarily good condition.

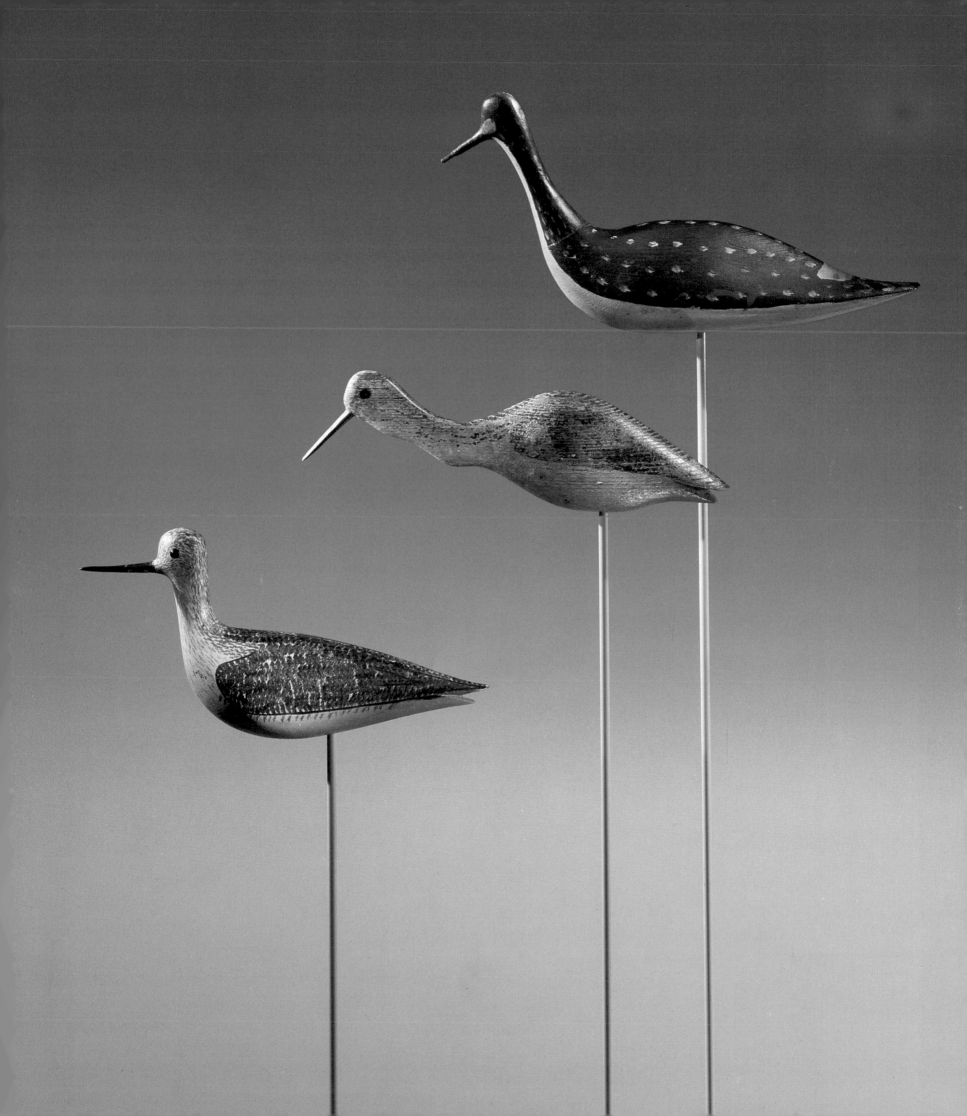

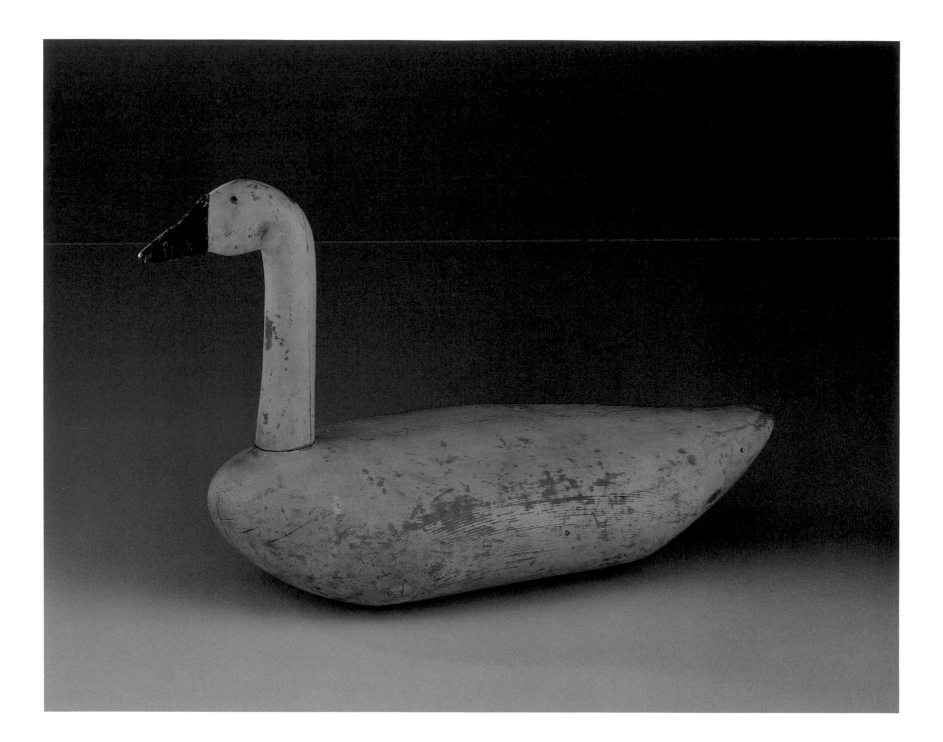

52
Attributed to John Vickers,
WHISTLING SWAN, *Cambridge,*
Maryland, 1930–1935, carved and
painted Atlantic white cedar with
glass eyes, 15³/₄ × 28 × 11 inches
(62.702.1).

Sandhill cranes were market hunted from about 1875 to about 1900, by which time they had become nearly extinct. Federal legislation passed in 1924 prohibited the market hunting of this species and thus curtailed the need for decoys. These birds are still protected by law, and the sandhill crane population is experiencing a slow but important recovery.

Decoys, like other forms of folk art, reveal a good deal about American life, particularly as it was lived in rural coastal communities in this century and the previous one. Except for those produced by large "factories," most decoys were made by local citizens who resorted to carving birds as a necessity first and a business last. As hunters who knew local waters, feeding areas, and market demands, these makers used their craft to earn a living. They took considerable pride in their work and eagerly displayed their individualism, particularly as the market expanded and bird populations inversely diminished. Some makers became well known, their birds favored for their effectiveness. Different makers were cele-

brated for different types of birds and soon became specialists. And as these makers' reputations increased throughout the early years of the twentieth century, so did the popular appeal of their birds. Some makers of working decoys also began producing souvenir birds that were collected by sportsmen and others. Occasionally a maker adapted a design for home use; this was the case with the wood duck (plate 53) by John O'Neal, which he fitted with feet and legs as a decorative piece to amuse his family.

The age-old craft of making decoys, or stools, as they were sometimes referred to, underwent a gradual but dramatic change after about 1920, with the passage of legislation banning market gunning. Although the need for lures decreased, some old-time carvers continued to produce them for sportsmen; a history and study of the subject slowly emerged, and in 1923 the first decoy exhibition was held in Ballport, Long Island. Subsequent shows followed as these carvings began to be valued not only as useful objects but as ornamental and artful works.

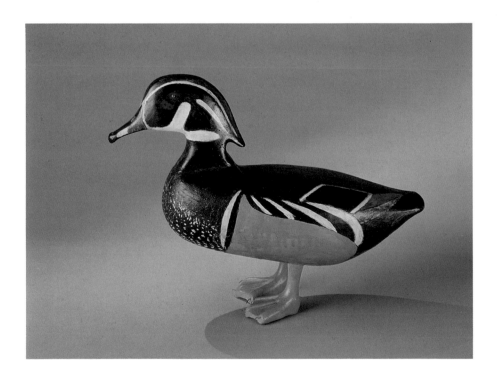

53
John O'Neal, WOOD DUCK,
Currituck, North Carolina, ca. 1945,
carved and painted wood, 8¹³/₁₆ ×
11¾ × 4⁵/₁₆ inches (84.701.1).

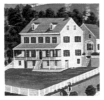

CHAPTER THREE

Places for Work and Living

Art historians divide American art into categories and discuss it in various ways because it was conceived and created for diverse reasons. The abstractions and distortions of modern art reflect ideas and emotions. Representational art of various periods captures the physical world of objects, places, events, and people. At different times in our history art has dealt with both the material and the spiritual world, and occasionally both are captured in the same work.

During the second half of the nineteenth century, photographs, readily available and inexpensive, became the chief competition for the art we now call folk. Photography produced, and created a taste for, very specific and factual images of people and places. Those nineteenth-century artists who had the technical ability to compete by rendering works in the highly realistic idiom now desired did so; those who did not often took up photography as an alternative source of income. Ironically, it was this representational art, imitating the appearance of things literally, that forced, in turn, the advent of modern art. By the early twentieth century art no longer had to be faithful to nature to be meaningful.

Appreciating the renderings of folk artists requires that we recognize the transition from realistic and representational art to abstract art, and that we understand the reasons for it. Most of the folk art featured in this book is neither wholly representational nor wholly abstract but combines elements of both. The views of places where average Americans lived and worked often express such common feelings as

pride of ownership and a sense of personal achievement; the objects associated with these places serve simple utilitarian functions. But while nineteenth-century views of towns and houses may appear to portray actual places faithfully, such scenes are usually devoid of the trash piles, dilapidated outbuildings, and other elements that might suggest social neglect or even poverty. Typically, middle-class, work-ethic values of accomplishment and growth pervade American house portraits and townscapes.

Many folk art objects portray the essence of their subjects rather than being faithful reproductions of them. We often credit this to a lack of skill and training on the part of the artists involved, which is certainly the case for many nonacademic painters, but this was not the only force that shaped pieces such as *The Preacher* (plate 72), or the Cheviot sheep weather vane (plate 66f). A weather vane, by virtue of its placement on the top of a building, was seen from a distance. Thus it functioned as a symbol as well as a signal. There was little need for weather vanes to be slavishly descriptive, as long as they were clearly directional. Surely the makers of vanes knew this; it is unlikely that, as craftspeople, they did not recognize how and to what purpose their labor was spent.

The Preacher and other similar objects whose provenances are now obscure pose related questions that are not easily answered. It may be noted that such pieces often seem more symbolic than realistic and may have been intended to spark the imagination or to aid memory and identification. Much early advertising art falls into this category.

Detail of plate 60

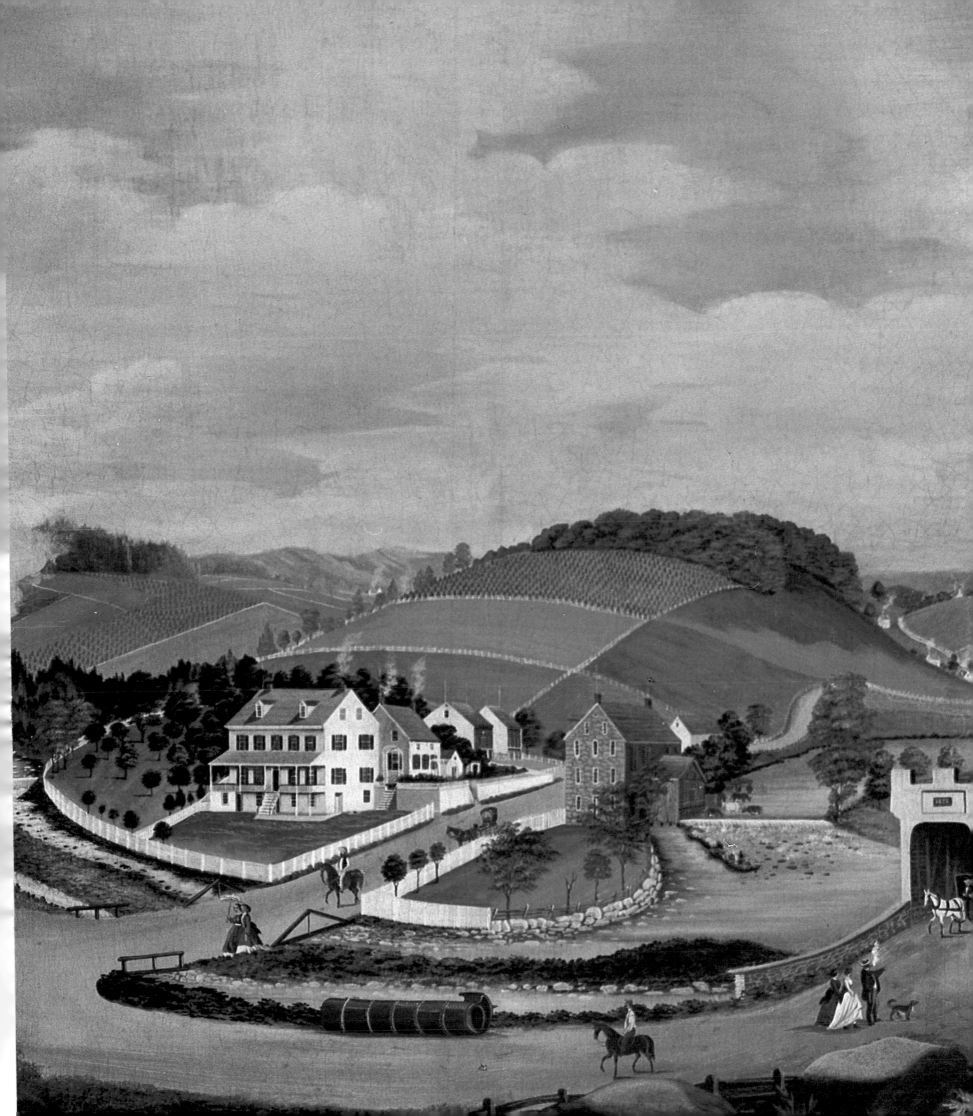

The sense of pride and accomplishment reflected in nineteenth-century townscapes is intricately tied to the invigorating effect of a frontier that was being pushed ever westward. Many historians and theoreticians have commented on the relationship of American expansion to the constant evolution of human endeavors, including the establishment of the governments, institutions, and systems of all sorts that shaped both the nation's and Americans' attitudes. Town views such as Hidley's offer evidence of man's energetic efforts to conquer or at least to control the land. The viewer's attention is usually focused on man's civilizing stamp, a settlement surrounded by plowed fields or cleared land, with an area of untouched, heavily wooded countryside beyond.

Even more obvious records of man's achievement are found in portrayals of individual edifices and structures, such as *Train on Portage Bridge* (plate 58) or *Berks County Almshouse* (plate 59). Much of what is known today about the painter John Rasmussen (1828–1895) is contained in the records of the Berks County (Pennsylvania) Almshouse, an institution that figures prominently in his known work (plate 59). By the second half of the nineteenth century, most Pennsylvania counties had public, tax-supported almshouses, or poorhouses, where elderly persons without families and the destitute were given simple accommodations and food for as long as they needed them. Rasmussen was born in Germany and emigrated to the United States in 1865. From 1867 to 1879 he described himself in the Reading, Pennsylvania, directories as a painter and fresco painter; for a time during this period he also was in the painting business with a son, Charles. He was first admitted to the almshouse in 1879; his problem seems to have been alcoholism, since he is listed in almshouse records as an "intemperate." It was also noted that he "had frequented houses of prostitution," was "sane" but "not able-bodied," and was suffering from rheumatism. The artist was discharged on July 10, 1893, but was readmitted on March 3, 1894, and this

time the records state that he "had been in jail." He died at the almshouse in 1895.

Before 1887, when his rheumatism made it difficult for him to paint, Rasmussen executed nine known versions of the complex that served as his home for many years. These pictures were probably intended for workers at the institution, and all of them were based on a similar composition created about ten years earlier by Charles Hofmann (1820–1882), the artist responsible for *Henry Z. Van Reed's Farm* (plate 60). Hofmann was also a German immigrant and had admitted himself to the Berks County Almshouse in 1872.

The nature of the relationship between the two artists can only be surmised, but it is known that Hofmann continued to execute views of this kind during the years when both men were residents of the institution. There are, however, striking differences between their styles. Hofmann rarely graded colors from light to dark, whereas Rasmussen consistently provided such shading. Both men used bright colors, and their precisely detailed, large landscape views depict an orderly environment that seems inconsistent with the dismal existence suggested by what is known of their lives. As evidenced in other scenes discussed in this chapter, the two artists portrayed their environment as they wanted it to be, rather than as it actually was.

All of Rasmussen's almshouse portraits are painted on zinc- or tin-coated sheet iron, a support that Hofmann had adopted in 1878 and that apparently was available in the wagon shop of the complex. The institution's paint shop probably furnished paints for both men. The subjects in the corner vignettes and at the top of Rasmussen's view show almshouse properties; clockwise from lower left, these are tenant house number 2; a west view of the new hospital; the grain barn; tenant house number 1; the kitchen, supplying spring, and reservoir; and tenant house number 3 and the cemetery.

∧
55
Attributed to Joseph Henry Hidley,
POESTENKILL, NEW YORK:
SUMMER, *Poestenkill, New York,*
1865–1872, oil on wood panel, 23¹/₂
× *22¹/₈ inches (58.102.17).*

56 >
Joseph Henry Hidley,
POESTENKILL, NEW YORK:
WINTER, *Poestenkill, New York,*
1868, oil on wood panel, 18³/₄ ×
25³/₈ inches (58.102.16).

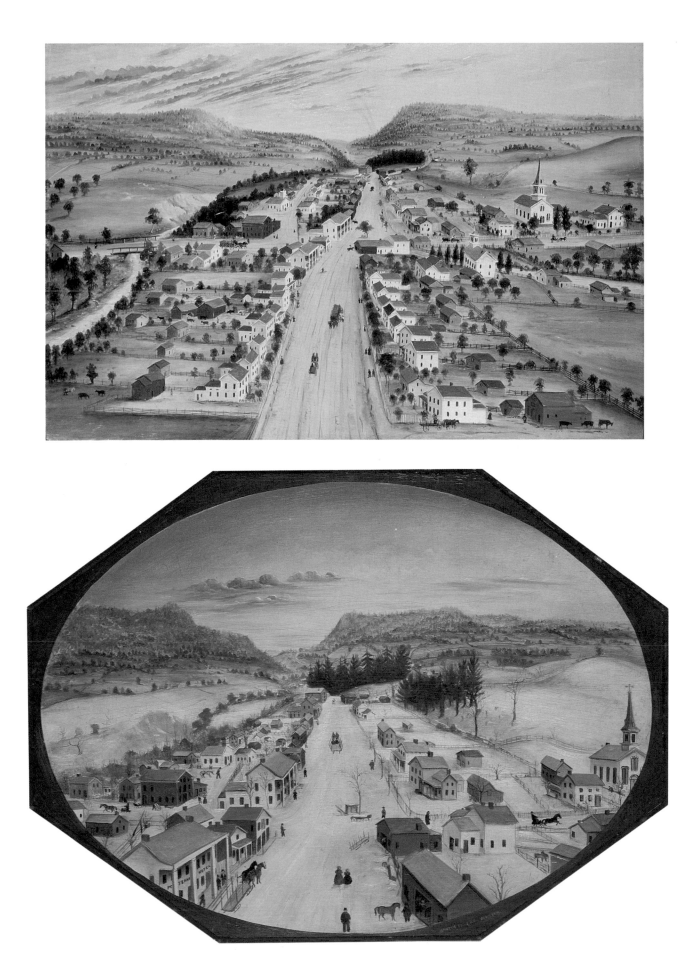

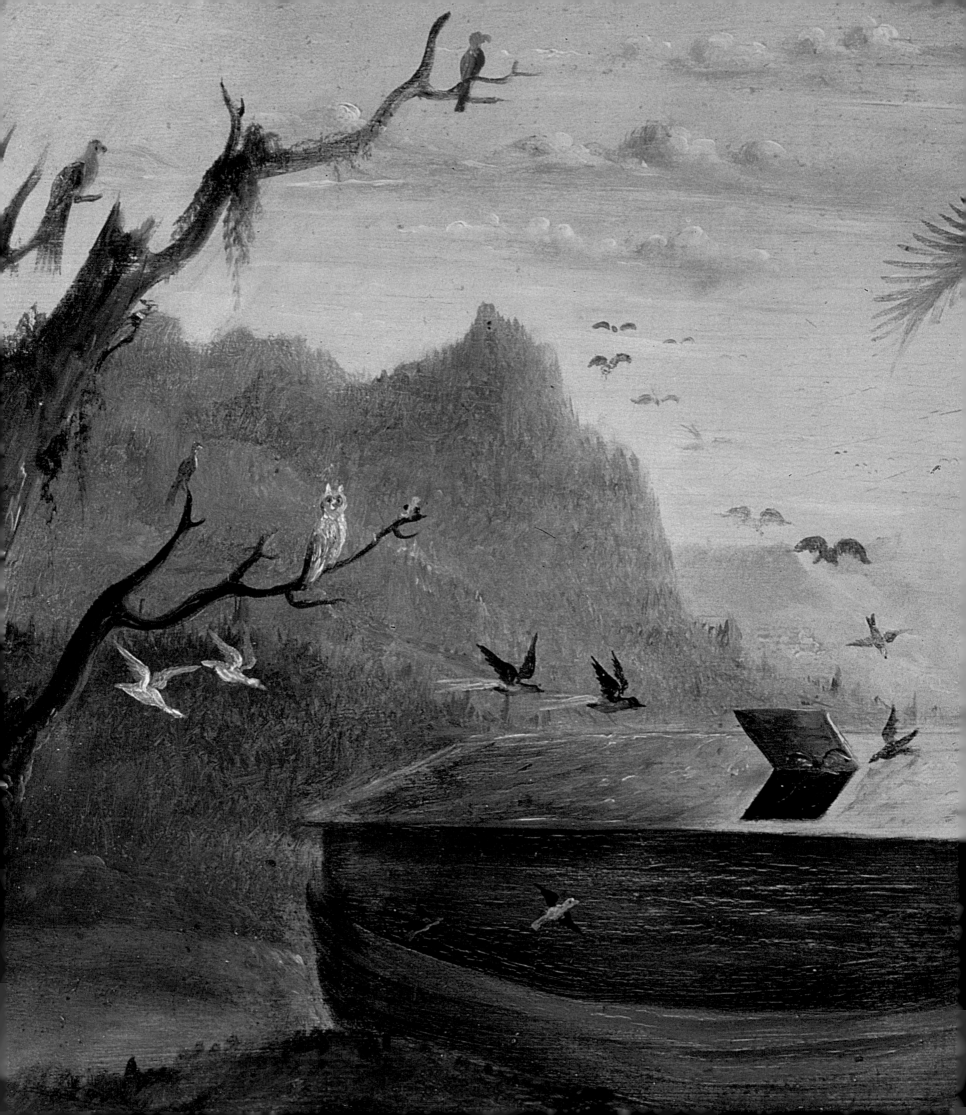

< Detail of plate 57

57
Attributed to Joseph Henry Hidley,
NOAH'S ARK, *Poestenkill, New York, ca. 1870, 25¾ × 26¼ inches (57.101.8).*

Like Rasmussen, Charles Hofmann is described in the almshouse records as intemperate and a vagrant. He died there of "dropsy" on March 1, 1882, and was buried in an unmarked grave in the paupers' lot on the hill behind the complex. His *View of Henry Z. Van Reed's Farm, Papermill, and Surroundings* (plate 60) is among his most notable paintings. This pristine fall landscape includes numerous informative details that illustrate the increasing industrialization of rural Pennsylvania during the third quarter of the nineteenth century, and it provides a visually pleasing and interesting record of the holdings of one proud Pennsylvanian. It also serves as an invaluable reference to the customs and practices of the day: note the lightning rods on all of the taller buildings, the ventilated cupolas that allowed heat to escape from some of the structures, the fashionable gingerbread decoration on the plum-colored dwelling on the far left, the variety of fence types, and the mule-drawn wagons that hauled rags from Reading to be made into paper at the mill.

The original Van Reed papermill in lower Heidelberg Township was built by a third-generation Dutch immigrant, Henry Van Reed (b. 1780), but was soon left to his son, Charles. Later the operation was leased to Charles's son, Henry Z. (1828–1879), who assumed ownership of the property in 1859. Five versions of this picture were created by Hofmann for Van Reed. According to a local legend, Van Reed paid the artist five dollars and a quart of whiskey for the first painting, then requested four more— one for each of his children— paying five dollars plus another quart of whiskey for each subsequent canvas.

The view of *Eagle Mills* (plate 61) is somewhat similar to the Van Reed picture in its quality and detail, though it was created not in Pennsylvania but in New York, not far from Poestenkill, where the artist Joseph H. Hidley worked. Former owners of this picture ascribed it to Thomas Wilson, and in one record stated that it was signed by him. (No signature has been located on the front of the painting, and the reverse is now obscured by lining canvas.) There was a Thomas Wilson (active 1847–1855), a painter, in Albany as early as 1847–1848; sometime between 1850 and 1855 he moved to Greenbush, in Rensselaer County, where he was listed as a carriage painter. Presumably this was the artist of *Eagle Mills.* The picture's intricate grapevine border indicates the hand of a skilled decorative painter and relates to embellishments used on carriages and household furnishings during that period.

At the time the picture was painted, the village shown was known as Millsville. It was a typical country town, with 125 inhabitants, twenty houses, a store, a tavern, a carriage shop, and a mill complex. It has changed little since, and a visitor today would immediately recognize the intersection shown here, except that the mill, which burned in 1911, survives only as a brick foundation. As its painted signs note, the Eagle Mill originally produced "flour by the barrel," but it was later converted into a hoe factory. Research indicates that the picture may have been commissioned by Edward L. Roberts (1811–1879), who lived in the house in the far distance. Roberts was a carriage painter at one point, and perhaps Wilson was a colleague.

The sentimentality expressed in town and home views is especially evident in the work of such twentieth-century folk artists as Grandma (Anna Robertson) Moses, Mattie Lou O'Kelly, and Queena Stovall, but "memory pictures," as they are sometimes called, have existed for many years. For example, *The Residence of David Twining 1787* (plate 62) was painted by Edward Hicks (1780–1849) sometime between 1845 and 1848. Hicks, who is better known for his many depictions of the Peaceable Kingdom, is discussed in some detail in chapter 5. He was born in Attleborough, Bucks County, Pennsylvania, on April 4, 1780, the son of Isaac and Catherine Hicks. After Catherine's death in 1781, Isaac Hicks was unable to keep the family

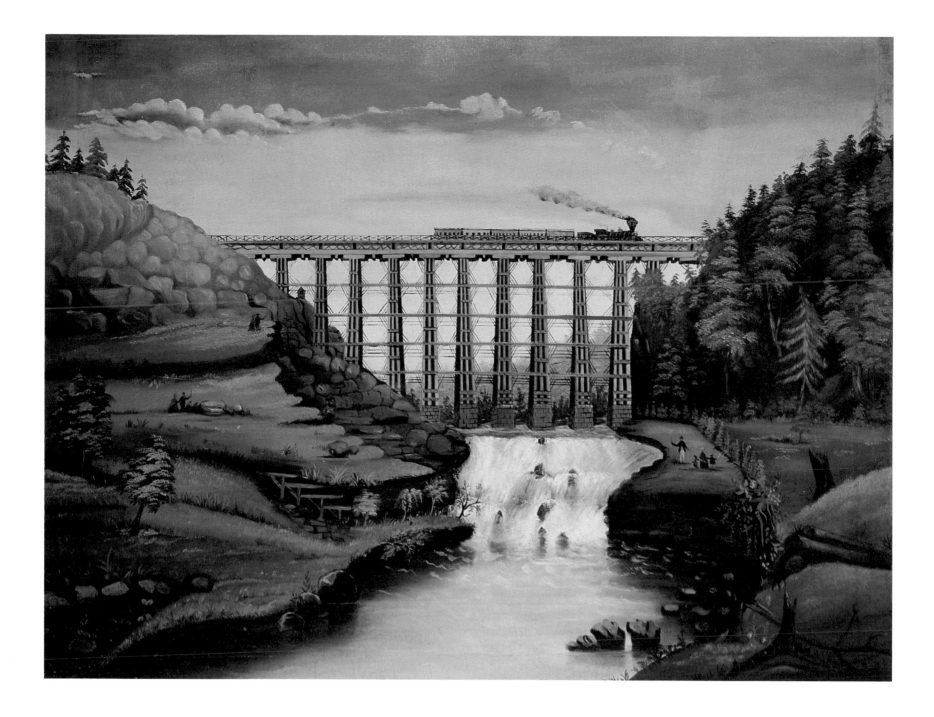

58
Unidentified artist, TRAIN ON
PORTAGE BRIDGE, *possibly New
York State, 1852–1875, oil on
canvas, 33 × 42 inches (58.102.5).*

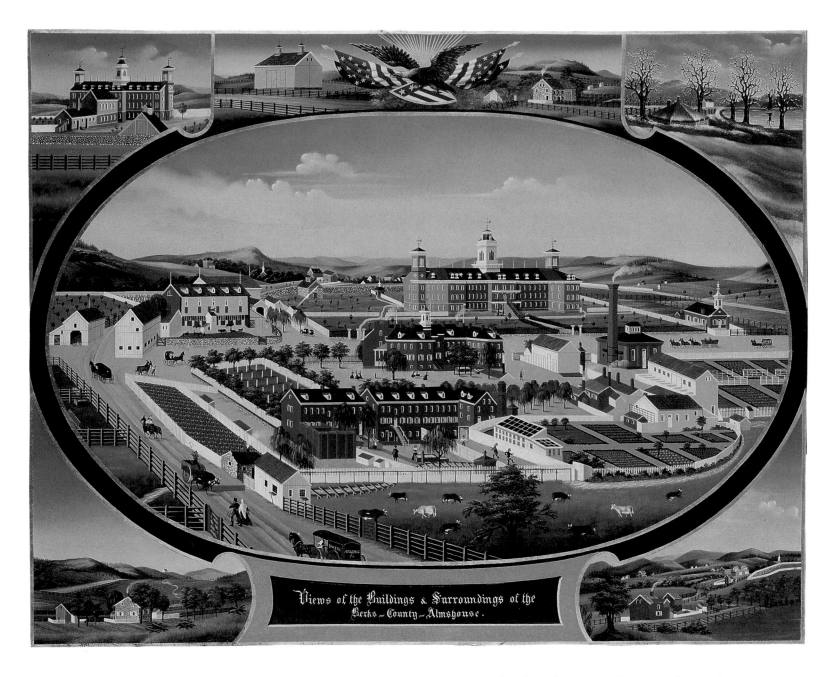

Views of the Buildings & Surroundings of the
Berks—County—Almshouse.

together, and in 1785 David and Elizabeth Twining took the boy to live with them and their children at their farm. The Twinings were staunch Quakers, as was Edward's paternal grandmother, and the artist himself eventually became a Quaker preacher.

The Twining farm, located on Buck Road in Newtown Township, Bucks County, looks today much as it looked in the artist's lifetime. During his later years Hicks painted several versions of this scene from memory in remembrance of what he considered the happiest period in his life. The Twining

family was close, and Edward was raised as one of them.

In the doorway of the stone farmhouse at right in the painting stands the Twinings' daughter Beulah, whom the artist claimed as his favorite "adopted sister." David Twining is shown standing at the gate, with his wife seated nearby, reading from the scriptures to young Edward Hicks. Mary Twining and her husband, Jessie Leedom, with their horses, are at the center of the composition, surrounded by the outbuildings and farm activities of a prosperous

∧
59
Attributed to John Rasmussen,
VIEWS OF THE BUILDINGS &
SURROUNDINGS OF THE
BERKS-COUNTY-ALMSHOUSE,
Berks County, Pennsylvania, 1880–1881, oil on zinc- or tin-coated sheet iron, 31 × 39 inches (60.102.2).

60 >
Charles C. Hofmann, VIEW OF
HENRY Z. VAN REED'S FARM,
PAPERMILL, AND
SURROUNDINGS, *Berks County, Pennsylvania, 1872, oil on canvas, 39 × 54½ inches (67.102.2).*

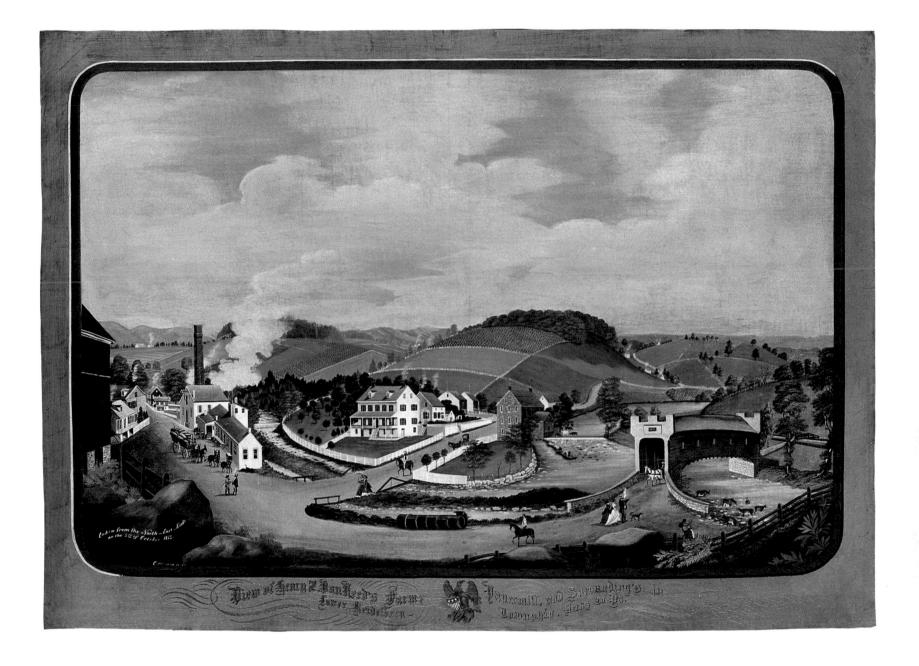

Pennsylvania homestead. All aspects of the scene are neat and orderly. There is even a tidy row of clean pigs in the left foreground, reflecting both the Quaker belief in order and cleanliness as godly qualities and Hicks's idealized notion of how the world should not only look but also be. The precision or preoccupation with order and detail evidenced here is typical of most "memory" pictures of this time and of later years: because the images also functioned as recognizable descriptions of places, people, and activities, they needed to be clear to be understood.

Edward Hicks's several versions of the Twining farm and others like it in Bucks County were created principally for his friends and family. His easel painting, regardless of its type, was generally aimed at the same audience, and his reputation as a painter was confined to his hometown area. Ironically, the paintings for which he is celebrated today represent only a tiny portion of his production as an artisan. He was a carriage painter by trade and practice and combined this with other, similar work, such as painting fire buckets and Windsor-style furniture, grain-painting woodwork in local

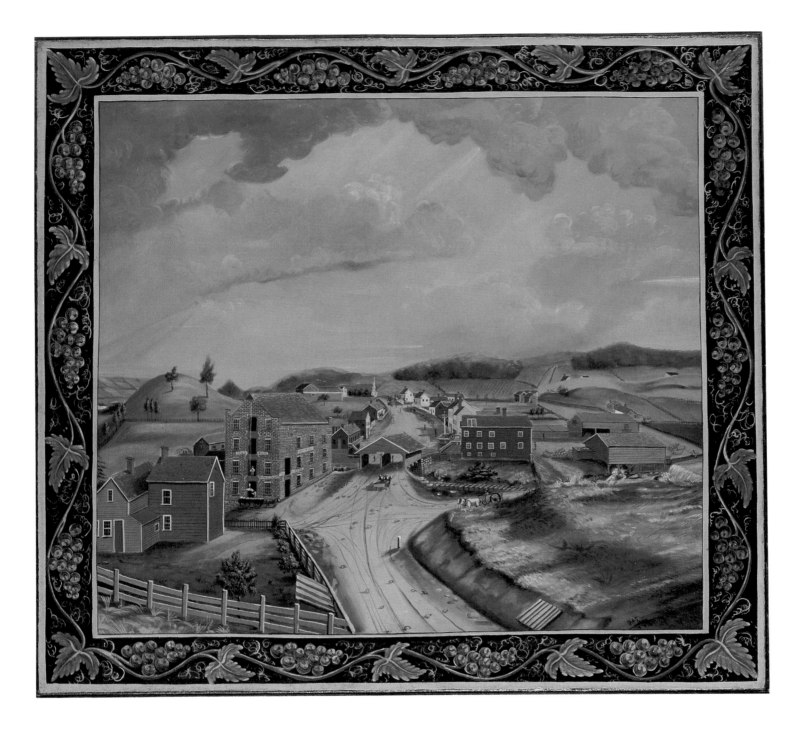

houses, and painting signs. A sign that hung in Newtown, made for Henry Van Horn, is attributed to Hicks (plate 63).

Signboards such as that for Van Horn and the Josiah Turner boot sign (plate 64), as well as the other advertising art seen throughout this book, were an integral part of a town's appearance during these years. Many different materials were used to

fashion early advertising symbols, but the most prevalent forms were simple board signs embellished with brightly colored letters and bold pictorial designs that reflected the nature of the business or of the goods sold.

According to family tradition, the very graphic sign made for Van Horn advertised his full range of expertise in woodworking. The sign was originally

61
Possibly Thomas Wilson, EAGLE MILLS, *Eagle Mills, New York, 1845, oil on canvas, 34⅞ × 40 inches (58.102.20).*

62 >
Attributed to Edward Hicks, THE RESIDENCE OF DAVID TWINING 1787, *Bucks County, Pennsylvania, 1846–1847, oil on canvas, 26½ × 31⁹/₁₆ inches (33.101.1).**

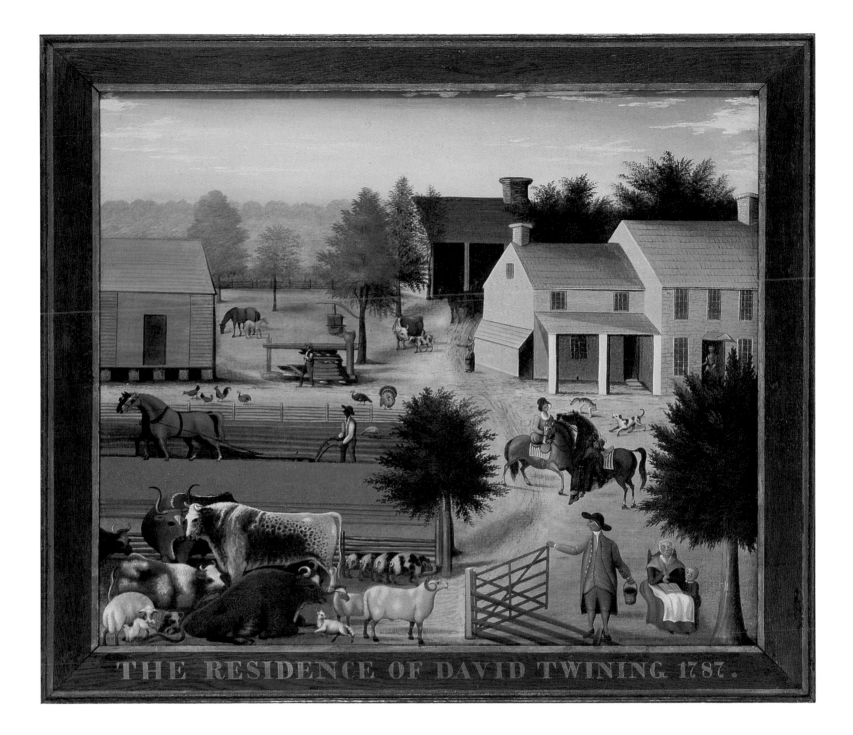

THE RESIDENCE OF DAVID TWINING. 1787.

nailed to the front of a frame workshop that stood across from Newtown Common from 1796 to 1798, at which point Van Horn relocated his joinery to another site. The sign was lovingly preserved by four generations of Van Horns as the work of "a famous Quaker minister," which Hicks surely was; in fact, Edward Hicks was Newtown's best-known Quaker. In 1796 he would have been about sixteen, just completing his five-year apprenticeship with a carriage- and coach-making firm. The sign itself makes use of the "cradle to grave" theme, a clever device indicating that Van Horn's carpentry work could serve his customers' needs throughout their lifetime.

Hung in position, the Van Horn sign, mounted flat against the building rather than suspended from a bracket affixed at a right angle to the wall, might small town. While the rooster, a traditional symbol of watchfulness, ranks among the most popular icons, there were many others. Consumers frequently selected specific forms because they related to the functions of the buildings on which the vanes were to be placed, or because of an association with local industry. For instance, large fish weather vanes survive that are known to have topped fish houses and seafood markets in coastal areas.

Sheep such as the example in plate 66f, made between 1875 and 1900 out of cast zinc (for the head) and copper (for the body and ears), may have been chosen for vanes used on farms where they were a significant portion of the livestock holdings. By the end of the nineteenth century copper became a favored material for weather vanes because it was easy to work as well as durable. The stylized, simple ribbing on this sheep was an economical and effective means of representing the animal's fleece.

The butterfly vane in plate 66d is made entirely of copper and brass; traces of its original yellow paint are still visible. Butterfly vanes do not survive in great quantity, though weather vane manufacturers' catalogues in the late nineteenth century (see figure 9) advertised them in several sizes. The several spots or dents noticeable on the butterfly's wings and on the surface of the Indian hunter vane (plate 66a) were caused by people shooting at the vanes to make them spin, a common pastime.

The horse weather vane and the Indian hunter shown in plate 66 are fine examples of manufactured vanes dating from the last quarter of the nineteenth century. The Indian represents Massasoit, the Wampanoag Indian chief who gave aid and counsel to the early colonists. The molds used to produce this vane originated with Harris & Company of Boston in the 1870s but were sold to the W. A. Snow Iron Works, also of Boston, in 1883. Snow in turn sold the molds to E. G. Washburne & Company of New York (late of Danvers, Massachusetts) in about 1940.

Surviving material documenting the American South and its towns, farms, and homes during the eighteenth and nineteenth centuries, either through folk or through formal pictorial renderings, is proportionately small compared to what survives from the mid-Atlantic region and from the Northeast. There are several important and revealing examples in the Center's collection, however, including a rare depiction of negro slaves making music and dancing on a yet-to-be-identified plantation (plate 68). This small watercolor was probably executed about 1795–1800. It was found in Columbia, South Carolina, and scholars believe that the plantation was located between Charleston and Orangeburg. The paper's watermark indicates that it was made by an English paper-maker, James Whatman, Jr., between 1777 and 1794. The costumes, which are depicted in considerable detail, are an extraordinary source for students of late-eighteenth-century American black culture.

Scholars continue to debate the meaning of the activities shown in *The Old Plantation*. The string instrument has been identified as a molo, and the drum as a Yoruba instrument called a gudugudu. Drumming as a form of entertainment and of communication among slaves was common in much of the South until the 1870s. The dance might be nonsecular and of Yoruba origin, and the stick and scarves apparently have a significance tied to the dance.

There seem to be no other examples of American genre painting of the late eighteenth to early nineteenth century to equate with *The Old Plantation*, which was collected in 1935 by Holger Cahill for Mrs. Rockefeller. In 1940, however, Mrs. Rockefeller added another early work, an intriguing Southern view, to her collection: Joshua Tucker's watercolor *South East View of Greenvill S. C.* (plate 67) was given to her by the artist's great-nephew.

Joshua Tucker (1800–1881), the son of Seth and Jane Payson Tucker, was born in Winchendon,

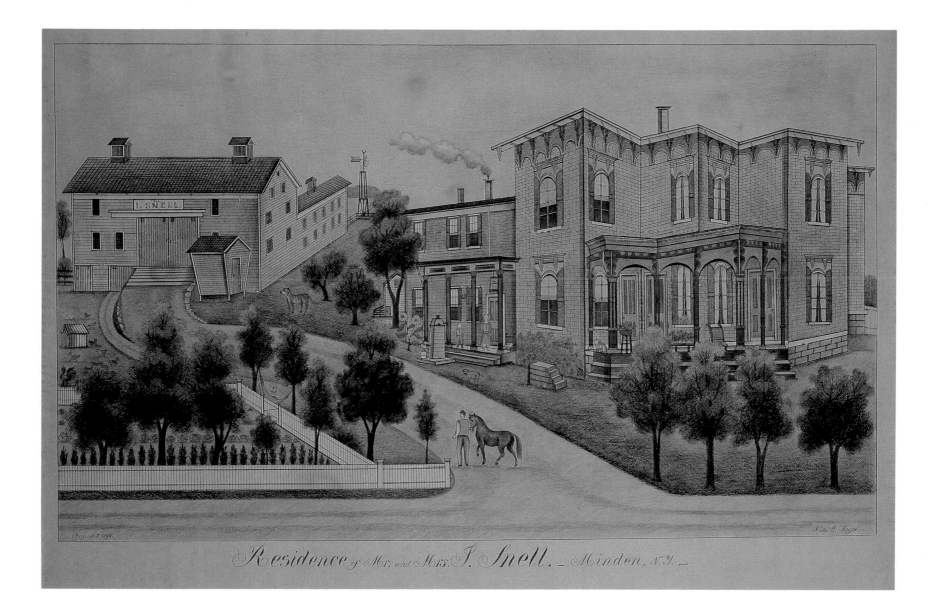

65
Fritz G. Vogt, THE RESIDENCE
OF MR. AND MRS. I. SNELL,
Minden, New York, August 4, 1896,
graphite and colored pencils on
wove paper, 26^{15}/$_{16}$ × 39^{1}/$_{2}$ inches
(78.202.1).

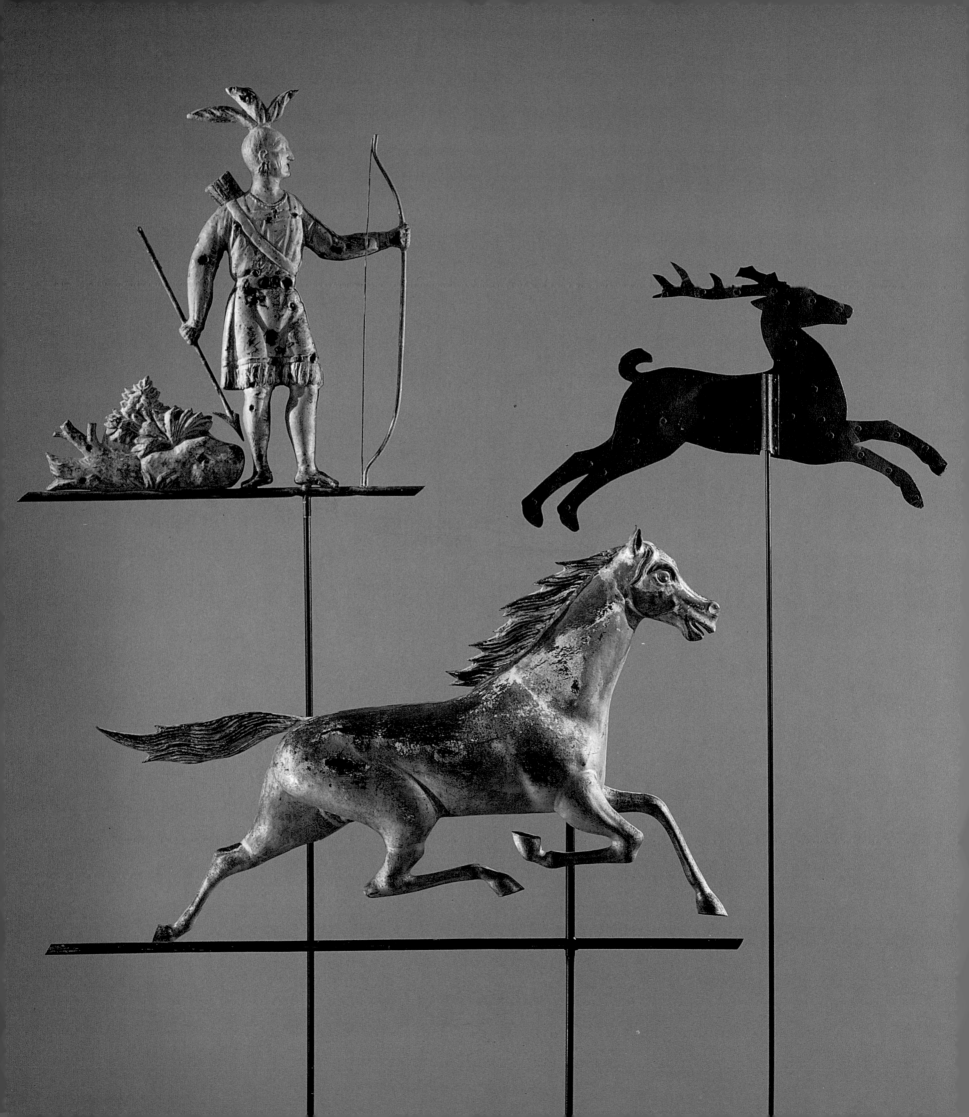

From left to right:

66a
Unidentified maker, INDIAN HUNTER, possibly Boston, Massachusetts, 1875–1900, painted copper, 32¼ × 30½ × 2¼ inches (58.800.2,1).

66b
Unidentified maker, HORSE, United States, 1870–1890, gilded copper and lead, 29⅛ × 48 × 6 inches (66.800.4).

66c
Unidentified maker, RUNNING DEER, possibly Quakertown, Pennsylvania, possibly 1890–1910, sheet and bar iron, 20¾ × 32¼ × ¾ inch (31.800.5).*

66d
Unidentified maker, BUTTERFLY, United States, 1875–1900, painted copper, 17 × 17 × ½ inch (62.800.2).

66e
Unidentified maker, ROOSTER, United States, 1850–1875, painted sheet copper, 18½ × 23 × 1½ inches (72.800.2).

66f
Unidentified maker, CHEVIOT SHEEP, United States, probably 1875–1900, copper and zinc with gilt, 20 × 29½ × 3 inches (32.800.6).*

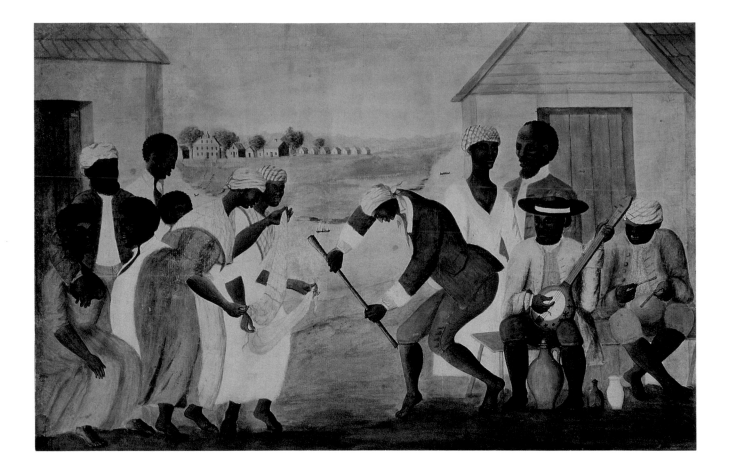

are shown carrying baskets of vegetables on their heads, a small boy sells papers, food vendors assist customers, and other descriptive elements give the viewer a lively impression of street life in an urban center. On close examination the individual figures look more like caricatures than real people and are reminiscent of the carvings Hamilton executed. One wonders whether it was what his painterly eye saw that influenced his carving or whether it was the quality of caricature found in his carvings that influenced his painting.

Lady of Fashion (plate 70e) is a fine example of the rich variety of tobacconist art. She may have been made in New York City and presumably represents a Cuban lady advertising cigars. In some Latin American societies a rose worn behind a certain ear indicates that a woman is married; one worn behind the other ear shows that she is seeking a hus-

band. Whether or not this is the specific symbolism intended here, it cannot be denied that symbolism in its broadest sense dominated the selection of the figural types for tobacconist carvings, and often dictated their gestures and details of their costumes as well.

The ideal trade sign is self-explanatory, and the *Turk* (plate 70a), by an unidentified maker who may have been from Monmouth County, New Jersey, is readily associated with the sale of Turkish or imported cigars. In this case the stocky, cylindrical form of the figure deliberately mimics the shape of the product he advertises.

Although the function of this figural carving (plate 70b) is uncertain, the man with the cigar continues to be appreciated as a delightful caricature. He is smaller than most tobacconist figures, but the cigar

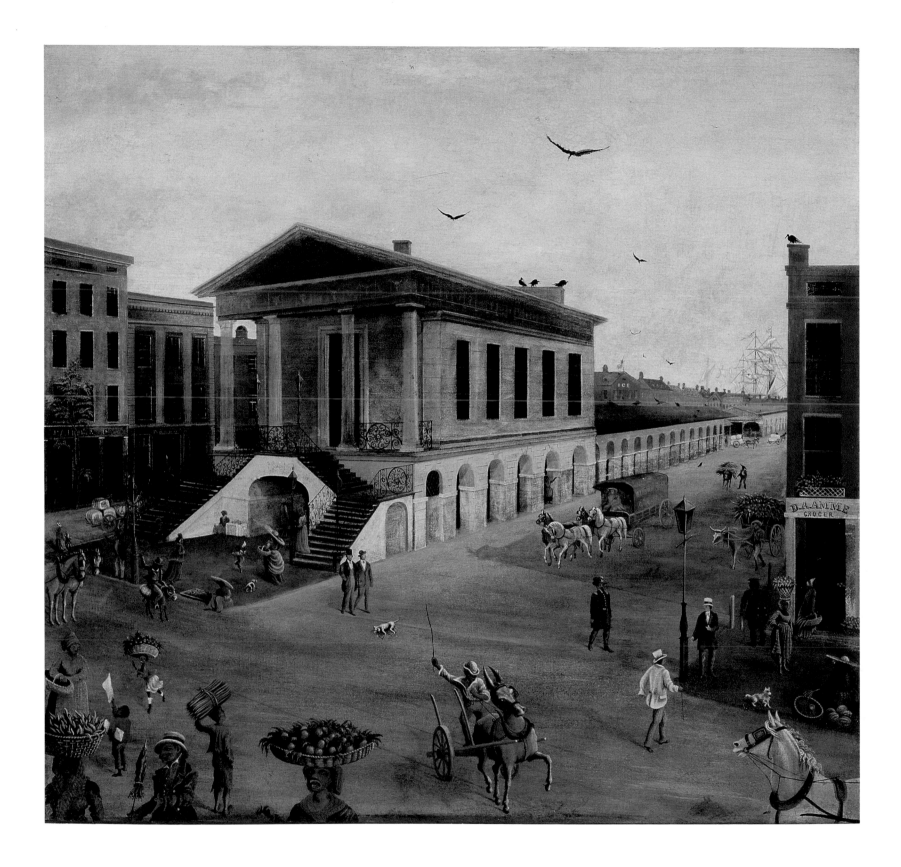

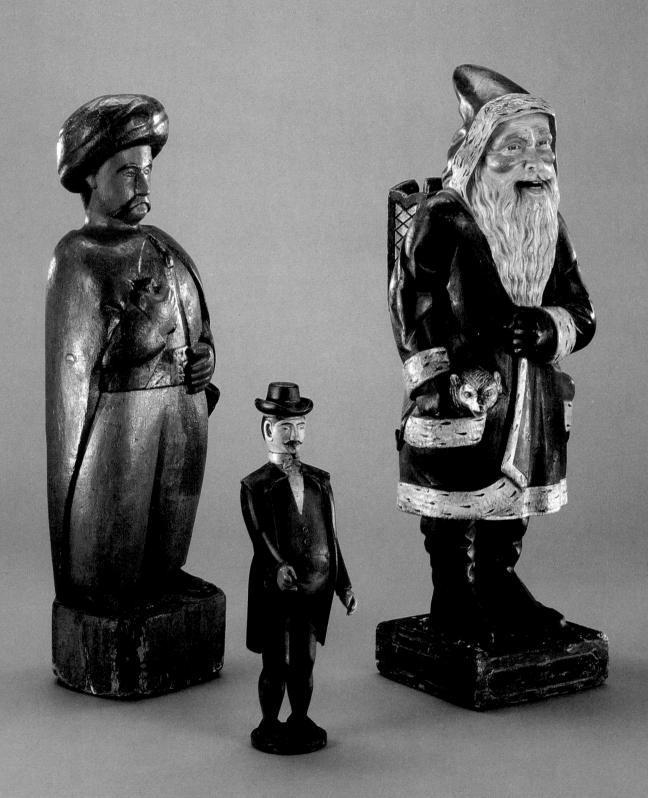

From left to right:

70a
Unidentified maker, TURK, *possibly Monmouth County, New Jersey, 1875–1890, carved and painted wood, 42 × 11 × 10½ inches (32.705.1).**

70b
Unidentified maker, POLITICIAN, *United States, 1875–1900, carved and painted wood and leather, 23⅞ × 7 × 9½ inches (63.705.1).*

70c
Attributed to Charles Robb, SANTA CLAUS, *probably New York City, 1875–1900, carved and painted wood, 45 × 14 × 13 inches (61.705.1).*

70d
Unidentified maker, OFFICER, *United States, probably 1875–1890, carved and painted wood and metal, 60½ × 11 × 17 inches (57.705.2).*

70e
Unidentified maker, LADY OF FASHION, *possibly New York City, 1870–1890, carved and painted wood, 68 × 11½ × 28 inches (57.705.3).*

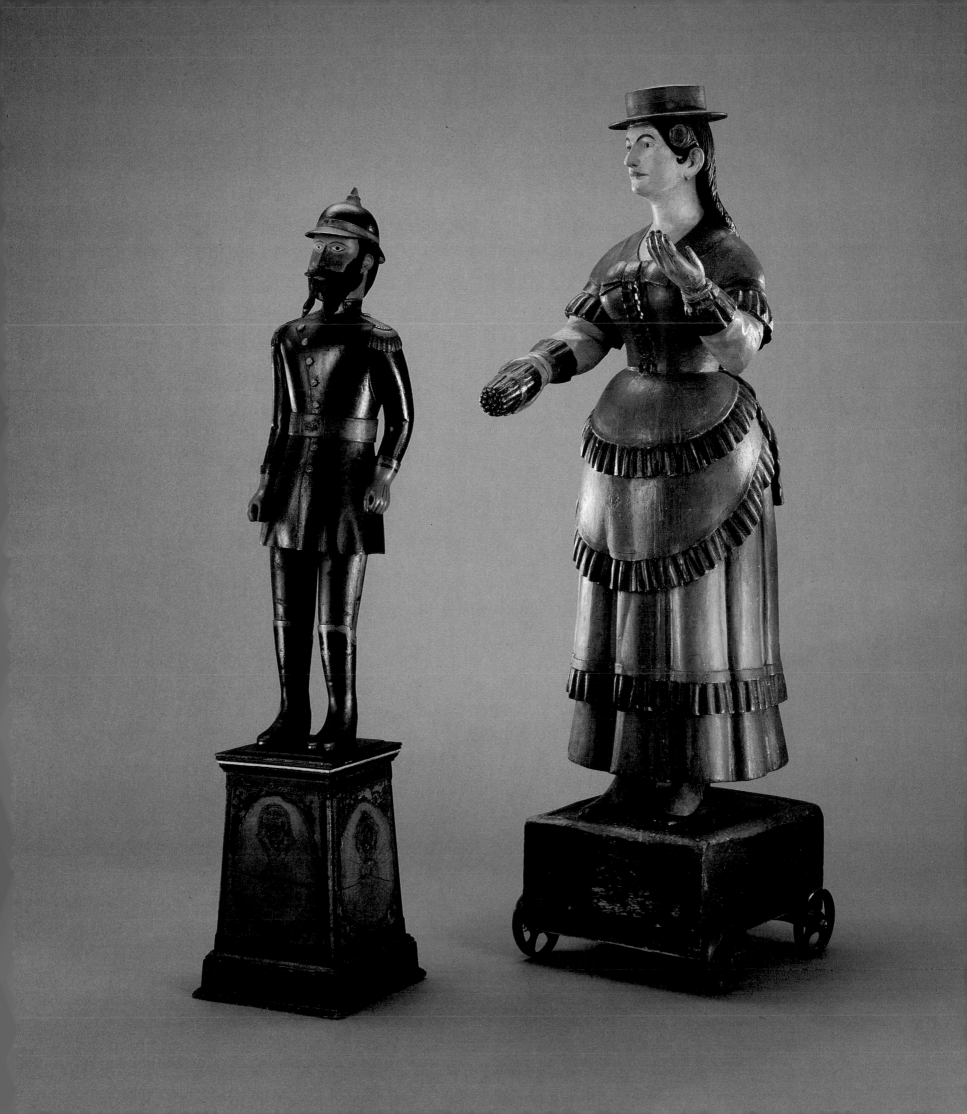

may indicate that he served as a countertop advertisement. Some speculate that the figure's rotund shape and dapper dress may have identified him as a politician.

The late-nineteenth-century carved figure of an officer (plate 70d) may have been a tobacconist figure or may have represented some other product or trade, while the Santa Claus (plate 70c), attributed to the celebrated carver Charles Robb (1855–1904), had an entirely different and quite unusual function. This figure originally belonged to a Lutheran church located on Bleecker Street in New York City. Charles Robb lived near the church and may have been married there. For more than forty years Santa's pack held programs, sermons, and notices of interest to the congregation. Then, when the church ran short of funds in the 1940s, the figure was given to an electrician in payment for work rendered. This use of a carved Santa in an established church may seem peculiar today, but in nineteenth-century society the deeds of Saint Nicholas, or Santa Claus, were closely associated with moral values and the promulgation of good works.

Related to tobacconist figures and other large, three-dimensional advertising art of the period were carousel figures; the Bactrian camel (plate 71a), attributed to the Charles W. F. Dare Company of Greenpoint, Brooklyn, New York, is an important example of the form. Dare was a maker of "toys, phaeton goats, carousel figures, and amusement devices of various kinds, including equipment for shooting galleries, swings, and cane boards." The factory was well known, and in 1899 the *New York Times Illustrated Magazine* stated in a story about the firm that "twenty-five carvers were kept at work all year round." The Center's camel, originally much lighter in color, wears a green and yellow blanket with a band of red and with gilt fringe.

We know little about the original function of *The Preacher* (plate 72). Perhaps, like other pieces illus-

trated here, the figure decorated either the front of a store or a store window in some late-nineteenth-century town; or possibly it may have been used in a house of worship, like the Santa figure. *The Preacher*, long a favorite among visitors to the Center, was collected by Mrs. Rockefeller in 1931. It was first thought that he represented Henry Ward Beecher, though the figure relates quite closely to a German monument to Martin Luther that was erected in Worms in 1868; Americans were familiar with the statue through pictures and replicas in metal. Here the figure has been reduced to the simplest terms, resulting in an image that is far more powerful than its source.

Signage, an important part of the American townscape, could be both symbolic and whimsical—tickling the fancy of viewers, generating associations and smiles then as now. Two fine examples of this include the barber pole (plate 71c), dating from between 1870 and 1890, and the *Elf at Shaving Horse* (plate 74), made in Pennsylvania about 1900.

The spiraling red-and-white-striped barber pole originated in England and served to indicate that the shop within was also a surgeon's office. When barbers ceased to practice bloodletting, they retained the traditional shop sign and its colors. The clever addition of the patriotic white stars on a blue ground at the top of this pole must have caused many a passerby to stop, scratch his head, and smile.

A surprising variety and number of folk art renderings reflect workaday tasks, and this is especially noticeable in advertising art. The elf sitting at his shaving horse exemplifies this impulse, and the unknown carver managed to treat a common activity in a lively and amusing manner. It originally functioned as a shop sign, and as such it was also meant to entertain; it is mechanical, and the arms and legs of the elf move.

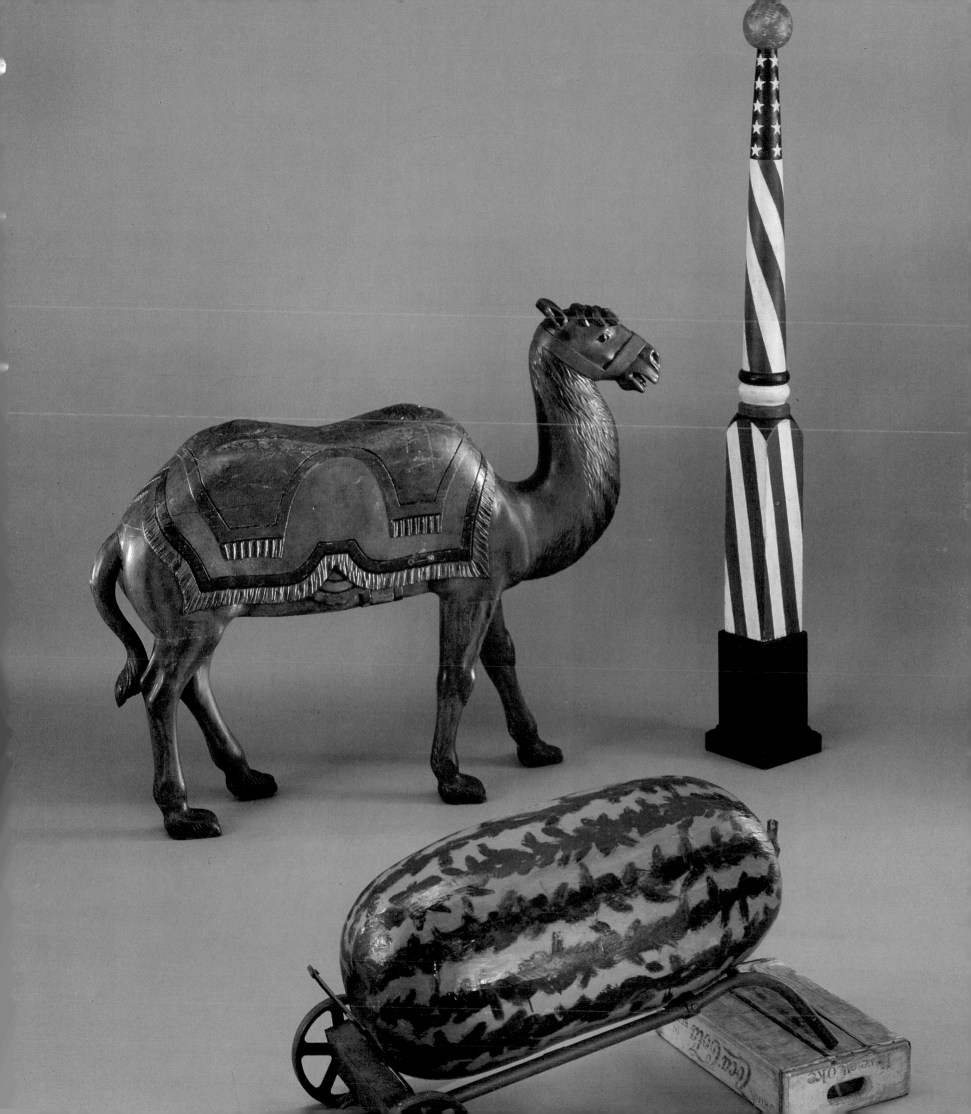

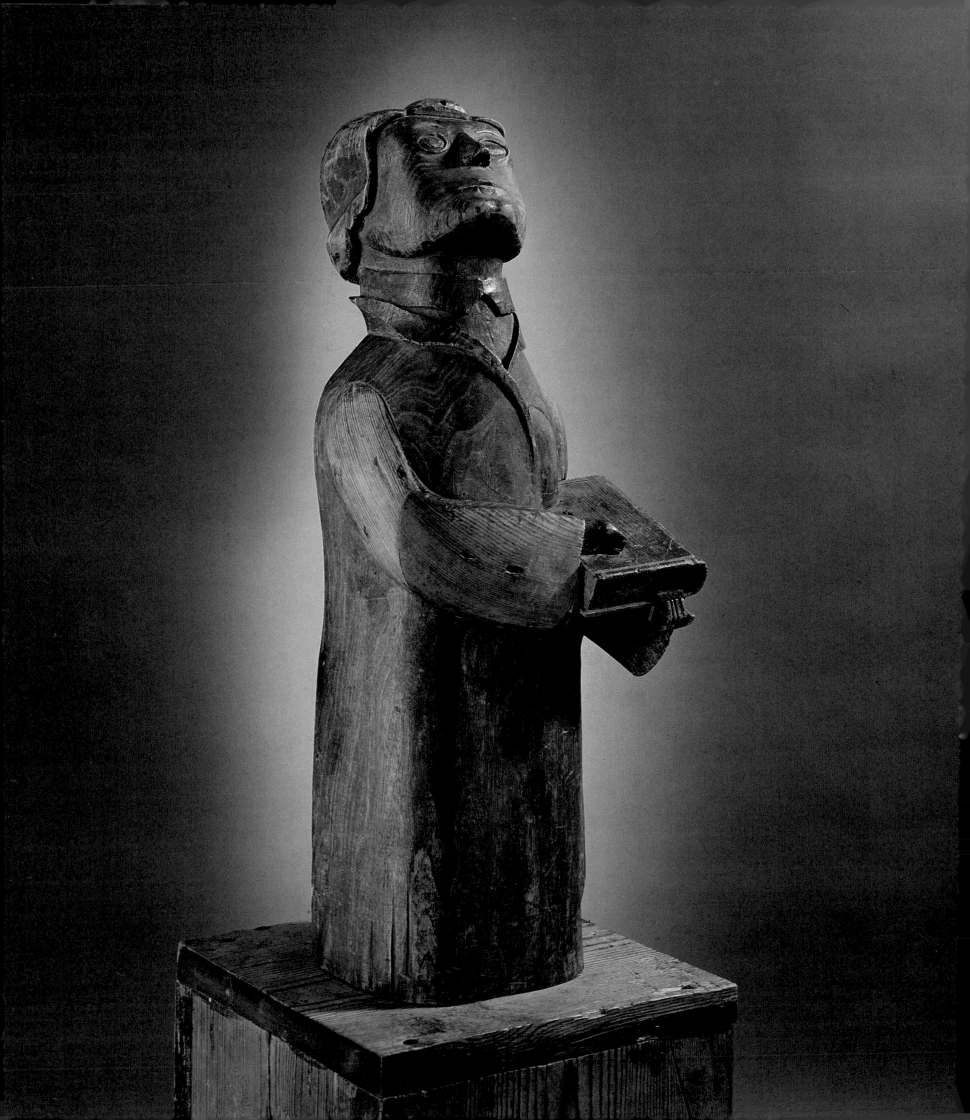

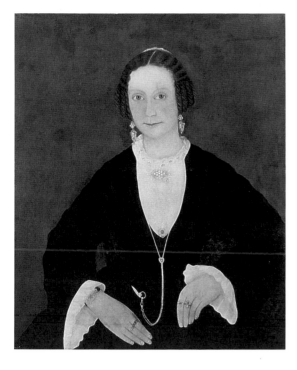

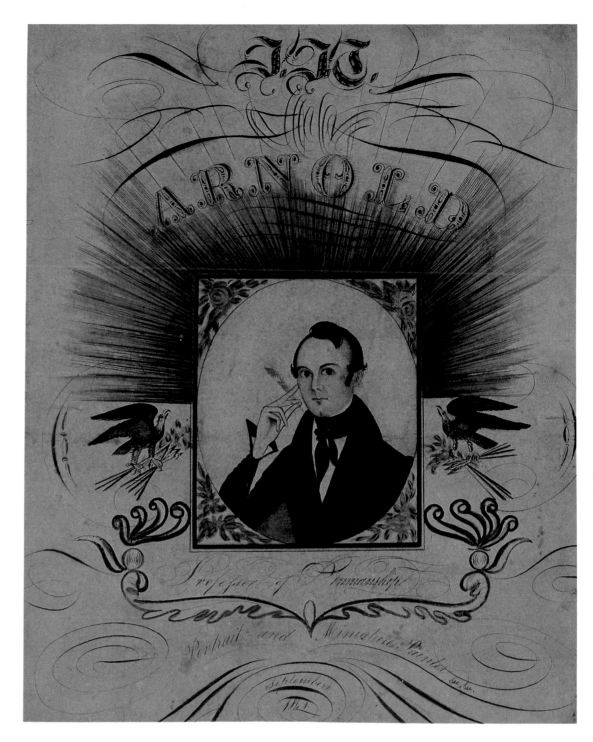

∧
Figure 10
Attributed to John James Trumbull Arnold, SQUIRE'S WIFE, *probably Pennsylvania, Maryland, Virginia, or West Virginia, ca. 1850, oil on canvas, 34⅛ × 28 inches (37.100.3).*

< 72
Unidentified maker, THE PREACHER, *United States, ca. 1870, carved butternut and eastern white pine, 21 × 7½ × 7¼ inches (31.701.5).**

73 >
John James Trumbull Arnold, SELF-PORTRAIT, *probably Pennsylvania, Maryland, or Virginia, 1841, watercolor, pencil, and ink on wove paper, 9⅞ × 7⅞ inches, Gift of the Antique Collectors' Guild (77.300.4).*

One of the most whimsical signs created by a twentieth-century folk artist is the watermelon (plate
71b) carved by the late Miles Carpenter (1889-
1985). It requires two strong persons to move the
oversized but naturalistic wooden fruit, which was
created in 1960 to attract customers to Carpenter's
icehouse and produce stand, in Waverly, Virginia,
during watermelon season. In 1963 Carpenter
began to fill the back of a pickup truck on the road-
side with additional examples of his carved work;
he had started carving in the early 1940s to amuse
himself when his sawmill business was slow.

Another type of signage that was commonly found
in early towns in America during the eighteenth
and nineteenth centuries but that seldom survives is
the wide variety of ephemeral paper broadsides and
placards. These were usually portable and were
often used by traveling salesmen and even artists,
including John James Trumbull Arnold (1812–
ca. 1865), to promote trade. Scholars believe that
Arnold's miniature self-portrait (plate 73) doubled

as such an advertisement. It is the most elaborate
example of his work discovered to date, and it offers
ample evidence of his considerable ability with pens
and brushes. The inscription "Professor of Penmanship," perhaps understandable in an advertisement, conveys a rather boastful and pretentious
self-description. Although small in size and perhaps
viewed as less than grand by Arnold's contemporaries, who were used to far more imposing, eye-
catching signage mounted both outside and inside
public places, it reflects the same concerns and aspirations as those more sophisticated pieces.

The identified examples of Arnold's large-scale
portraits date from about ten years after his promo-
tional watercolor. Although other portrait painters
had begun assimilating techniques that allowed
them to compete with the photographic processes
that were beginning to encroach on their business,
Arnold's work remained refreshingly original and
personal (see figure 10, *Squire's Wife*).

74
Unidentified maker, ELF AT
SHAVING HORSE, *probably
Pennsylvania, ca. 1900, carved and
stained wood, 33¼ × 11¾ × 30⅞
inches (80.701.2).*

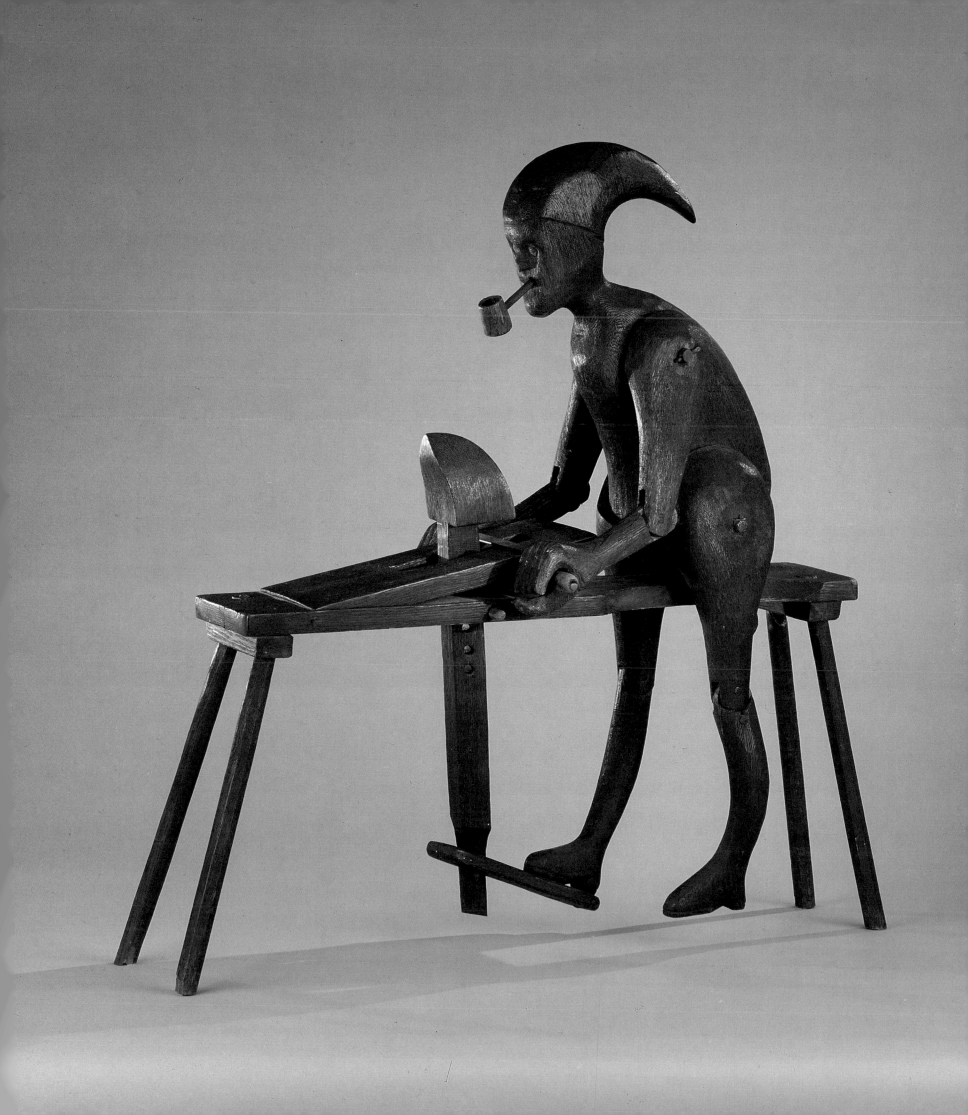

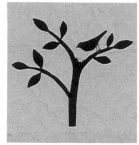

CHAPTER FOUR
Home Sweet Home

The study and appreciation of American folk art can be both rewarding and frustrating because the material is so diverse and is often intrinsically ironic and contradictory. For instance, the neat and rather plain exteriors of the buildings seen in townscapes and in portraits such as that of Deborah Richmond (plate 76), or the simple, abstracted surfaces of some three-dimensional pieces such as *The Preacher* (plate 72), seem at odds with the profusely patterned interior decoration found in many homes of the period. But it is this rich diversity, as well as the imaginative and sometimes incongruous merging of traditional forms with new trends inspired by advancing technologies, that can make the material both useful as documentation and satisfying as art. Many of the objects in this book display this tension between the old and the new, but nowhere is it more evident than in paintings that illustrate both household activities and furnishings.

A particularly remarkable pair of small portraits by Jacob Maentel (1763–1863), of Jonathan and Rebeckah Jaquess of Posey, Indiana, sets the stage for this chapter. These two inscribed portraits (plates 77 and 78) were painted in 1841, when Maentel was seventy-eight years old. Jonathan's portrait includes a fully rigged ship that, as the inscription makes clear, symbolizes his religious beliefs, and also his service at sea during the American Revolution. The pious statement at the bottom of the picture reads: "There all the ships company meet. Who sail with their saviour beneath. With shouting each other they greet. And triumph over sorrow and death."

The companion portrait, of Jaquess's third wife, Rebeckah Fraser Rankin, provides a splendid illustration of a colorful midwestern interior replete with boldly stenciled walls, a woven carpet, and a pinstriped, writing-arm Windsor chair. The couple's piety is again attested to by the Bible, with its tiny inscription, that Mrs. Jaquess has just laid aside. While the scene may seem contrived, it was probably based on the old lady's daily routine. Holding her spectacles in one hand— indicating that she has been reading— she sits by a window, with the curtains pulled back to provide better light, which casts a strong shadow beneath the arm of her chair.

Writing-arm Windsors were a popular furniture form in middle-class households during the first half of the nineteenth century, but they are usually associated with writing rather than reading. Some chairs of this type are fitted with small drawers beneath the flat arm surface or under the seat for the storage of writing implements and paper. The fancy and unusual example illustrated in plate 79 was probably produced in New England, though research thus far has revealed nothing about the maker or about the area in which the chair was made. Strictly speaking, it is not a Windsor chair, since it features fashionable aspects of the neoclassical style in its upper back, above supports that are basically Windsor. No other examples of this particular form have been located, which suggests that the chair was designed especially for the original owner, perhaps to match a set of neoclassical side chairs.

75
Unidentified maker, ALBUM QUILT, *United States, probably ca. 1850, various cottons with some silk details, 80¾ × 68¾ inches (85.609.5).*

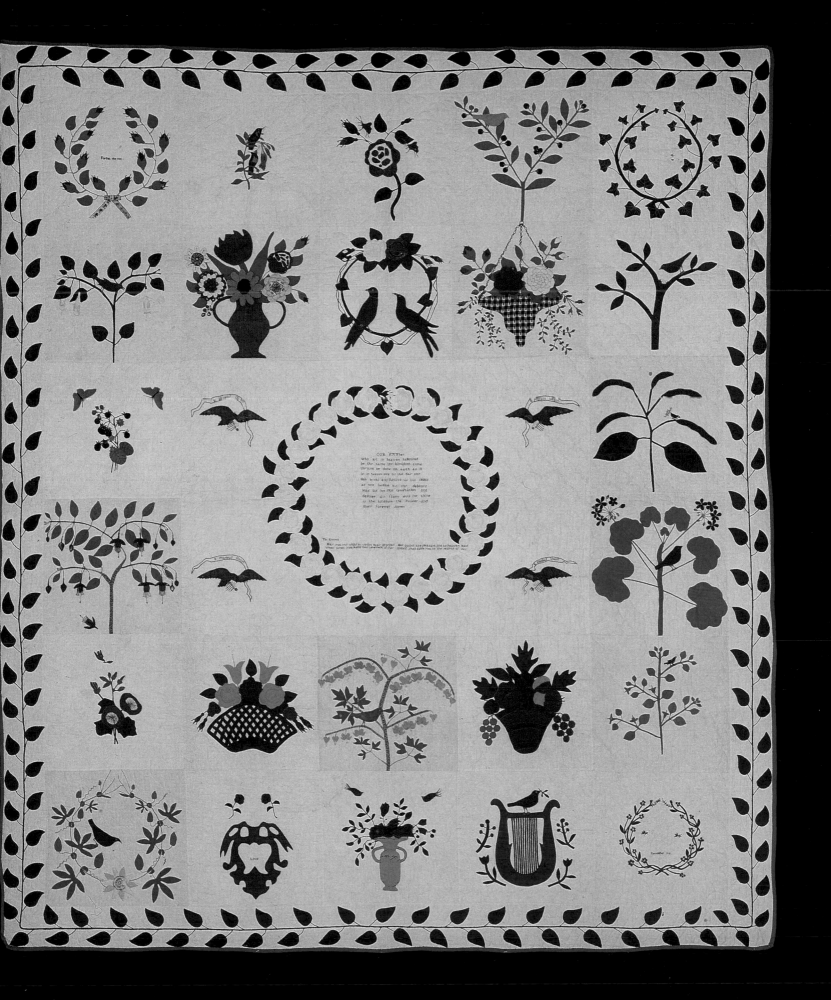

The decorative details on Mrs. Jaquess's chair indicate that it, too, was painted, though not as boldly as the fancy example. Together, the chair in plate 79 and the interior in Mrs. Jaquess's portrait reveal the variety of decorative techniques and the combinations of pattern and color common in the homes of average Americans before 1850.

Similar furnishings are seen in the 1832 painting of the Talcott family by Deborah Goldsmith (plate 81). This small picture is prized for its pictorial documentation of costumes and furnishings, as well as for its naive charm. The artist's preoccupation with small detail— the portrait was meant to provide this Hamilton, New York, family with a recognizable depiction of their home— is evident in Goldsmith's efforts to render the decoration on the ornamented chair backs, the figured edging on the fichu at Betsey Talcott's neck, the coloring and the striped pattern of what was then called the Venetian carpeting, and the graining on the cupboard in the corner. Even the brass hardware on the case piece is simulated, through the use of gold paint.

For several years before her marriage, Deborah Goldsmith (1808–36) supported her aging parents by traveling to towns and villages in rural New York and seeking commissions for watercolor portraits. This engaging record of three generations of Talcotts, all dressed up and seated in their well-furnished parlor, is among her most ambitious compositions.

The watercolor of the Tilton family at home (plate 80) by Joseph H. Davis (active 1832–1837) illustrates a similar taste for what to modern eyes is a disarming assortment of figured designs and surface decoration. Although his loose rendering makes the vivid, abstract patterning found on the furniture and in the geometric design of the colorful floor coverings in most of Davis's portraits seem exaggerated, this type of decoration was, in fact, a reality in many middle-class households. Although Davis's interiors do feature actual forms and styles

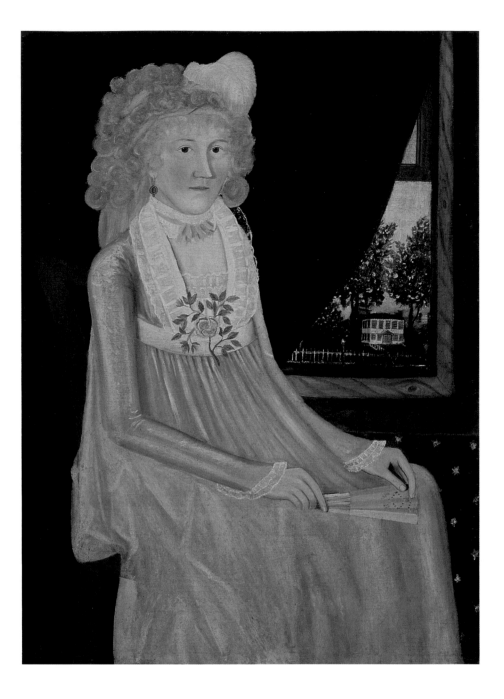

76
Unidentified artist, DEBORAH RICHMOND, *probably Sheffield, Connecticut, probably 1797, oil on canvas, 45³/₄ × 34³/₄ inches (74.100.3).*
Painted about 1797, this portrait is of a twenty-five-year-old New England schoolteacher who died unmarried in 1802. Many folk portraitists started their careers as housepainters or furniture painters and turned to portraits to make extra money; the unidentified painter of Deborah Richmond's portrait may well have been one of these. The attention lavished on the architectural features visible through the window, and the literal rendering of certain details of costume and interior decoration— including the early wallpaper and the grain-painted woodwork— suggest that the artist was deliberately trying to compensate for his inability to correctly handle perspective and three-dimensional forms. The fan Deborah holds descended with the painting and is also in the Center's collection.

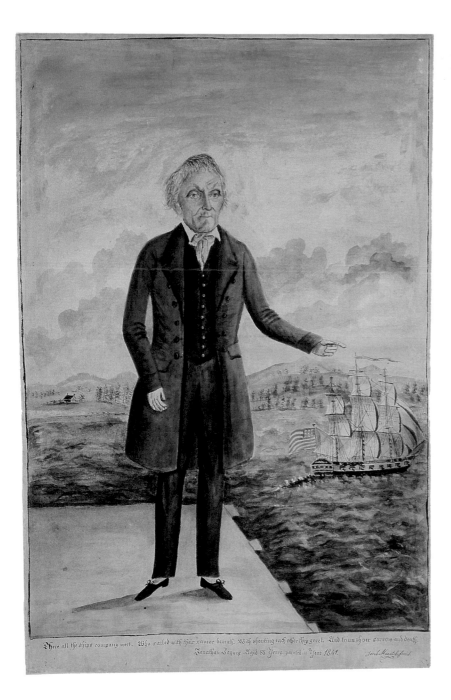

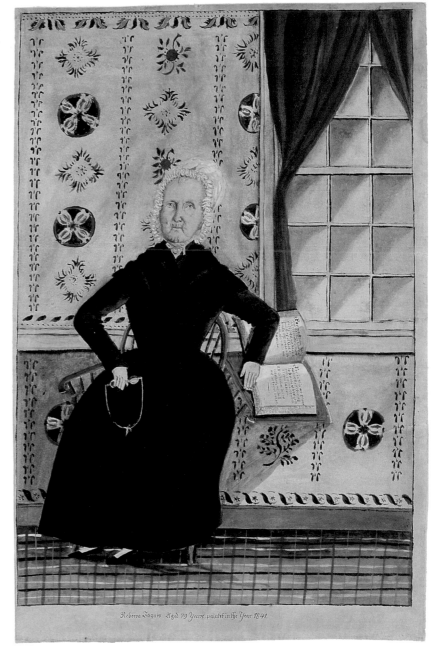

77
Jacob Maentel, JONATHAN
JAQUESS, *Posey County, Indiana,*
1841, watercolor and ink on wove
paper, 17⅝ × 11¼ inches
(59.300.6).

78
Jacob Maentel, MRS. JONATHAN
JAQUESS (REBECKAH FRASER
RANKIN), *Posey County, Indiana,*
1841, watercolor and ink on wove
paper, 17¾ × 11⅜ inches
(59.300.7).

of furnishings of the period, however, they really only function as decorative foils for his figures.

Some of Davis's portraits bear dates; the Tiltons' picture, for example, is dated January 1837 in a festooned foliate wreath behind the figures, a framing device that was used frequently by the artist. John T. Tilton and his wife, Hannah, lived in Deerfield, New Hampshire, at this time. Their daughter Isabelle is shown handing some flowers to her mother while her father reads the *New Hampshire Patriot and State Gazette.* The scene is one of domestic tranquillity, complete with a playful cat about to pounce on its young mistress. Few facts are known about Davis's life, but research on more than 130 watercolor portraits inscribed by him indicates that between 1832 and 1837 Joseph H. Davis, the "Left Hand Painter" (as he inscribed one of them), traveled extensively along the Maine–New Hampshire border.

The portrait of William Howard Smith (plate 83) at age five years and seven months, by Joseph Whiting Stock (1815–1855), is another fine visual document of one home's interior decoration. A companion portrait of William Howard's sister (plate 82), who stands on the same beige carpet with its meandering green vine, is also in the Center's collection. Stock's characteristic use of props to indicate the interests and personalities of his subjects is abundantly evident in both of these portraits. The hoop visible through the open door to the left of William Howard suggests one of the child's preferred outdoor activities. The schoolbook he holds is open to an engraving showing a battle between British troops and Indians; Stock actually glued it to the surface of the canvas, probably to reflect the boy's interest in soldiers or military campaigns. William Howard, who lived in Springfield, Massachusetts, eventually succeeded his father in the manufacture of carriages and stagecoaches.

Thanks to newspaper advertisements and a personal journal that covers his first fourteen years as a busy portrait painter, a good deal is known about Joseph Whiting Stock, an itinerant artist who lived for most of his forty years in or near Springfield. Crippled by an accident in childhood, Stock learned painting from a pupil of one of the leading American painters of the time, Chester Harding. Although his portraits appear to lack depth and his subjects seem rather rigid, Stock had the ability to record acceptable likenesses, whether from life or from daguerreotypes, even posthumously. His output was extraordinary. His journal entries reveal that he earned $740 during a nine-month period in 1842–1843, having "painted to order 37 portraits and 18 miniatures besides several landscapes, etc." Stock's prices for oil portraits varied depending on the size of the canvas and the number of subjects; thirty by twenty-five inches seems to have been the most popular size and generally cost six dollars.

The Quilting Party (plate 84) is another kind of domestic view, this one successfully capturing the spirit of a festive occasion. This composition, like many others produced by American folk painters, was derived from a popular printed image; the artist had obviously seen the black-and-white illustration that appeared in *Gleason's Pictorial* on October 21, 1854 (figure 11).

Genre works that were drawn from life naturally offer the most revealing glimpses of how our ancestors lived, but the more generalized printed works and the copies they inspired can also provide information about commonplace activities. In this example, the copy surpasses the original source in its color and design, though the details were closely duplicated. It represents a mid-nineteenth-century quilting bee at an unknown location in western Virginia. Bees offered the ambitious housewife an opportunity to get the season's quilting done quickly with the help of many hands. These events were also important social occasions, replete with rituals that varied from region to region. Oral traditions and documented histories note that after a day of intense sewing and exchanging of gossip, the

From left to right:

79a
Unidentified maker, WRITING-ARM CHAIR, *probably New England, ca. 1820, painted wood, 45¼ × 38 × 32⅞ inches (81.2000.2).*

79b
Unidentified maker, SIDE CHAIRS, *probably New York, 1815–1825, painted wood with rush seats, 32¼ × 18⅞ × 18⅝ inches (74.2000.1,4, and 5).*

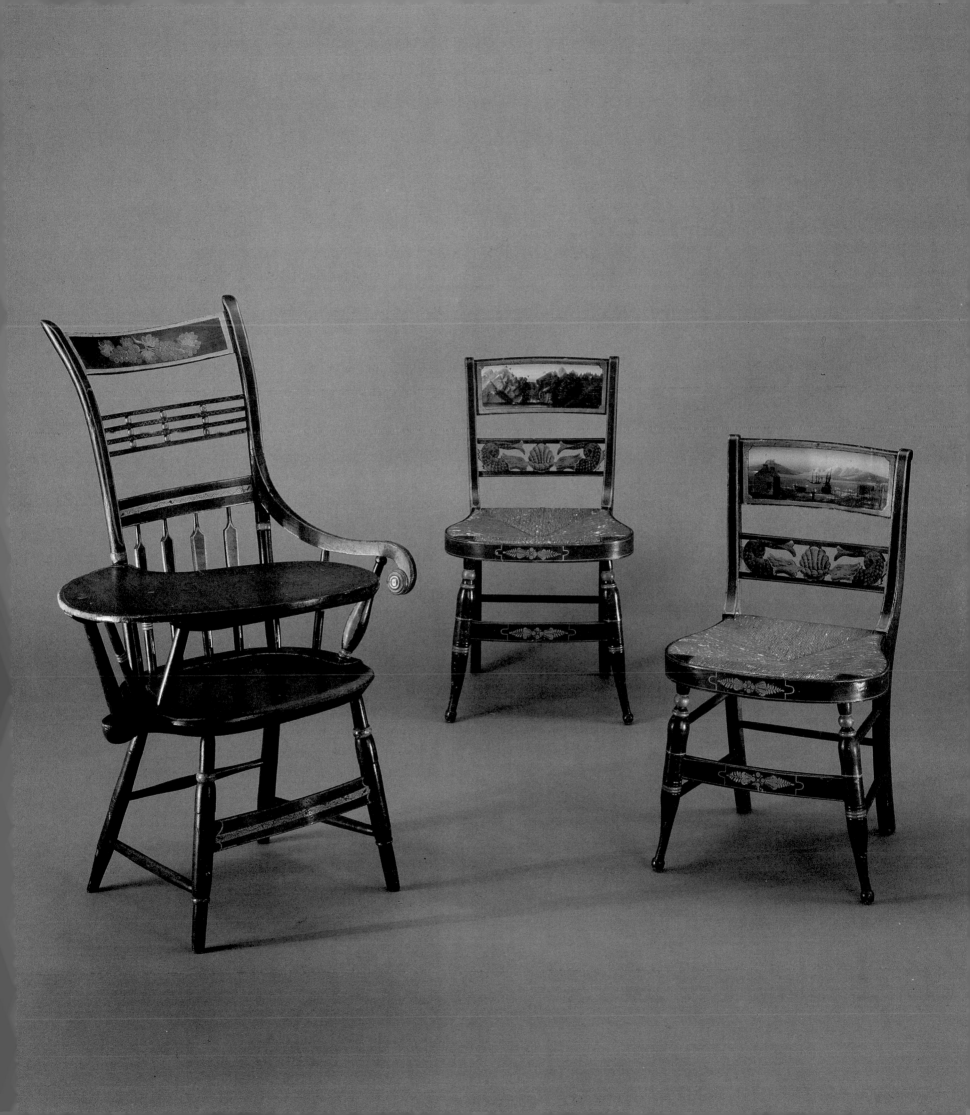

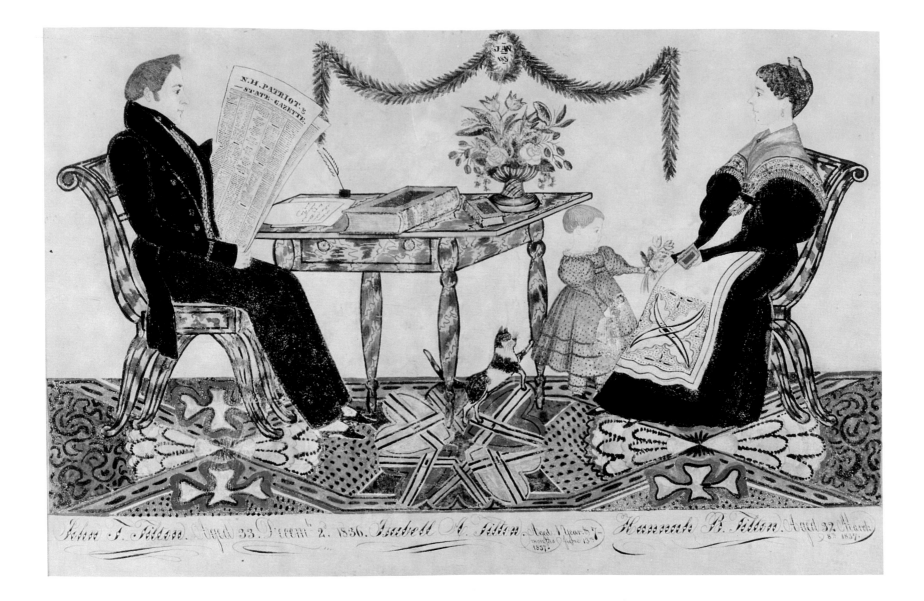

women were often joined by their men for supper and singing and dancing.

The household accessories seen in pictures such as this one— woven and highly patterned fabrics and floor coverings, colorfully painted furniture, and the bedcover being quilted here— provide a quick visual inventory of some of the things found in nineteenth-century American homes. Obviously, not all homes were filled with color and with painted surfaces. Between 1825 and 1880, more formal furniture made of mahogany or other exotic woods, in

the French style or the Greek, often stood in the same room with painted pieces, usually on brilliantly patterned carpets or floor cloths rather than on more subdued floor treatments. The best porcelain probably existed side-by-side on pantry shelves with locally made earthenware and stoneware, and those paintings that we now call folk sometimes hung in the same room with works by European-trained artists. The typical American family's household often contained a range of objects that varied widely in quality, sophistication, style, and date of manufacture.

∧
80
Attributed to Joseph H. Davis, THE TILTON FAMILY, *probably Deerfield, New Hampshire, January 1837, watercolor, pencil, and ink on wove paper, 10 × 15 1/16 inches (36.300.6).* *

81 >
Deborah Goldsmith, THE TALCOTT FAMILY, *probably Hamilton area, New York, 1832, watercolor, pencil, and gold paint on wove paper, 14 1/4 × 17 3/4 inches (57.300.2).*

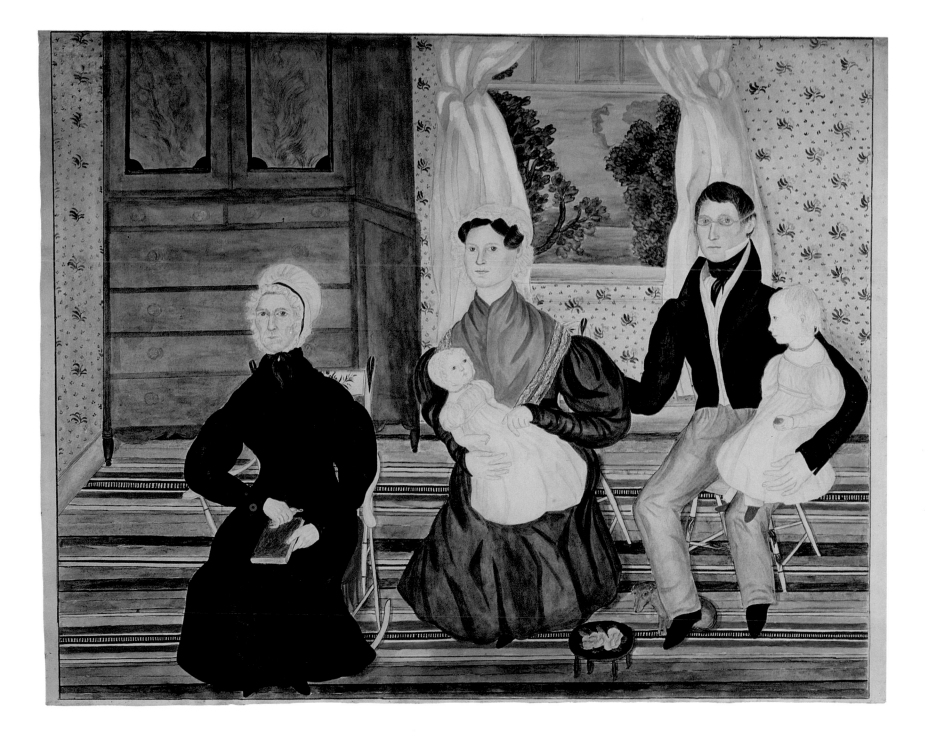

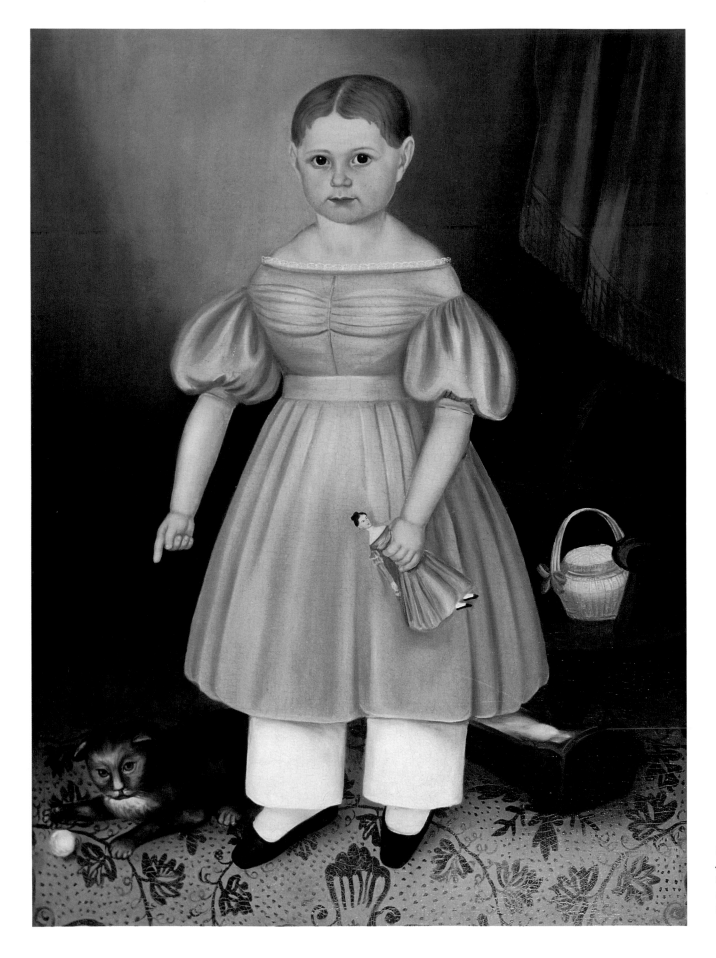

82
Joseph Whiting Stock, MARY JANE
SMITH, *Springfield, Massachusetts,
1838, oil on canvas, 41⁷/₈ × 30³/₁₆
inches (41.100.9).* *

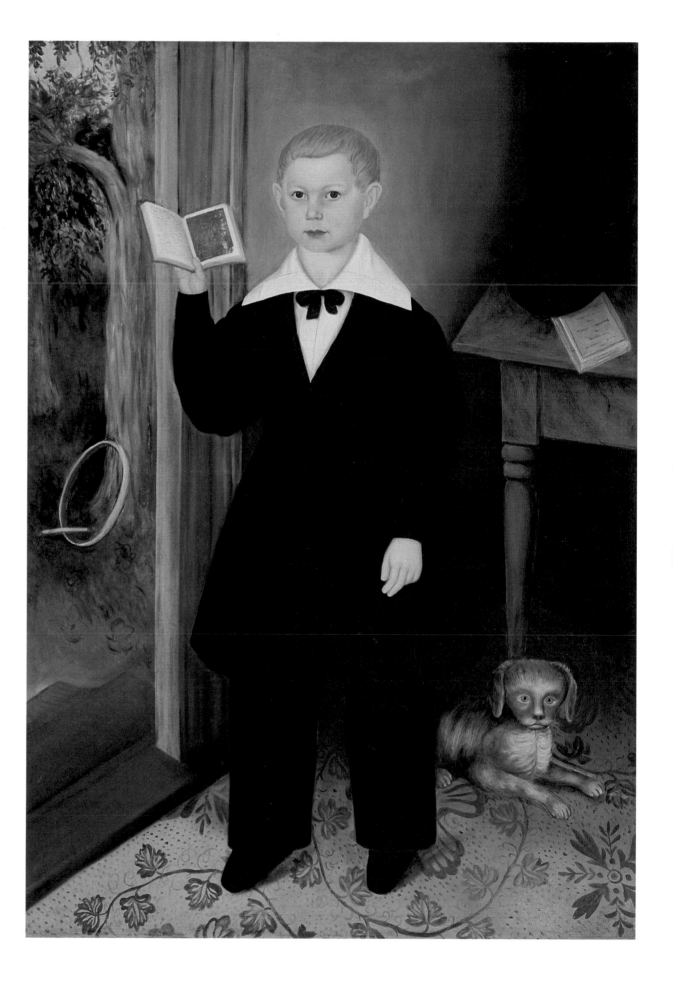

83
Joseph Whiting Stock, WILLIAM
HOWARD SMITH, *Springfield,
Massachusetts, 1838, oil on canvas
with engraving glued onto canvas,
52¹/₄ × 35⁷/₈ inches (41.100.8).*

In Pennsylvania-German communities, the dower chest, or *ausschteier kischt*, was a very popular form, given to girls— and occasionally boys— sometime between their eighth and their tenth year to hold the accumulation of household items, clothes, and small furnishings that would be taken to a new home after marriage.

The example illustrated in plate 86a, dated 1769, is believed to have been used as a dower chest, though certainly not all chests of this form were created to serve this function. Chests were basic and common storage units for linens, clothes, and other items; the form itself can be traced back for many centuries in Europe and elsewhere. But what is important and aesthetically exciting about many of the Pennsylvania examples, as well as a few southern ones, is their bold painted decorations, which relate to those used earlier in Germanic areas of Europe. The hands of certain decorators, most as yet unidentified, can be distinguished, and the chests can thereby usually be grouped and categorized as to regional style and origin. Hearts, urns, flowers, unicorns, religious symbols, exotic birds, and animal figures are among the most popular motifs seen on these chests. This example is among the earliest dated ones that survive.

The way in which the decoration was achieved on such pieces is sometimes difficult to ascertain without a fair amount of experimentation with the same tools available to early decorators. Graining brushes and other materials used in the twentieth century and perhaps earlier by tradesmen who practiced true *faux* painting (surfaces actually intended to fool the eye, as opposed to the decorative surface effects most common on folk art pieces) may have been quite unlike the simple, traditional equipment used by the craftsmen who decorated locally made blanket chests and other woodenwares. The more sophisticated tools included specially sized brushes (often quite thin and delicate in profile), as well as stamps and other devices that when pressed against the wet painted surface would leave an imprint re-

sembling a wood knot, or burl. Combs for graining, sometimes made of metal, became quite common in the twentieth century. Today most grainers use oil-based paints, but a large percentage of the pieces surviving from eighteenth- and nineteenth-century America were embellished with water-based paints.

Prior to 1870, the skilled decorator's tools might include such items as feathers, wadded paper (which made an interesting pattern when dabbed on wet paint), a corncob, some putty, brushes trimmed and shaped along their end to create toothed profiles, a few natural sponges— and even his fingertips. The process began with a base coat of paint, usually of the casein variety. The base coat was as important for the final look of the piece as the decorative glaze of water-based paint, which would be applied and worked with one or more of the tools cited while it was still wet. Rosewood effects, like that seen on the dressing table in plate 85 and on the writing-arm chair in plate 79, usually required a medium-red base coat; yellow, chiefly ocher, was often used for the base coat when another wood was being simulated. The painted surface of the small chest illustrated in plate 86b does not imitate wood but instead makes use of its pale-ocher ground for a "thumbprint" design. Pale-cream grounds were also chosen to mimic stone and to facilitate other fanciful effects.

The Pennsylvania dower chest in plate 86a has a pale-cream or ocher background over which the ornamentor applied a glaze coat of burnt siennas and umbers to create the principal decorative areas. The effect on the drawer fronts was obtained with brushes, while either putty or a sponge created the swirling burled designs in the background. The interiors of the two hearts on the front and the stars on the chest's ends were worked in a similar fashion. Other details, such as the borders around the hearts, stars, circles, and moldings, were deftly executed with brushes. After the glazed figural design coat had dried, the artist probably sealed the sur-

∧
84
Unidentified artist, THE QUILTING PARTY, *United States, probably 1854–1875, oil and pencil on paper adhered to plywood, 19¼ × 26⅛ inches (37.101.1).* *

Figure 11 >
Print from Gleason's Pictorial, *October 21, 1854, showing the source for* THE QUILTING PARTY *(plate 84).*

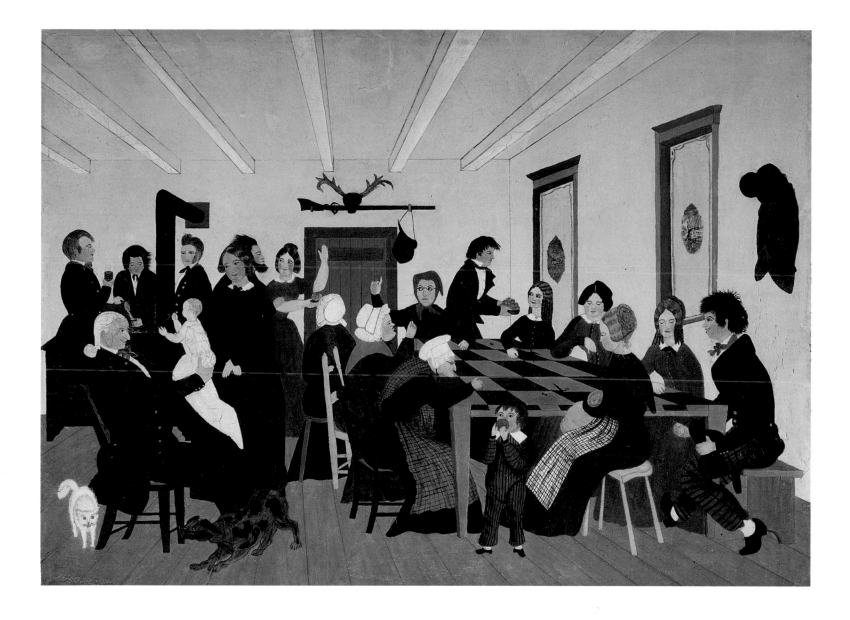

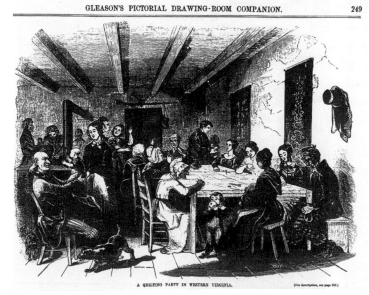

A QUILTING PARTY IN WESTERN VIRGINIA.   [For description, see page 252.]

face with a coat of varnish or shellac before executing the outlined hearts, the date block, and the tangential circles surrounding the keyhole.

Pattern was critical to the success of such pieces, but it had to be created quickly and with a sure hand since the glaze coat set up and dried quickly. Usually a decorative painter completed one side or a single surface element of a piece before going on to another. It would have been difficult to work the front, sides, and top of a full-size blanket chest simultaneously, unless several hands were employed in the task. The little box in plate 86b, however, probably had its top and sides worked all at once, and it boasts one of the strongest patterned surfaces of any piece in the Center's collection. Its condition is remarkable, considering that it was made about 1835.

The decoration of the slightly larger New England box with a dome lid (plate 86c) was created by a somewhat different process, erroneously called smoke graining. The decoration does not imitate wood, as "graining" implies, but is a fanciful panorama of humorous figures, including horses, a bird, some dancers, and a clown riding a lion. Smoke decorating was a simple and dramatic method of ornamentation used during the first half of the nineteenth century; it is rarely done today, except by craftsmen interested in practicing historical techniques.

The piece was first painted with a light-colored base coat; then a varnish was applied, and before this was completely dry, a lighted candle was passed near the surface so that soot in the smoke would adhere to the fresh varnish. In this case, the stenciled silhouettes of circus figures were made by cutouts placed on the box during various stages of the smoking process.

While *graining* is not an appropriate term for the techniques used to create the decorative surfaces on the blanket chest in plate 86 or on some of the

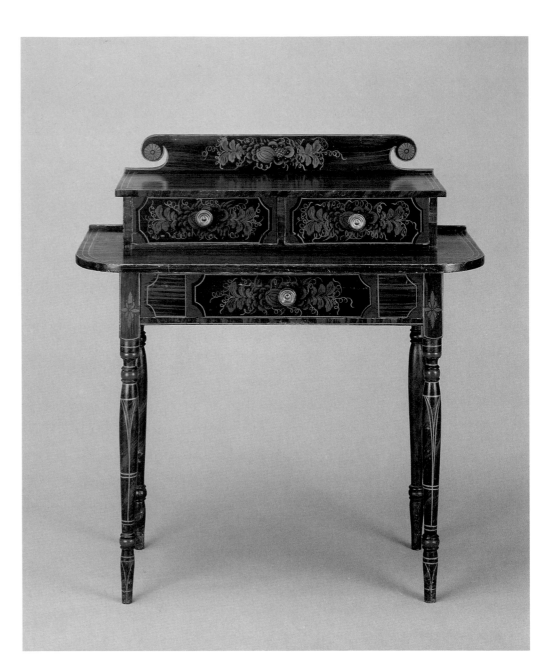

85
Unidentified maker, DRESSING TABLE, *probably New England, ca. 1825, painted wood and brass, 39 1/16 × 36 × 18 inches, anonymous gift (73.2000.2).*

Clockwise from bottom:

86a
Unidentified maker, DOWER OR BLANKET CHEST, *probably Dauphin County, Pennsylvania, 1769, painted wood, iron, and brass, 29 1/8 × 50 3/4 × 22 3/4 inches (72.2000.5).*

86b
Unidentified maker, BOX, *probably New England, possibly 1825–1850, painted wood, 9 5/8 × 13 3/8 × 7 1/4 inches (60.708.1).*

86c
Unidentified maker, DOME-LID BOX, *probably New England, 1825–1850, painted, smoked, and stencil-decorated wood, 23 3/4 × 11 3/4 × 10 3/4 inches (61.708.2).*

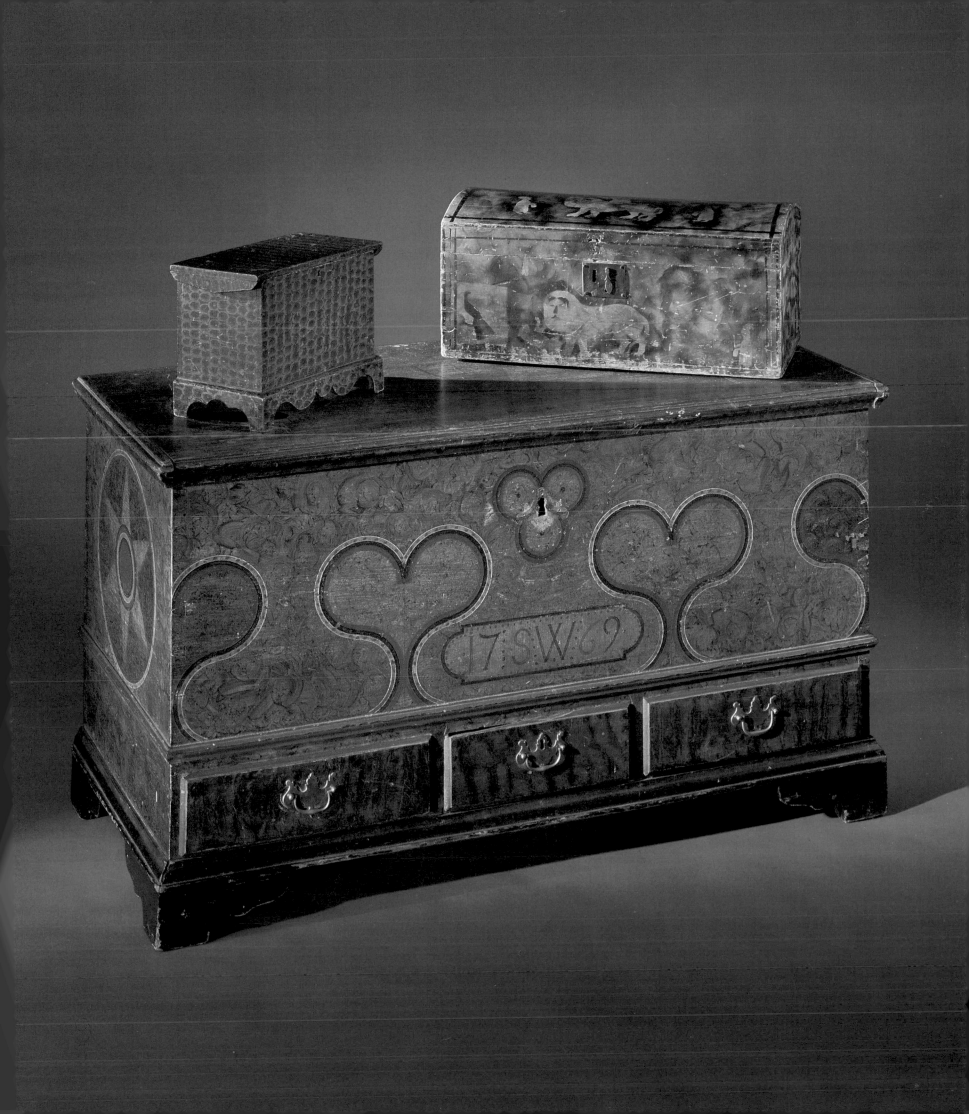

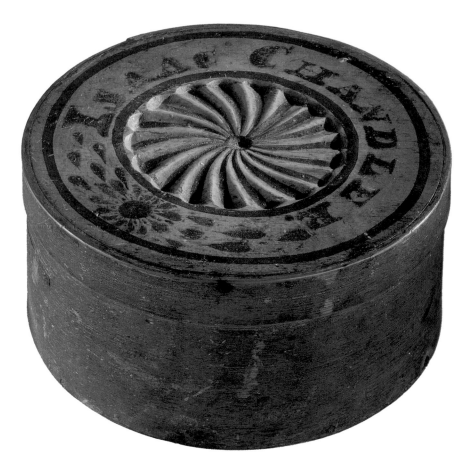

other pieces discussed here, the word does accurately describe the technique employed for the surface of the dressing table in plate 85, made in New England about 1835. Here the surface imitates the exotic and expensive rosewood used in more formal furniture. This particular example also has red and yellow banding to simulate inlaid stringing, as well as gilt bronze stenciling to simulate the brass and gilded mounts found on furniture of the Empire style.

Painted furniture dating from the first half of the nineteenth century could be boldly decorated with solid colors or embellishments other than *faux* or grained work. The two chairs from New York State (plate 79b), dating from about 1815, were undoubtedly painted by a skilled professional ornamentor, as evidenced by the fine landscape scenes on their crest rails. The scenes appear to be imaginary, and some relate to views published in popular drawing books of the time. Ruins, pseudo-Gothic architecture, "rustic" cottages, and stylized rock

formations are often featured in these instruction manuals.

The small two-drawer chest shown in plate 88 is perhaps the simplest of all the furniture included in this book, but it makes a very strong visual statement. The maker used both paint and chip carving to ornament this piece, which has several inscriptions in pencil, including "Catherine Bothers" and "Lowell." Perhaps Catherine was the original owner, and Lowell was either her last name or the town where she lived. It is not easy to determine the use of such small case pieces, since documentation rarely survives from the original owner. One can imagine that Catherine may have stored small trinkets, jewelry, or sewing implements in the chest.

Painted and unpainted boxes in all shapes and sizes were used for storing household goods and other items— foods, sewing equipment, seeds, dried vegetables, powders, and spices. Most of these are plain and unadorned but for a coat of varnish or

∧
87
Unidentified maker, ISAAC CHANDLER'S BOX, *United States, possibly 1825–1845, painted wood, 3¹/₂ × 7⁵/₈ inches in diameter (79.708.1).*

88 >
Unidentified maker, MINIATURE CHEST WITH TWO DRAWERS, *possibly New England, ca. 1840, painted wood, 10 × 6 × 4¹/₂ inches, bequest of Effie Thixton Arthur (79.2000.5).*

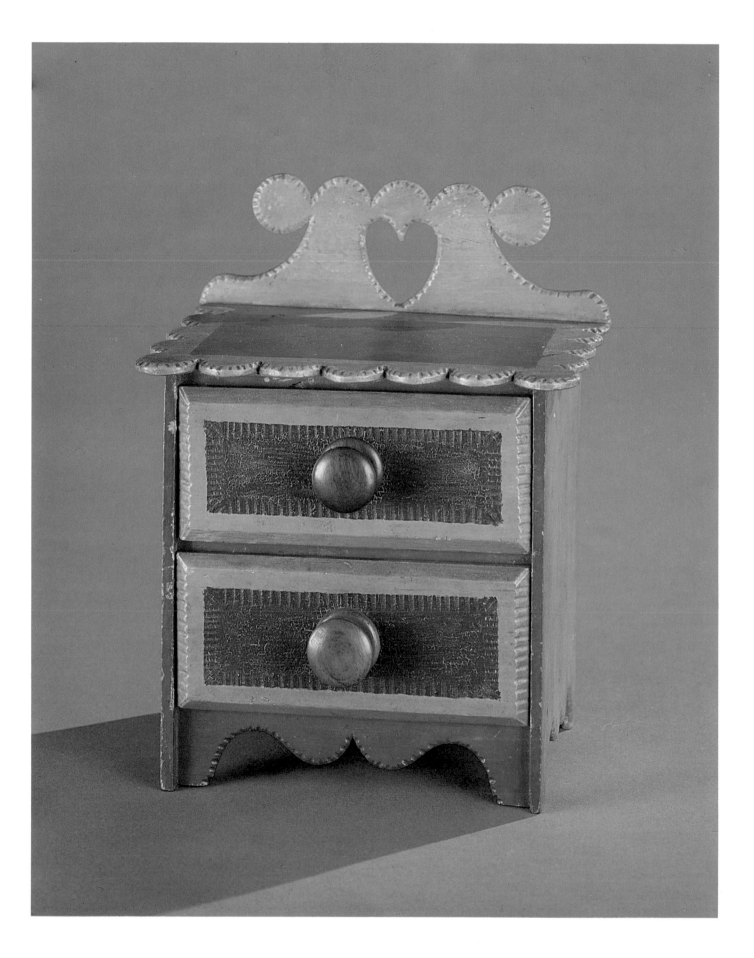

paint. Isaac Chandler's round box (plate 87) is of a form that generally remained unadorned, but here the maker carved a swirling sunburst in the center of the lid and accented the top surface by inscribing the owner's name in black and adding a variety of designs in dark-green paint over a background coat of yellow.

The polescreen with a landscape painting attributed to Edward Hicks (plate 89) is an extraordinarily rare example of an early-nineteenth-century piece of furniture with a painted design element. The stand was probably constructed in a local Bucks County cabinet shop, and then Hicks was hired to paint the panel, of tulip poplar framed in mahogany, the same wood used for the pole. Scholars have known for years that Edward Hicks painted furniture, but none of the surviving records for his shop mention this particular form.

Early American homes contained all sorts of woodenware. Besides furniture, there were interior architectural elements, kitchen utensils, storage pieces, and a miscellany of other objects. Native-grown woods were usually cheap, readily available, and easily worked, both by local craftsmen and by less skilled amateurs. The walking stick illustrated in plate 90 was made in 1846 by an amateur carver, Thomas Purkins (1791–1855) of Virginia, who carved the stick and then picked out the fine details of the carving with inks. His present-day descendants report that Purkins was a huge man, weighing 350 to 400 pounds; if this is true, it may explain his devotion to the sedentary activity of cane carving. About a dozen walking sticks fashioned by Purkins are known, and at least three of them, including this one, bear inscriptions claiming they were made from holly wood taken from Wakefield, George Washington's birthplace in Westmoreland County, Virginia. Purkins had a 1,740-acre plantation, called Hollywood, in nearby Stafford County.

This example is the earliest dated stick recorded for the artist thus far. Many of its well-executed indi-

vidual carvings, such as the hound's head, reveal Purkins's considerable talent for carefully rendering naturalistic forms, while others, such as the eagle, the cat, and the lion, show a more stylized approach. It appears that Purkins made his canes only for family members; he was not a professional carver.

Hundreds of other carvers produced and sold more common items, such as the butter print with anchor in plate 91 or the J. Q. Adams pastry board in plate 92. The latter, which may have been made in Pennsylvania about 1825–1830, commemorates a series of events that preceded and resulted in the War of 1812. John Quincy Adams was President from 1825 to 1829; from 1817 to 1825 he served as secretary of state under James Monroe. The emphasis in the new republic was on the use of America's own products and manufacturers, as indicated here by the inscription "Peece [sic], liberty, J.Q. Adams, Home Industry." On the back of the board is a carving showing an Indian holding a bow and arrow in each hand.

Butter molds were used throughout the nineteenth century to decorate butter and sometimes— when the butter was sold at the market, for example— to identify the kitchen where it was made. Anchors rarely appear on butter prints, making this example unusual. More common designs included cows, flowers, acorns, wheat sheaves, and pineapples.

Naturalistic design motifs, particularly flowers, leaves, and fruit, were used to decorate virtually all types of domestic equipment from the seventeenth through the nineteenth centuries, and the same themes continue to serve as sources of interior ornamentation today. References to the earth's abundance, to the seasons of the year revolving around planting and harvesting times, and to man's historic reliance on the land and the sea for food and other provisions appear in art of all types nearly all the world over. But these motifs were especially common in the art of nineteenth-century America, with its largely rural population. The bond between man

89
Attributed to Edward Hicks and an unidentified cabinetmaker,
POLESCREEN, *probably Bucks County, Pennsylvania, ca. 1830, mahogany pole and frame with oil paint on yellow poplar panel, 57¼ × 22 × 18½ inches (86.2000.1).*

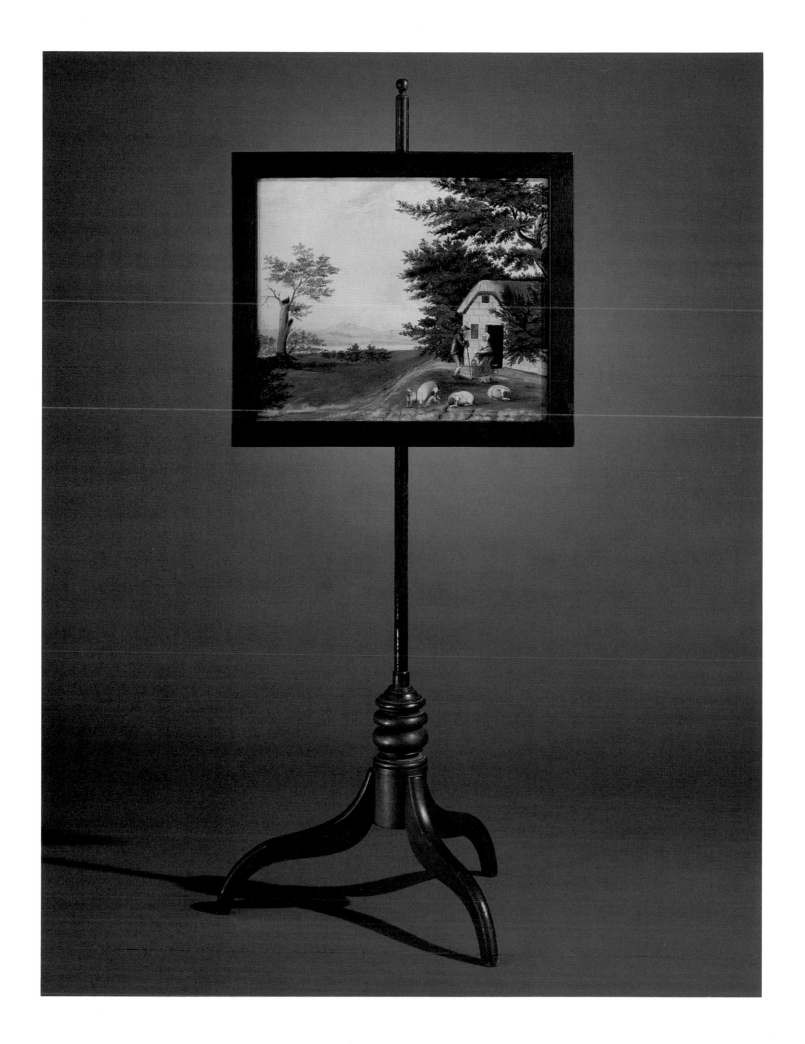

and the land and sea in America, necessarily close, is particularly clearly reflected in the fashioning of tools, the founding of small towns, and the creation of household furnishings— in short, in the material world. The abolition of slavery made the bond with the land even stronger for those white Americans who previously had relied on slave labor for large cash crops.

These designs based on flora and fauna, as well as the equally compelling designs reflecting national pride and historic events, resulted in some highly colorful and distinctive household furnishings. The album quilt in plate 93, for instance, effectively combines all of these sources of inspiration. Circular wreaths of flowers and foliage, common to quilts of this and other styles, are interspersed with fruit and other foliated designs. The obelisk in the upper left is the Ringgold monument, erected in Baltimore as a memorial tribute to Major Samuel Ringgold (1800–1846), a valiant Maryland soldier who died in the Mexican War. The building at upper right is a loose interpretation of the national capitol in Washington, D.C.

The style of this quilt links it to a number of others of Baltimore origin. A tradition in the previous owner's family supports the intriguing theory that the squares comprising the interior design were made for and sold by the Order of Masons in Baltimore. A certain Mary Evans is believed to have been responsible for many of the more complex quilt blocks. Sarah Anne Whittington Lankford (1830–1898), whose initials are cross-stitched in the center of the apple wreath at lower left, was the sister of Henry Smith Lankford (1823–1905) of Baltimore, who is said to have purchased the squares. Sarah— perhaps with several of her friends and family members— is believed to have assembled and quilted the squares and provided the outermost floral border.

Album quilts are usually the product of a group of people, each contributing and often signing one or

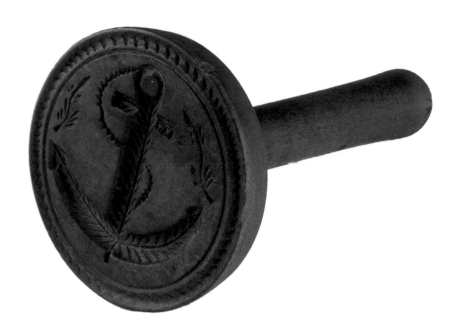

< 90
Thomas Purkins, WALKING STICK, King George County, Virginia, 1846, carved wood with ink decoration, 37 × 2 inches in diameter (81.708.1).

91 ∧
Unidentified maker, BUTTER PRINT, United States, 1850–1870, carved wood, 5⅝ × 3¹/₁₆ inches in diameter, Gift of Mr. and Mrs. Foster McCarl, Jr. (82.708.4).

92 >
Unidentified maker, J.Q. ADAMS PASTRY BOARD, probably Pennsylvania, 1825–1830, carved wood, 10³/₁₆ × 5⅞ × ¾ inch (59.708.2).

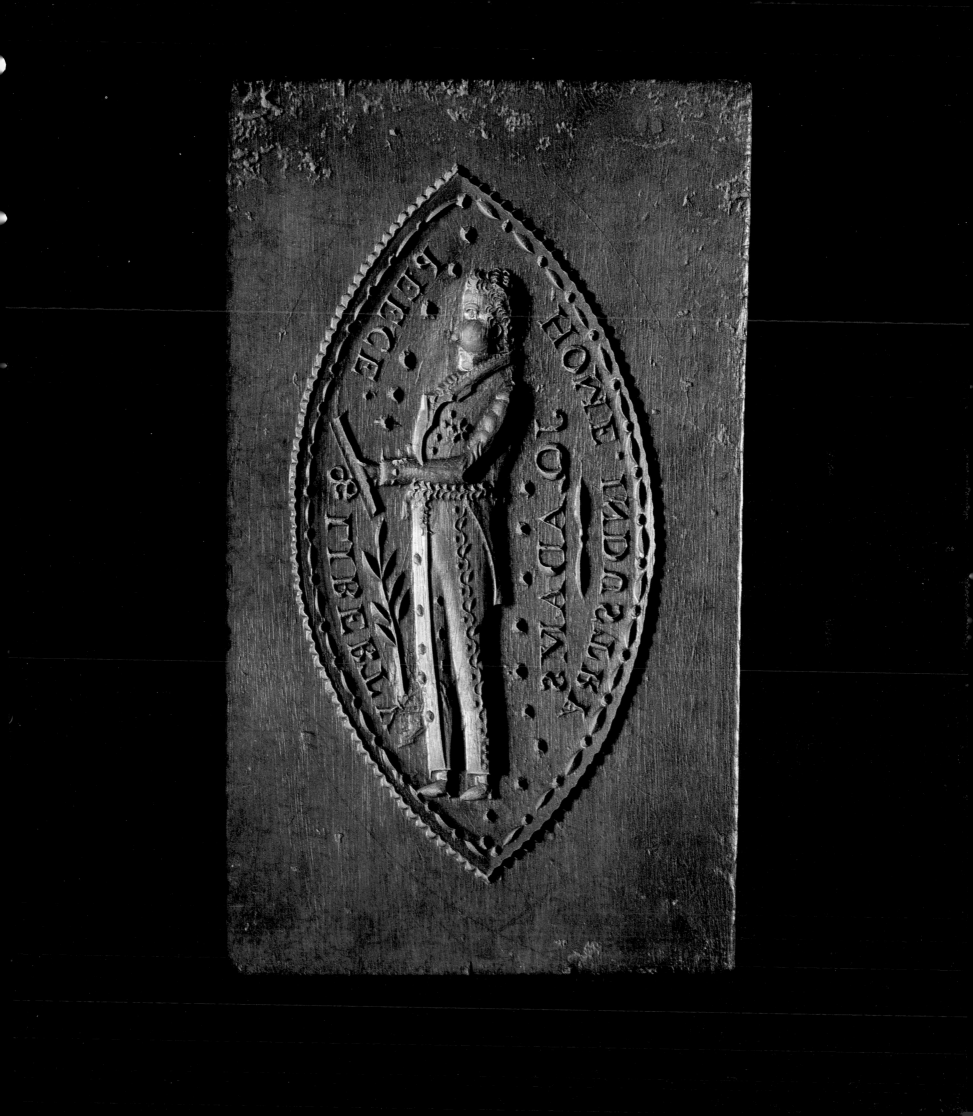

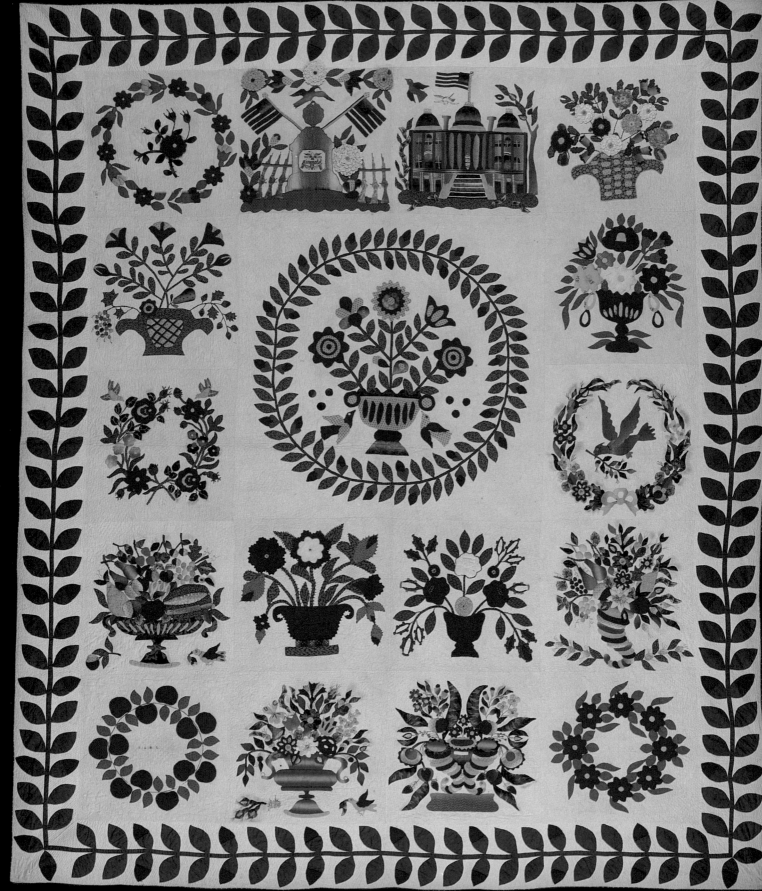

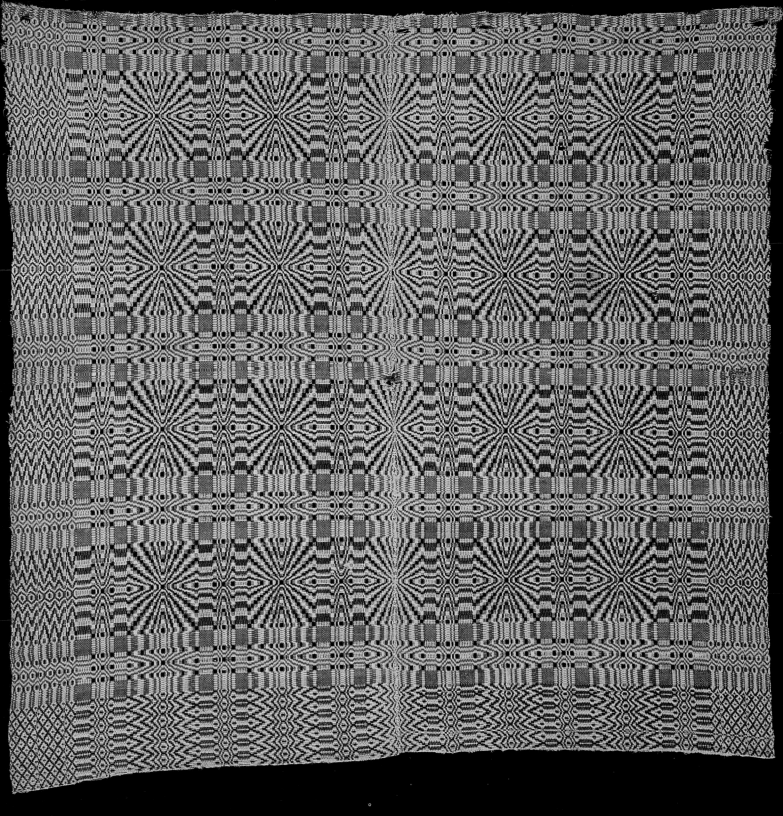

93
Sarah Anne Whittington Lankford,
probably Mary Evans, and possibly
others, APPLIQUÉD QUILT,
Baltimore and Somerset County,
Maryland, ca. 1850, various cottons
with inked details and silver metallic
thread, 84 × 99 inches, Gift of
Marsha C. Scott (79.609.14).

94
Unidentified weaver, OVERSHOT
COVERLET, *probably Pennsylvania,*
1825–1850, red, green, and dark-
blue wools with natural cotton, 70
× 68 inches, gift of Mrs. William
John Bovaird (73.609.8).

more of the blocks or squares that typify this type of bedcover and are the source of its generic name. The Lankford quilt is something of an exception, since the squares were probably bought from a single source, though they may have been quilted by a group. The number of individuals who worked on the album quilt in plate 75, which dates from about 1850, is unknown, but the repetition of some stitching details and the sharing of some of the fabrics among the various motifs suggest that the effort was limited to a small, close-knit group, or perhaps even a single person. The quilt is inscribed "to Emma" and "Louise Present" (meaning "Louise's Present"?), but no other identification has been made. It includes motifs rarely found on mid-nineteenth-century album quilts, including fuchsia, bleeding heart, and geranium plants. This example is quite realistic in its details, as are some areas of Lankford's quilt, where fabrics that had been specially dyed or chosen for their shades were pieced together to create depth and form for the flowers and other elements.

While realism is characteristic of many Baltimore-area album quilts, the vast majority of American-made quilts feature bold colors and nonrepresentational patterns, as in the Amish quilt in plate 98 or the small crib quilt in plate 95, by Alma Richter, with its highly stylized flowers, foliage, and birds. The motifs in the crib quilt are characteristic of Pennsylvania-German quilts, which may be an indication of Mrs. Richter's family background. The Amish quilt, like others of its kind, relies entirely on its precise geometric patterning and the contrast between its bright and dark colors for its success. The subtle, meticulously quilted pattern in this example includes baskets and hearts along the outer border.

The extraordinary pieced table cover in plate 99, probably made in New York State about 1835, is also based on the popular floral motifs of its day, though it is distinctive in both its technique and its palette. Black-ground textiles were popular in the eighteenth century but relatively rare during the

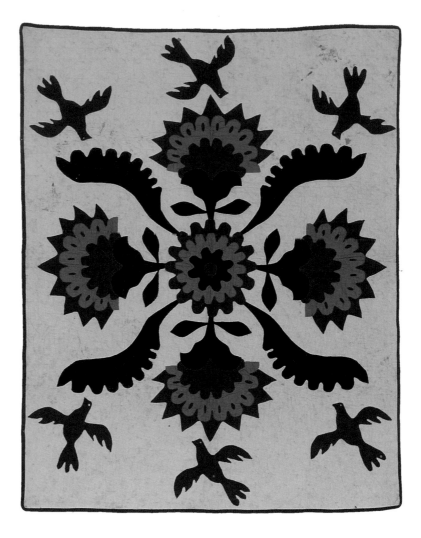

95
Attributed to Alma Richter, CRIB QUILT, *Sunman, Ripley County, Indiana, probably 1854, various cottons, 45¹/₈ × 35¹/₈ inches (85.609.1).*

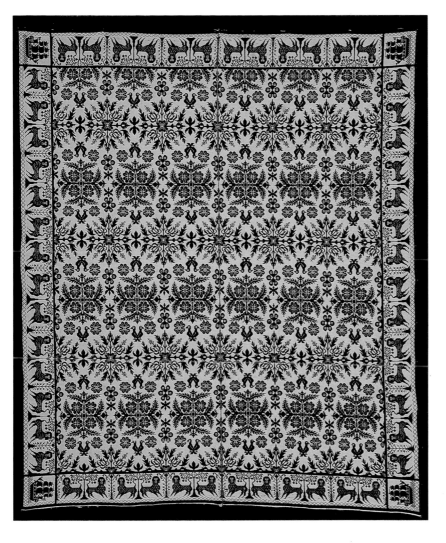

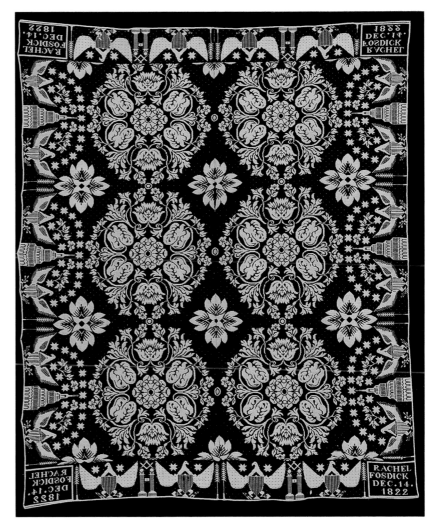

96
Unidentified weaver, DOUBLE-
WOVEN COVERLET, *probably
New York State, ca. 1835, blue wool
with white cotton or linen, 86 × 73
inches, Gift of Mr. and Mrs. Foster
McCarl, Jr. (82.609.1).*

97
James Alexander, DOUBLE-
WOVEN COVERLET, *near New
Britain, New York, 1822, dark-blue
wool with white cotton, 95 × 76½
inches, gift of Mr. and Mrs. Foster
McCarl, Jr. (78.609.5).*

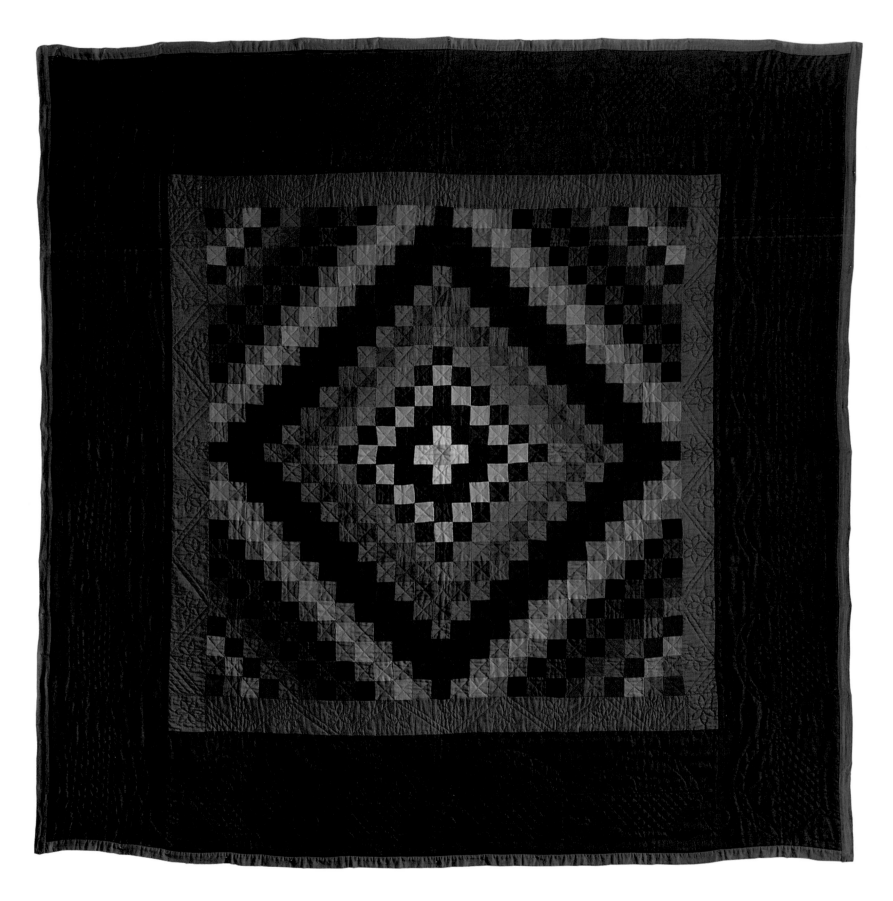

98
Unidentified maker, PIECED QUILT, *Lancaster County,*
Pennsylvania, probably 1900–1920, cotton and wool, 78 × 79 inches (80.609.2).

99
Unidentified maker, TABLE COVER, *probably New York State,*
probably 1830–1845, pieced wools with supplementary silk embroidery, 65³/₄ × 64⁷/₈ *inches (74.603.1).*

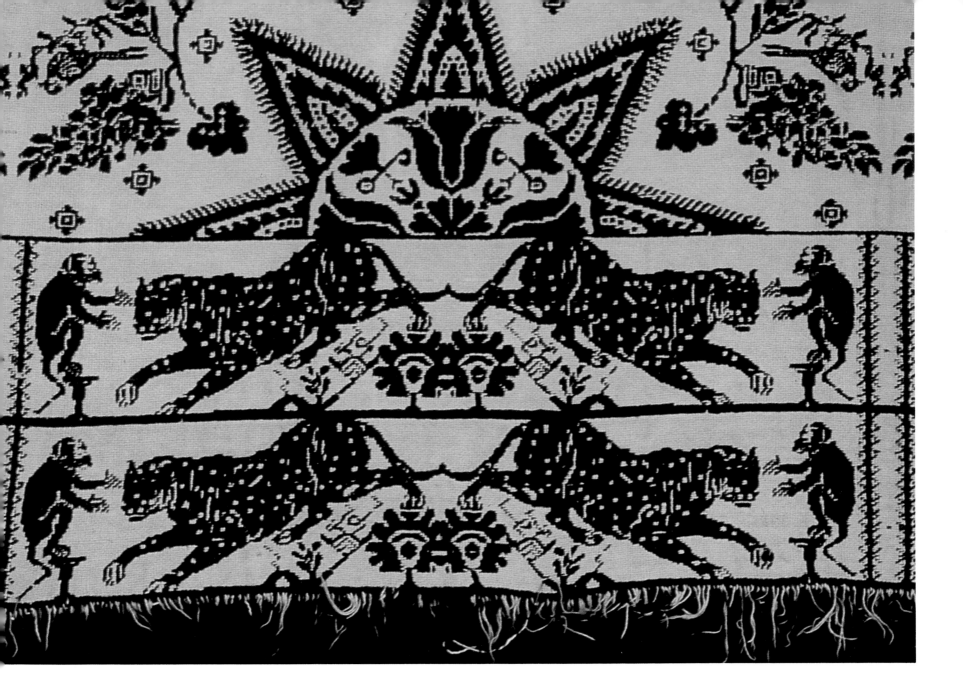

nineteenth century. Except for the supplementary embroidery, all of the designs on this cover were pieced into— that is, laid in, rather than appliquéd on— the black ground, making this an exceptional feat of workmanship.

Similar motifs are found on nineteenth-century woven textiles and decorative wallpapers, including the endless variety of coverlets and carpets produced on Jacquard looms. The Jacquard-type attachment for drawlooms was an outgrowth of many years of experiments aimed at simplifying the weaving process. The apparatus was named

after Joseph-Marie Jacquard (1752–1834), a Frenchman who perfected the mechanism in the early nineteenth century. It was introduced into the United States in 1824, and after it was widely marketed in the late 1820s, European weavers familiar with its use immigrated in large numbers. Many American weavers were also trained in the Jacquard weaving process and became professional loom workers.

Because of the range of patterns and the ease of production afforded by the new invention, the Jacquard coverlet soon displaced the more restrained

∧
Detail of plate 100

100 >
Unidentified weaver, DOUBLE-WOVEN COVERLET, *possibly Ohio or Indiana, probably ca. 1845, dark-blue wool with white cotton, 81 × 77½ inches, Gift of Mr. and Mrs. Foster McCarl, Jr. (78.609.2).*

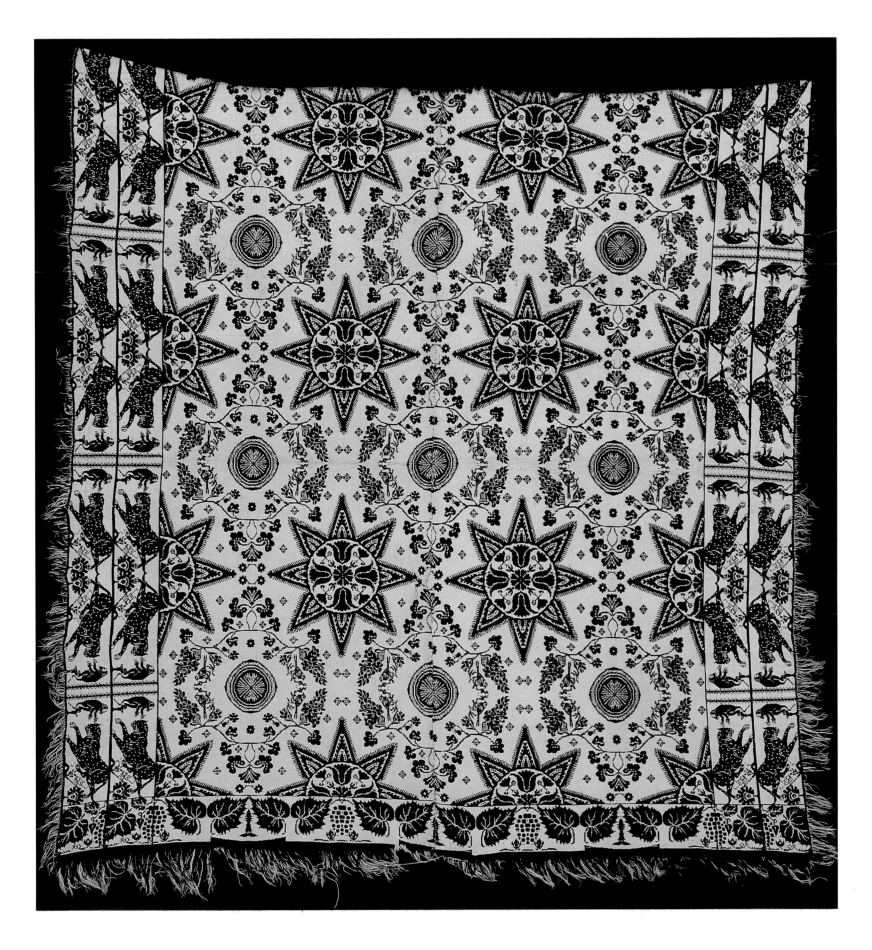

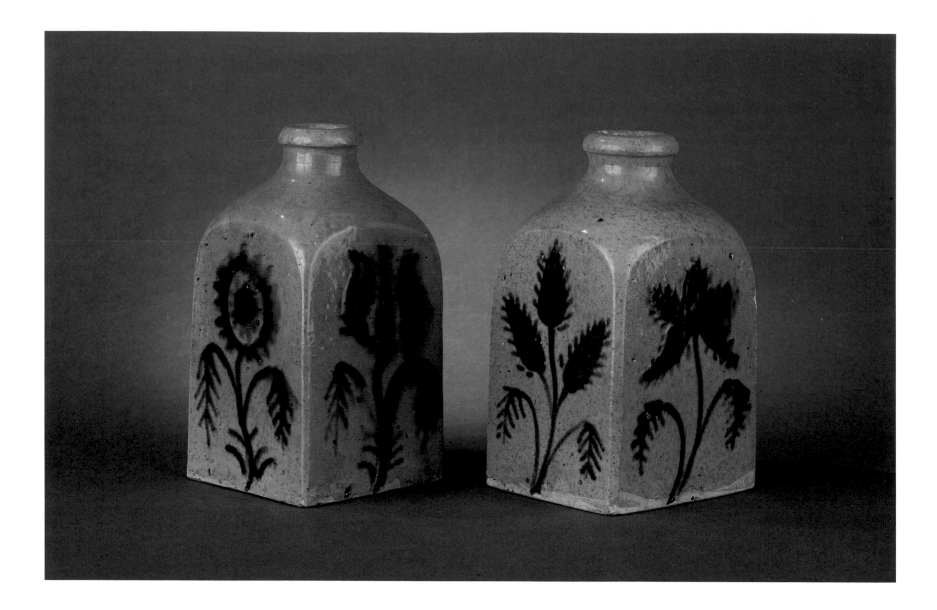

yet equally appealing overshot and double-woven geometric coverlets, which had been produced for years in America. The overshot example in plate 94, dating from about 1835, is woven in the "Sunrise" pattern for the main design and in "Bonaparte's March" for the seven-inch-wide border at the bottom. A more open, bolder geometric pattern is seen in the double-woven coverlet in plate 100.

The two Jacquard-type coverlets illustrated in plates 96 and 97 are characteristic of the form in their highly sophisticated interior medallions of foliage and fanciful flowers, but examples such as these are today prized for their decorative and more abstract border designs, which often incorporate traditional folk motifs. A three-masted sailing ship appears in all four corners of the first coverlet, and all four borders show a repeating design of a doglike animal, perhaps a poodle, alternating with foliage. The second coverlet, dated 1822, is attributed to James Alexander (1770–1870), a professional weaver.

Domestic life for most early Americans required a good many labor-intensive household chores, since churning butter, washing, cooking, and so forth had to be done without the conveniences of the modern

101
E. White, TEA CADDIES, *Mercer, possibly Pennsylvania, 1848, lead-glazed earthenware with dark-brown slip decoration, 7¹/₂ × 4¹/₈ × 3⁷/₈ inches (76.900.2).*

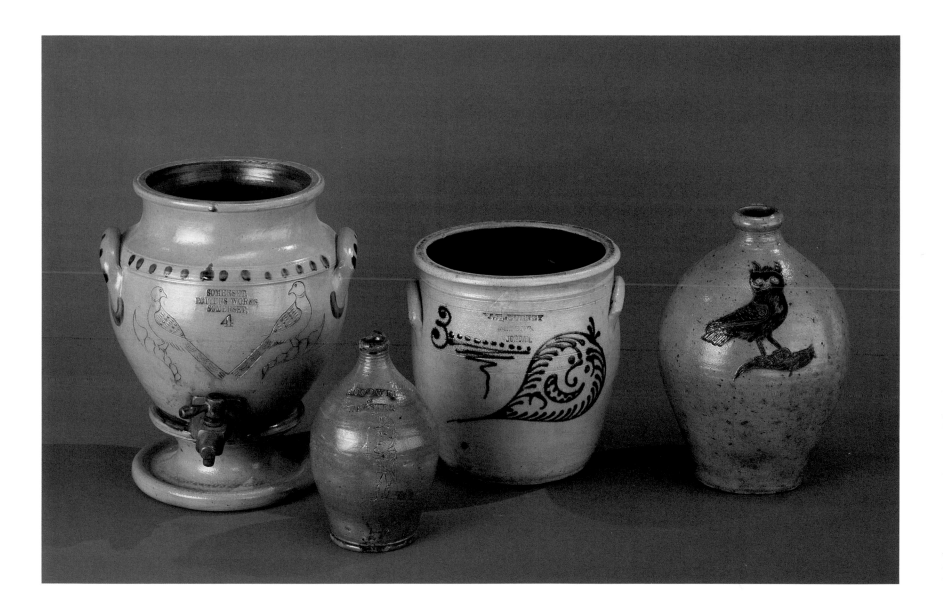

From left to right:

102a
Somerset Potters Works,
WATERCOOLER, Somerset,
Massachusetts, probably 1847–1860,
salt-glazed stoneware with incised
and cobalt decoration, 16 × 13¹⁵/₁₆
× 13 inches (75.900.1).

102b
Goodwin and Webster, JUG,
Hartford, Connecticut, probably
1810–1840, salt-glazed stoneware
with incised and cobalt decoration,
10¹/₁₆ × 6⁵/₈ × 6⁵/₈ inches (59.900.2).

102c
James McBurney & Sons, CROCK,
Jordan, New York, ca. 1855, salt-
glazed stoneware with cobalt
decoration and Albany slip interior,
14 × 9³/₄ inches in diameter
(75.900.4).

102d
Unidentified maker, JUG, probably
New York or New Jersey, 1790–
1810, salt-glazed stoneware with
incised and cobalt decoration, 14¹/₈
× 10 inches in diameter (84.900.2).

world, notably without the benefit of electricity, which was not in widespread use in this country until the 1930s. But the seemingly mundane tasks involved in preparing meals, clothing a family, and generally maintaining a household were enlivened by many brilliantly colored or whimsically ornamented objects. Humor regularly invaded these areas of human endeavor, and probably with good reason: it helped lighten the burden of repetitive, everyday tasks.

Decorated tinware and pottery were common to most households; these objects, closely associated with the activities of food preparation, show great variety in their decoration and themes. Coffeepots and teapots were among the first household articles to be fashioned from tinplate. Though similar, the two forms frequently were distinguished from each other by differing spout designs: a teapot typically had a one-piece, curving spout, while a coffeepot usually sported a "gooseneck" spout made of two separate pieces that formed a sharp elbow joint. Many coffeepots and other decorated tinware, such as the pieces in plate 103, were first given a ground coat that looks like black paint. The glossy finish and rich reddish- to golden-brown sheen, however, indicate that the material was in fact asphaltum. This was a refined form of asphalt that could be mixed with varnish and was favored by decorators because of its velvety smooth finish. This type of prepared surface facilitated the addition of the stylized flowers, foliage, and fanciful flourishes that characterize much of the painted tinware produced in America during the nineteenth century.

Not all tin was decorated in this manner; tinsmiths frequently embellished plain, uncoated ware with pierced and "wriggle-work" designs. Most tin lanterns of the period, such as the one illustrated in plate 104a, were pierced in simple geometric patterns to allow the light to shine outward. The stylized faces on this example transform a common household article into a rather unusual and whimsical object. Piercing tools of at least three different

shapes were used to create the faces around the top, the ones on the body, and the ornamental border. The door panel is fitted with horn, a material translucent enough to allow the light to penetrate to the exterior.

The tinware coffeepot (plate 104b) was made sometime between 1820 and 1850 and decorated by the "wriggle-work" process. Designs were worked into the spout, handle, lid, and body with a graver, or V-shaped cutting tool, using a rocking motion of the hand and wrist. The spout bears both straight and serpentine lines of wriggle-work, the lid features three tulip plants, and the handle sports a twining snake, his head placed close to the hinged lid. One side of the pot has the patriotic eagle, perched with wings spread on a flowering vine in front of a flag, while the other shows a brave, small soldier raising his sword toward two oversized tulip blossoms!

Military figures such as the one on the coffeepot abound in American folk art, either as single objects, as elements of isolated representational designs, or as parts of overall and sometimes unrelated motifs. No doubt these figures were associated with specific American military engagements, but their identity is often vague and generic. Or perhaps we have simply lost the knowledge of their identities, since they were so commonplace in the nineteenth century that no one needed a literal guide or inscription to recognize them. The profile of a soldier appears, for instance, on a Goodwin and Webster salt-glazed stoneware jug dating from 1810–1840 (plate 102b). He is crudely incised but fearless in his expression. Perhaps he commemorates the War of 1812, with its intensely nationalistic aftermath. Goodwin and Webster (active 1810–1840) produced other pieces with symbolic and representational decorations, including a Masonic jug bearing a tri-square and divider. The symbols used on such pieces reflect the same concern for visual shorthand and immediate recognition as those found on the exterior signage of the period.

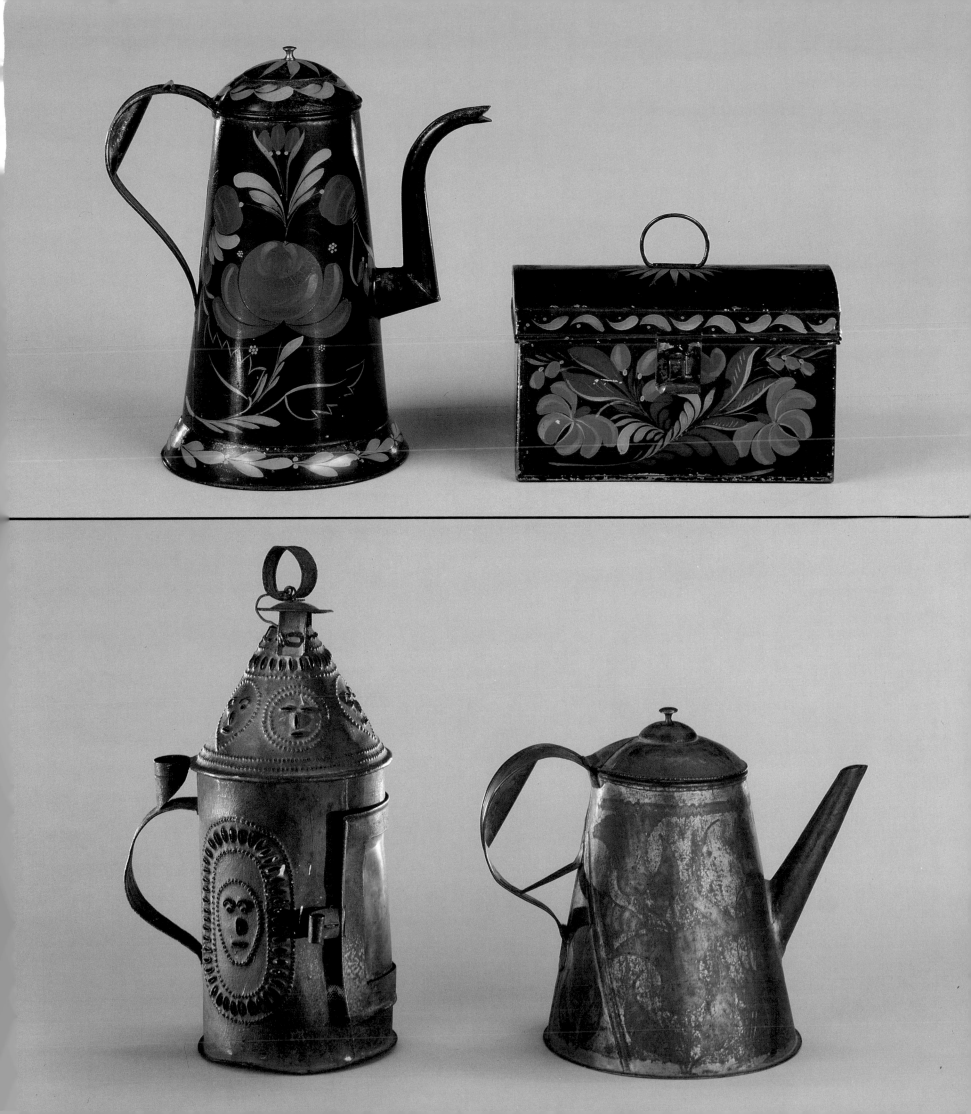

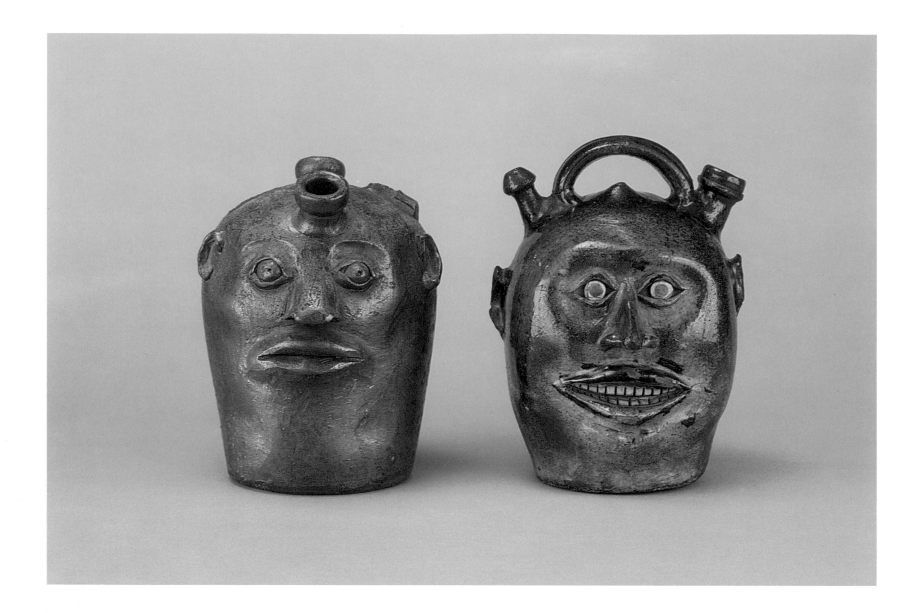

Ornamentation on pottery runs the gamut of the design elements seen on other household objects, from flora and birds (as in plates 101 and 102a) to humorous elements that could bring a smile to the weariest cook. The stoneware crock illustrated in plate 102c, with its smiling turnip, is a particularly fine example of whimsy.

Other motifs featured included all sorts of animal forms, such as the owl seen on the 1790–1810 stoneware jug shown in plate 102d. He may be questioning the wisdom of anyone who imbibes too much of the stuff within; similarly, the grotesque face on the jug in plate 105a clearly mocks the results of partaking of too much. This form of jug appears to be related to the "monkey jar," a type of plain earthenware vessel made to hold water and to cool it by evaporation, used in the West Indies and in the American South in the nineteenth and possibly the late eighteenth centuries. Other traditions indicate that such jugs are derived from objects and customs associated with voodoo and are called devil jugs because they stored liquor. In either case, the applied and molded facial features on many of these pieces may have originated in African sculptural traditions. The form, as it is known to us from surviving North American examples, appears to be unrelated to other American crocks. The larger, glazed earthenware example in plate 105b is attributed to John Westley (active ca. 1850–ca. 1870) on the basis of a signed and dated jug having a similar shape and arrangement of spouts. Little is known about Westley except that he lived in Philadelphia in 1850 and apparently made this signed-face harvest jug for Willa Frisby, whose name appears on the piece.

Perhaps the most ornate pieces of household pottery made during the nineteenth century were those used in the more public spaces of the home. It is unlikely that the elaborately incised and detailed pottery vessel in plate 106, featuring a comical little monkey, would have been kept in the kitchen or the pantry. This was a special piece, so special that no other examples like it have been located by the Center staff. Whimsical depictions of poodles, lions, birds, and other animals were made in many nineteenth-century American potteries, but these were often freestanding arrangements of two or more

figures that functioned purely as decorative items. The monkey's face in this example peers over the rim of a large cornucopia, the contents of which may have been the owner's pens or some other objects. The base the monkey stands on is hollow and pierced on its upper surface by a single hole with a slight rim, suggesting that it might once have held ink.

Whatever the utilitarian function of this object, the whimsy it embodies was one of the qualities valued by nineteenth-century Americans in their home furnishings. Both patterned and representational decoration were very popular, and the two were combined in various ways. The decoration itself could be expressive and highly symbolic; though some objects were only functional or purely decorative, others also served as communicators. Then, too, the ideas reflected in their decoration ranged broadly, from patriotism to status-consciousness and awareness of the intrinsic values of certain materials and forms, from simple humor to celebration of nature's bounty.

106
Unidentified maker, MONKEY
INKWELL, *possibly Pennsylvania,*
probably ca. 1875, stoneware, 7¾ ×
7 × 5 inches (79.900.5).

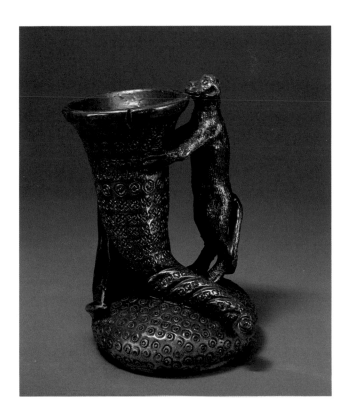

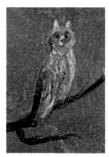

CHAPTER FIVE

A Virtuous Life
from Cradle to Grave

Studies of the social mores and religious values expressed in American art generally deal with theological principles and their academic interpretation. The folk art discussed in this chapter stems from a far less sophisticated but broader-based impulse— the traditional and popular conceptualizations of Old and New Testament stories, moralistic literary works, and memorable historical figures.

Through the late eighteenth and early nineteenth centuries, a thorough knowledge of the Bible, *Aesop's Fables*, *Pilgrim's Progress*, and similar didactic stories and teachings was taken as a fundamental sign of rectitude or, at the very least, of aspiration to a virtuous life. Parents and teachers took great pains to impart to children the precepts necessary for making correct moral choices, for enjoying social acceptance, and even for achieving eternal life. Sin was thought to tempt everyone, particularly the young, as was illustrated time and again in pictures portraying the parable of the Prodigal Son. One such scene (plate 108), dating from about 1790, shows the youth reveling with harlots, all in period dress. The unidentified folk painter who made this small picture created an atmosphere of decadence by including an abundance of wineglasses and by depicting the sticklike figures in suggestive poses. A gaunt cat lurks beneath the table and clutches a dead mouse, perhaps hinting at the evil and licentious undertones of this otherwise festive scene.

The stages of life were celebrated and memorialized by eighteenth- and nineteenth-century Americans in numerous ways, and some of these customs — such as baptisms and the building of funerary monuments— are still observed in the twentieth century. Others have disappeared from our culture, among them the making or commissioning of personalized birth and baptismal certificates with ornate decorations, as well as the creation of mourning pictures, a form that was introduced at the time of George Washington's death and flourished for some sixty years thereafter. Both traditions may fairly be described as ceremonial art, tied to the rites of passage in everyone's life, though sentiment played a stronger role in the production of mourning art than in that of birth and baptismal records. These documents were produced for friends and loved ones by amateur artists of both sexes, by clergymen and teachers, and by young boys and girls as classroom exercises.

Francis Portzline (1771–1857) was a teacher, among other occupations. Born in Germany, he immigrated to America sometime before 1800, when he was listed as an unmarried storekeeper in the York County, Pennsylvania, tax records for Monaghan Township. He moved several times within Pennsylvania, and his occupation was variously recorded as merchant, farmer, and schoolteacher. It was probably his teaching that inspired him to draw the colorful birth and baptismal certificate for Jonathan Schaffer in plate 109. Portzline's decorations are typically precise in execution, with dense applications of paint. The flanking peacocks seen in this example are among the most elaborate of his birds.

107
Unidentified maker, CATHOLIC FUNERAL PROCESSION, *possibly Vermont, ca. 1910, carved wood with leather, metal, and bone; priest, 9 × 3 1/2 × 3 1/4 inches; altar boy, 8 1/2 × 3 × 3 5/8 inches; bearer of cross, 8 × 3 × 5 inches; driver, 9 5/8 × 3 5/8 × 3 inches; sled, 2 3/4 × 13 1/4 × 6 1/4 inches; coffin carrier, 3 1/8 × 3 7/8 × 7 3/4 inches; coffin, 2 1/2 × 3 1/4 × 10 1/8 inches; horse, 9 7/8 × 3 × 15 inches; harness poles, 1/2 × 5 7/8 × 15 3/4 inches (80.701.3).*

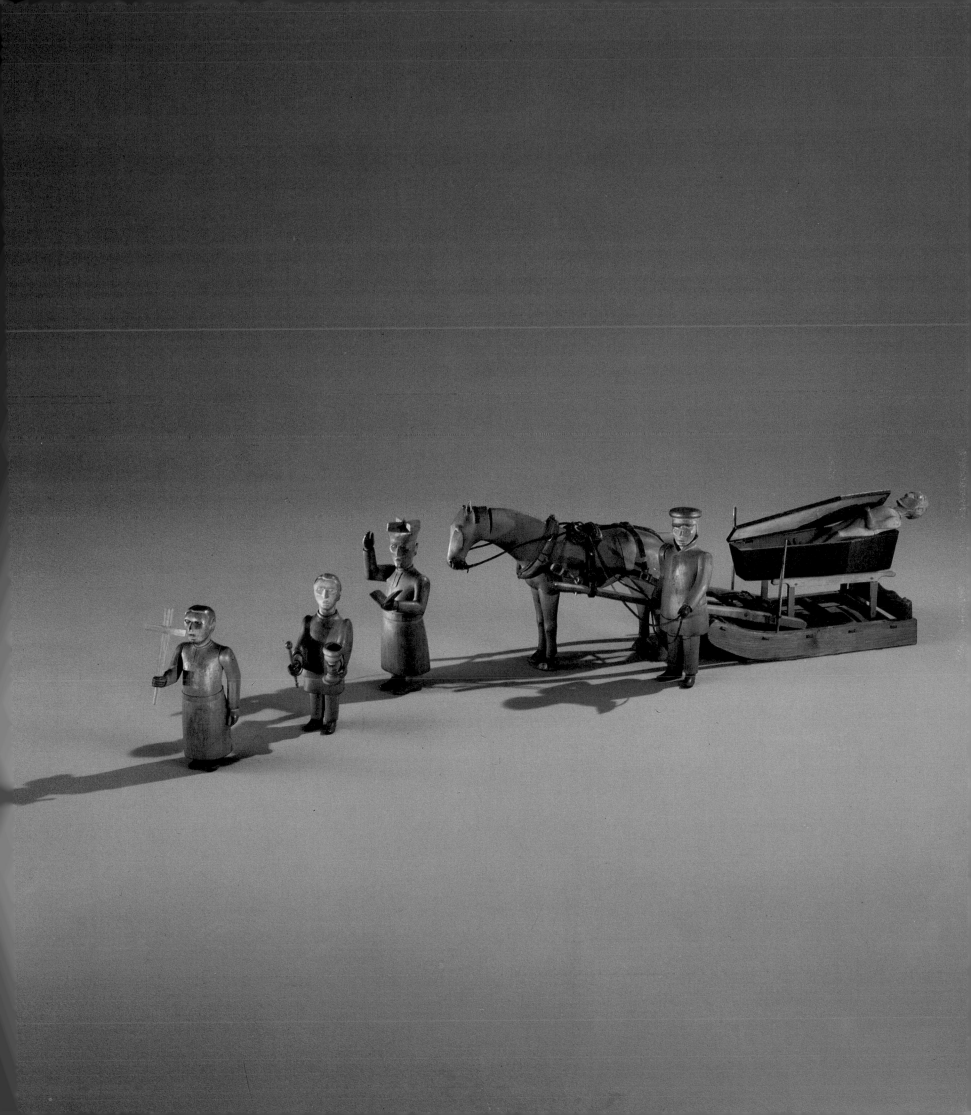

Here they attractively frame the main text within a heart shape, symbolizing love, and their tiny feet break into the heart's border to cleverly draw the viewer's attention to the written message.

The inscription is similar to those seen on most German-American fraktur. The term applies both to the ornamental calligraphy and to the traditional decorative motifs and geometric elements that frame the information provided by the lettering seen on most examples. The word is derived from the name of a fifteenth-century German type face called Fraktur, which the broken letters commonly used in these handmade illuminated records resemble. Fraktur was widely practiced by several generations of artists with German ancestry.

Portzline's fraktur records the fact that the child was born to lawfully wedded parents in the year "of our Redeemer 1844," was baptized by "Preacher" G. Erlemeier, and received the name Jonathan in holy baptism. Below this appears a description in German of the purpose of the ceremony that the certificate documents, and a clear reference to the child's intended path in the religious life: "Baptized into Thy name most holy, O Father, Son, and Holy Ghost, I claim a place, though meek and lowly, Among Thy seed, Thy chosen host. Buried with Christ and dead to sin, Thy Spirit now shall live within."

Another verse stressing the importance of God's guidance throughout life was included on Alexander Danner's certificate (plate 110), now attributed to Christian Mertle (b. 1802) and an unidentified scrivener. It reads, in translation: "God bless our going out and coming in, Your plowing and seed-time, . . . That the mountains bring you tidings of peace And the hills dance before you, . . ." There are few inscriptions on family records that use such plain yet poetic phrases to state the earnest desire, shared by all early Americans, for a good life.

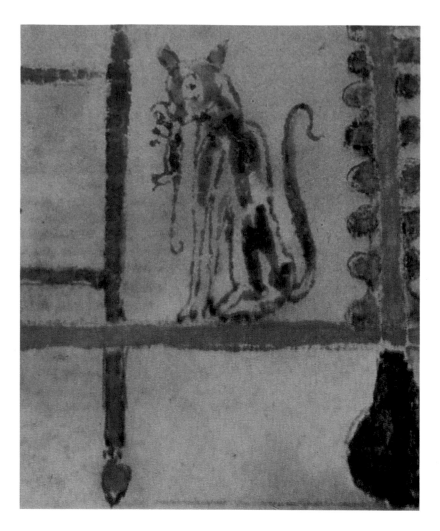

Detail of plate 108

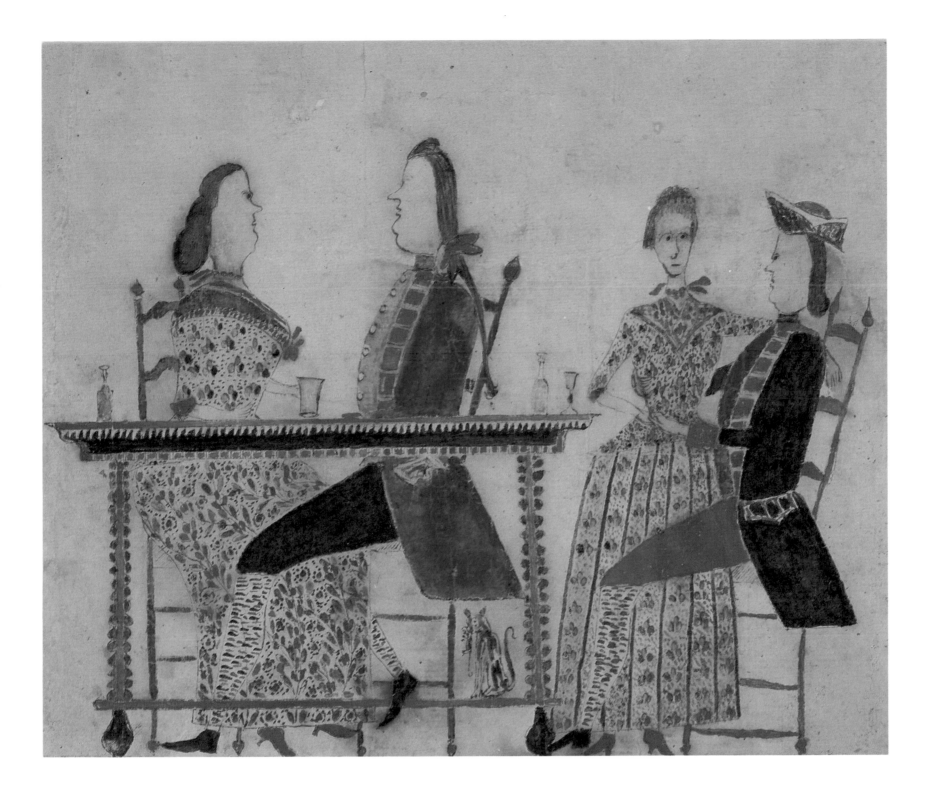

108
Unidentified artist, PRODIGAL SON
REVELING WITH HARLOTS,
*United States, possibly Connecticut,
ca. 1810, watercolor on wove paper,
11¾ × 10 inches (59.301.4).*

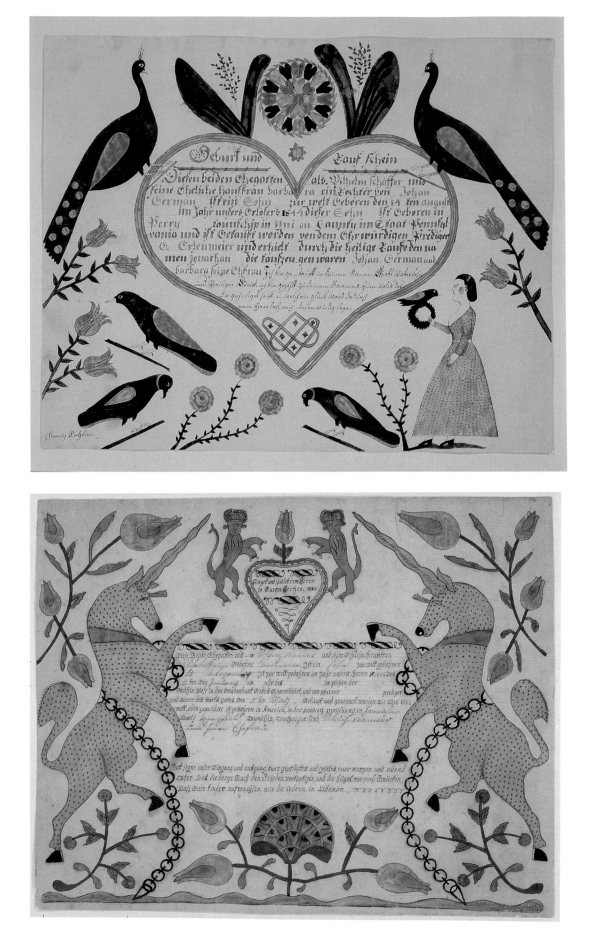

109
Francis Portzline, BIRTH AND
BAPTISMAL CERTIFICATE FOR
JONATHAN SCHAFFER, *probably
Snyder County, Pennsylvania, 1844,
watercolor, pencil, and ink on wove
paper, 12³⁄₈ × 15¹⁄₄ inches
(63.305.5).*

110
*Attributed to Christian Mertle and
an unidentified scrivener,* BIRTH
AND BAPTISMAL CERTIFICATE
FOR ALEXANDER DANNER,
*probably Lancaster County,
Pennsylvania, ca. 1800, watercolor,
pencil, and ink on laid paper, 12¹⁄₂
× 15⁵⁄₈ inches (35.305.1).**

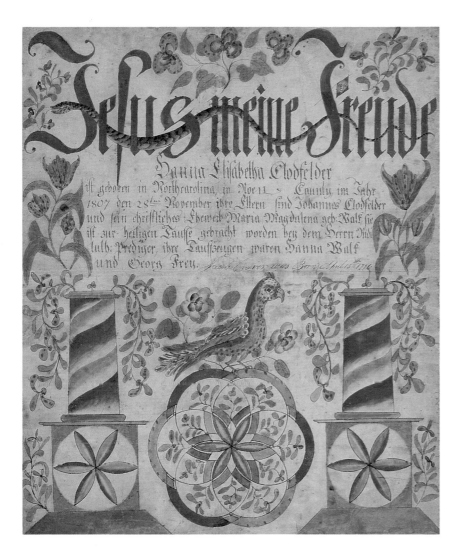

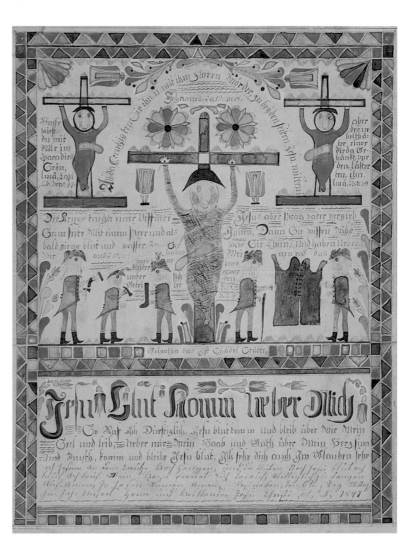

111
Attributed to the Ehre Vater Artist,
BIRTH AND BAPTISMAL
CERTIFICATE FOR HANNA
ELISABETHA CLODFELDER,
Rowan County, North Carolina, ca.
1807, watercolor and ink on laid
paper, 15 1/8 × 12 3/8 inches
(60.305.3).

112
Unidentified artist, THE
CRUCIFIXION, *Pennsylvania, 1847,*
watercolor and ink on wove paper,
13 7/8 × 10 3/4 inches (31.305.1).

The decorations on Danner's certificate, including the two rampant spotted unicorns, as well as the fine condition of the colors, make it an exceptional example of the work of Mertle, who was known only as the C.M. Artist until research by the fraktur scholar Pastor Frederick Weiser uncovered his identity. Only two other frakturs featuring spotted unicorns by Mertle are known.

The identity of the Ehre Vater Artist (active ca. 1785–1810), who drew Hanna Elisabetha Clodfelder's certificate (plate 111), in Rowan County, North Carolina, about 1810, still eludes scholars, as do the names of many other fraktur decorators. The pseudonym Ehre Vater Artist reflects this decorator's frequent use of the heading *Ehre Vater und Mutter* ("Honor Father and Mother") on his certificates, though phrases such as *Jesus meine Freude* ("Jesus my Joy") also appear as headings on other works by him, including the Clodfelder certificate. Here the letters are intertwined with and in some cases superimposed upon a snake, no doubt a visual reference to Satan. Other details in Hanna's certificate probably also had special meanings, though these are obscure to us today. Parrots, for instance, appear here and in the work of other decorators, but the symbolism intended by these colorful birds, if any, is unknown to us. The same may be said for representations of flowers, stars, and various architectural features. Were these simply decorative embellishments, or were there ideas associated with them? Scholars are still debating these issues, even though the fraktur drawings of early German-Americans were among the first forms of folk art to be systematically researched.

Some frakturs were explicit in meaning and intent. The *Crucifixion* in plate 112, created in 1847 by an unidentified Pennsylvania artist, depicts the events that occurred during the crucifixion of Christ. These are accompanied by verses from Luke 23 and John 19, describing what happened. The script in the arch above Christ's head cites the two thieves crucified with him, while Golgotha, the Place of

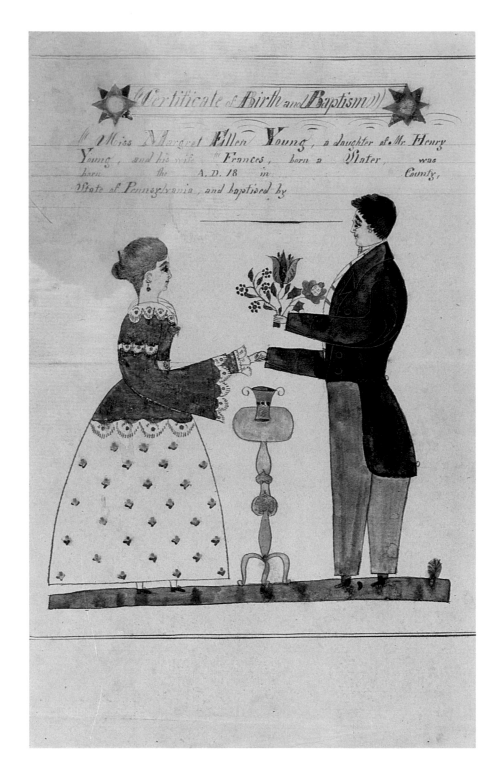

113
Attributed to Henry Young, BIRTH AND BAPTISMAL CERTIFICATE FOR MARGRET ELLEN YOUNG, *possibly Centre County, Pennsylvania, ca. 1840, watercolor and ink on laid paper, 12¾ × 7⅞ inches, gift of Mr. and Mrs. Stanford R. Minsker (78.305.1).*

114
Attributed to Henry Young, BIRTH CERTIFICATE FOR JOSEPH SCOTT FRITZ, *Lycoming County, Pennsylvania, possibly 1827, watercolor and ink on wove paper, 9¹⁵⁄₁₆ × 7⅞ inches (76.305.1).*

Joseph Scott Frits a son of Henry Frits and his wife Mary born a Scott, was born the 20th day of August A.D. 1821.

Mrs Yeaman vaulting.
In Fearfield Township Lycoming County State of Pennsylvania.

Skulls, is mentioned below Christ's cross. The three soldiers at left and the two at right are dividing Christ's garments, as in John 19:24. Only a few American frakturs illustrating the crucifixion survive; this example is one of three attributed to the same hand, two of them dated 1847. Such works served principally religious-inspirational purposes, and the ornamentation was as much didactic in intent as decorative.

Not all frakturs were dominated by religious or moral teachings, though the various types of birth, baptismal, and marriage certificates certainly were meant to document sacred commitments. The certificate for David Wetzel (plate 118), by Friedrich Bandel (active ca. 1810), illustrates a more contemporaneous approach to this kind of art. This example, like the birth certificate for Joseph Scott Fritz (plate 114), by Henry Young (1792–1861), combines what were then modern elements with old-world, traditional iconography and intent. The Wetzel record includes human figures— presumably the child's parents— wearing rather detailed costumes and seated in fashionable yellow Windsor-style chairs. Rarely are such elements seen in German-American fraktur. The equally rare and unusual certificate for young Fritz is, not surprisingly, the only known fraktur featuring a circus woman on horseback. The inscription below the figure reads: "Mrs. Yeaman vaulting." She was the wife of George Yeaman, known as "the Flying Horseman," who worked with various circus companies in America from 1816 until his death in 1827. His wife first exhibited her talents in horsemanship in New York City in December 1825.

More than 150 frakturs in thirteen formats have been attributed to Henry Young (originally Jung), who immigrated to Union County, Pennsylvania, from Germany in 1817. He worked as a church organist and a schoolteacher and supplemented his income by drawing frakturs. His *Certificate of Birth and Baptism* for his second-youngest daughter, Margret Ellen (plate 113), employs a design typical

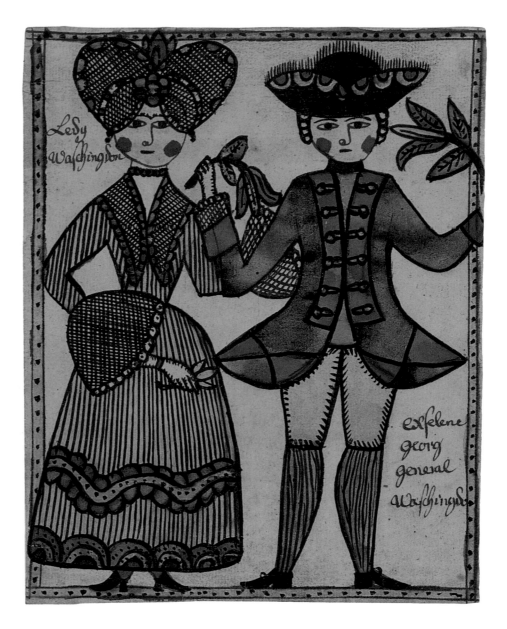

115
Attributed to the Sussel-Washington Artist, EXSELENC GEORG GENERAL WASCHINGDON AND LEDY WASCHINGDON, *probably Lebanon or Lancaster County, Pennsylvania, ca. 1780, watercolor and ink on laid paper, 8 × 6½ inches (58.305.18).*

116
Attributed to Polly Ann ("Jane") Reed, A PRESENT FROM MOTHER ANN TO MARY H., *New Lebanon, New York, 1848, watercolor and ink on wove paper, 14 × 14½ inches (62.305.2).*

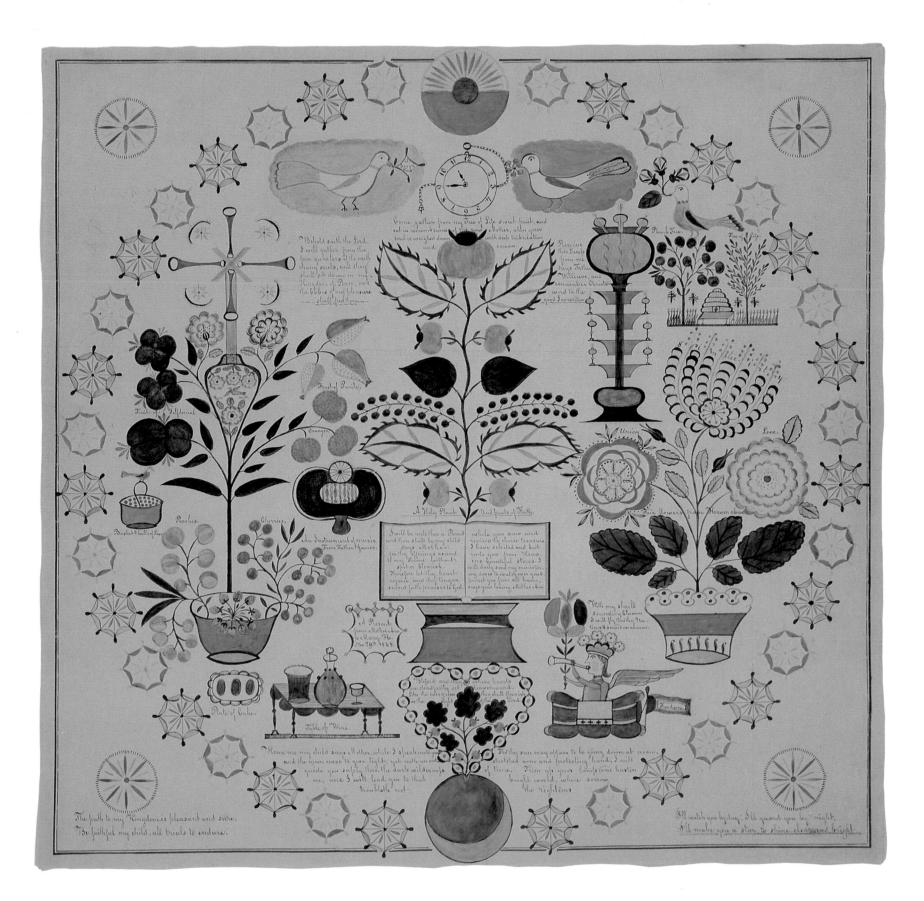

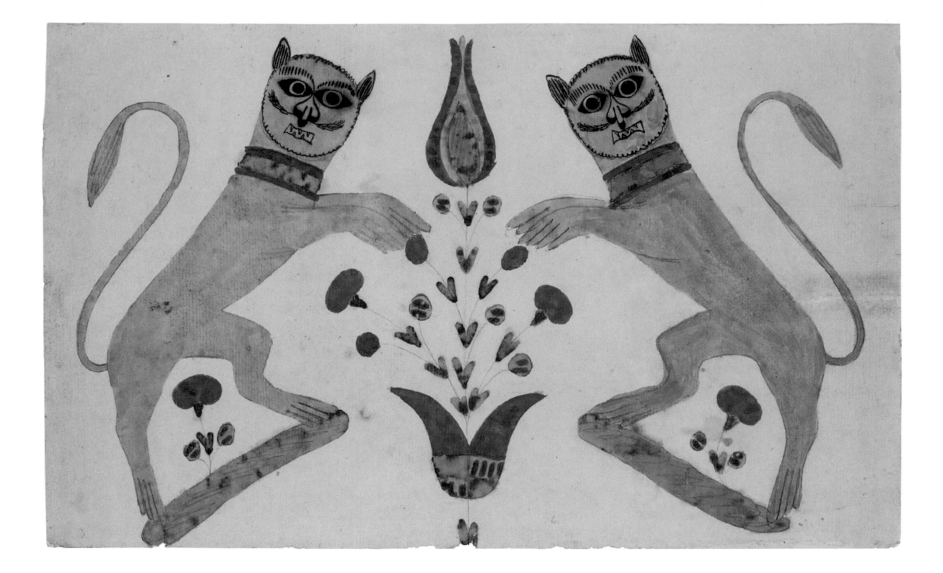

of his work, a man and woman in profile standing in front of a table, with the man holding a characteristic bouquet of flowers in his left hand. Curiously, Young neglected to cite the place and date of his child's birth, and the name of the person who baptized her.

Even further removed from the religious ideals of most frakturs are the decorative pictures produced by the very same hands, which were probably intended for public display within local homes. *Exselenc Georg General Waschingdon and Ledy Waschingdon* (plate 115) dates from about 1780;

while it is not religious in purpose, it represents two esteemed Americans who were immortalized in their own lifetimes. Although unidentified by name, the creator of this engaging work may well be America's best-known fraktur artist. Active from 1775 to 1800, he is occasionally called the Sussel-Washington Artist (after the former owner of this watercolor, the Pennsylvania collector Arthur J. Sussel) and is sometimes referred to as the bee-bonnet artist because of the elaborate crosshatched headdresses that frequently appear on his female subjects. His identity remains a challenging enigma.

∧
117
Attributed to Daniel Otto, LIONS AND TULIPS, *probably Pennsylvania, ca. 1820, watercolor, pencil, and ink on laid paper, 8¹/₈ × 13¹/₄ inches (59.305.2).*

118 >
Attributed to Friedrich Bandel, BIRTH AND BAPTISMAL CERTIFICATE FOR DAVID WETZEL, *probably Shenandoah County, Virginia, probably 1809–1815, watercolor and ink on laid paper, 12⁷/₁₆ × 15⁷/₁₆ inches (84.305.1).*

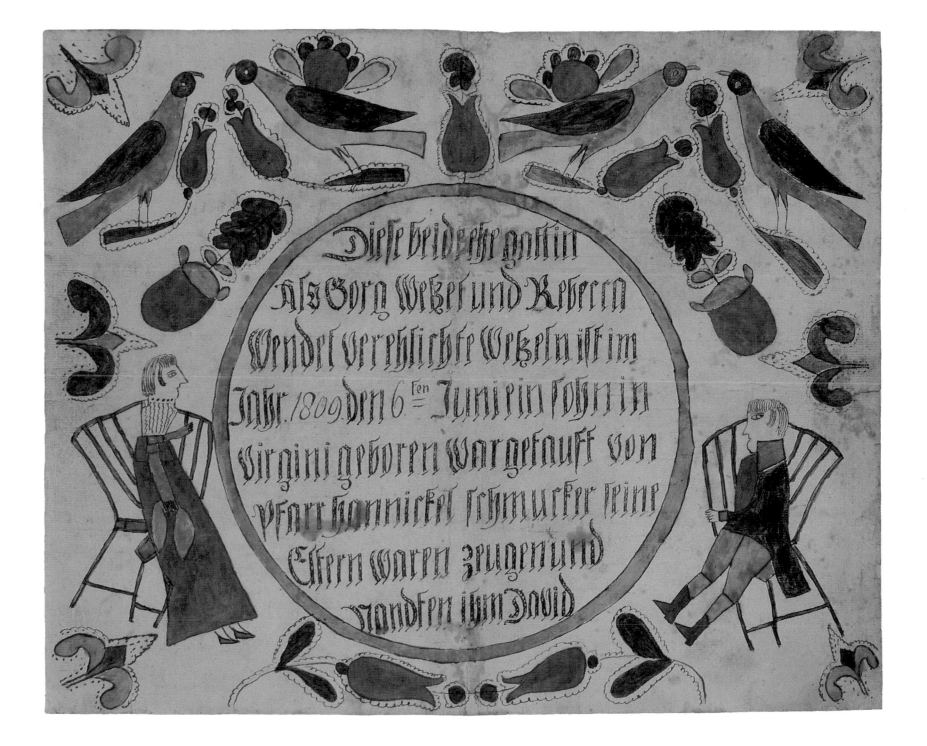

Lions and Tulips (plate 117) and the small picture featuring the merman (plate 46) are two examples of fraktur art based on myths or lore instead of religious themes. Abstraction and bold colors are essential to this kind of fraktur, and some pieces are characterized by playful humor. The merman, a mythical counterpart to the more common mermaid (see plate 44, for instance), has a smiling face and waves a cheery hello to the viewer. The lions, despite their fierce expressions, are dwarfed by the gigantic tulips, in a rather abstract but nonetheless dramatic arrangement. This little watercolor is attributed to Daniel Otto (ca. 1770–ca. 1820), whose fraktur birth and baptismal certificates are well known.

The Daring Hero (plate 120) is an example of a fraktur work that is rich in iconography and non-biblical in inspiration but obviously moralistic in theme. This powerful and bizarre drawing is signed by Jacob Strickler (1770–1842) and dated at the bottom 1792/1793. The title it was assigned comes from the artist's inscription in the upper left corner, though scholars theorize that the figure on horseback represents Saint George, another mounted "daring hero." In fact, one of the inscriptions on this piece states that the "hero," like Saint George, fought a dragon. Certain other details in this example may have been added after 1793, while other areas seem to have been left unfinished for no apparent reason. The bird at lower left, for instance, was never finished, and the arrangement and content of the inscriptions are curious and unclear. Perhaps the artist became dissatisfied with the drawing; an inscription on the back reads: "I have not done it right."

Strickler's *Daring Hero* may have been a companion piece to the *Winged Dragon*, plate 119, which is uncolored and also unfinished. From the fragmentary, disjointed inscriptions on both the front and the back, the dragon picture seems to have been regarded as a preliminary sketch by the artist.

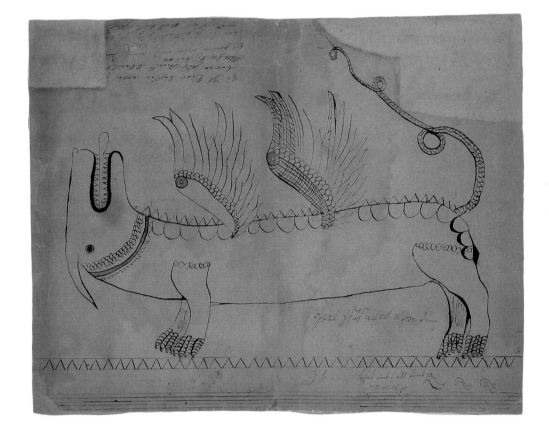

119
Jacob Strickler, WINGED
DRAGON, *Shenandoah (now Page)
County, Virginia, probably ca. 1803,
ink on laid paper, 13¼ × 16½
inches (74.305.6).*

120
Jacob Strickler, THE DARING
HERO, *Shenandoah (now Page)
County, Virginia, 1792, watercolor,
resin, and ink on laid paper, 13¼ ×
16½ inches (74.305.9).*

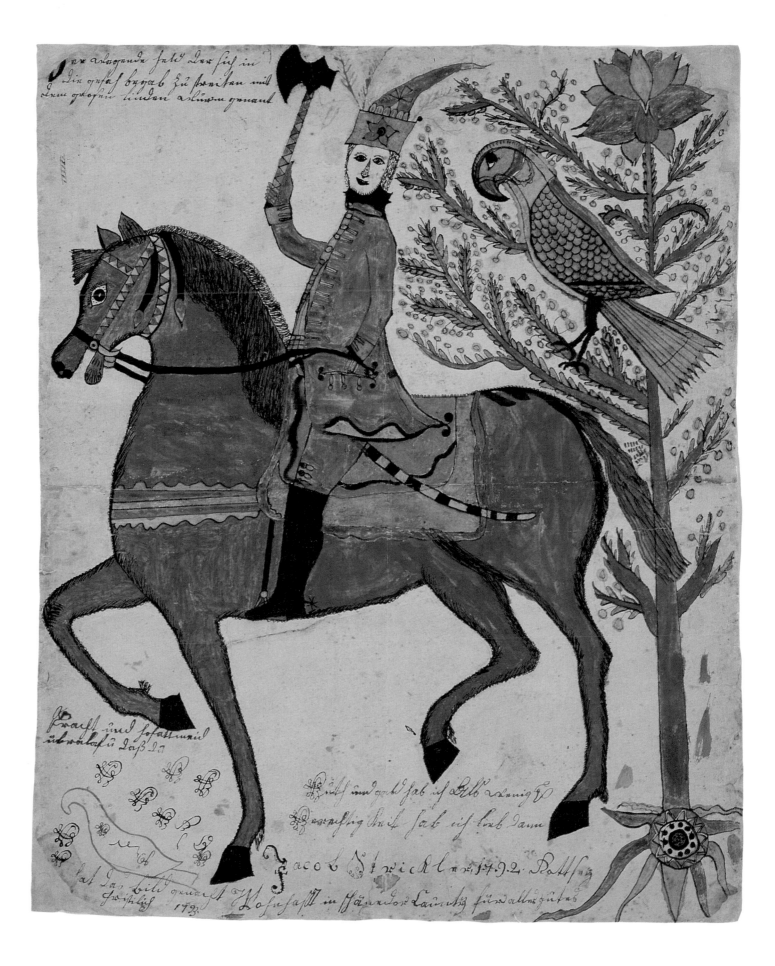

Nevertheless, it is boldly drawn and whimsical in its design.

Little is known about the relationship of German-American fraktur decorators and scriveners to those men and women of English-speaking descent who also produced a variety of ornamented family records; nor do we have much information on the tradition of such records in England, Scotland, Ireland, and other areas from which many Americans and their ancestors emigrated. The surviving American examples are, for now, the best evidence we have, and they suggest either that there was a shared knowledge of symbols and design motifs or that a cross-cultural blending of Germanic and Anglo-oriented designs took place in this country. The birth record for Sarah Harley (plate 121), by John Van Minian (active ca. 1790), was made in 1791 in either Maryland or Pennsylvania and is a fine example of a record in English that utilizes a number of Germanic-style elements.

No information regarding Van Minian's life has been located, though a number of highly decorative drawings by him are known. Most have either a Berks County, Pennsylvania, or Baltimore County, Maryland, provenance. Sarah's record typifies the best of Van Minian's drawing in its design elements and its overall composition. Nationalistic emblems — the eagle with wings spread, stars with the inscription "Epluribus [sic] Unium" below, and the all-seeing eye of God— are combined with traditional German flower, heart, and geometric devices. The sprouting vines with cloverlike foliage and small flowers are a common motif in Van Minian's work, as are the figures in profile, but both devices are unusual in German fraktur.

Mary E. Wheelock's birth record (plate 122) is the smallest and simplest of its type in the Center's collection but also one of the most appealing examples, with its crisp lettering and drawing and its well-preserved blue, pink, and yellow colors. The circular format is not often seen in either German

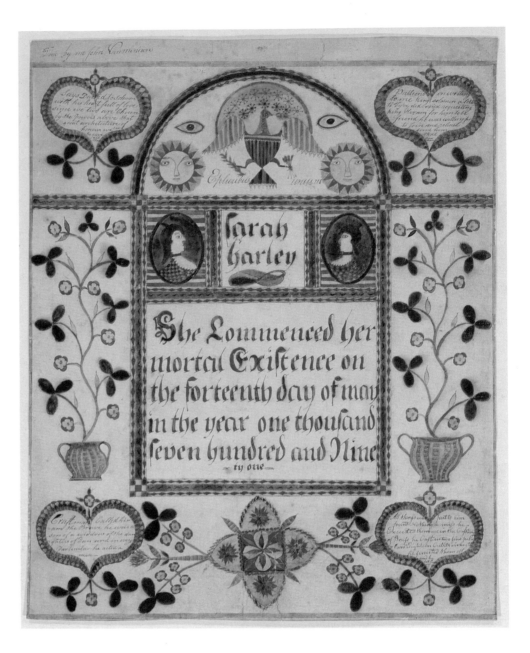

121
John Van Minan, BIRTH RECORD FOR SARAH HARLEY, *Pennsylvania or Maryland, 1791, watercolor and ink on laid paper, 15¼ × 12¼ inches (58.305.14).*

122
Unidentified artist, BIRTH RECORD FOR MARY E. WHEELOCK, *United States, 1830–1835, watercolor, ink, and pencil on laid paper, 5¾ × 7⅛ inches (58.305.23).*

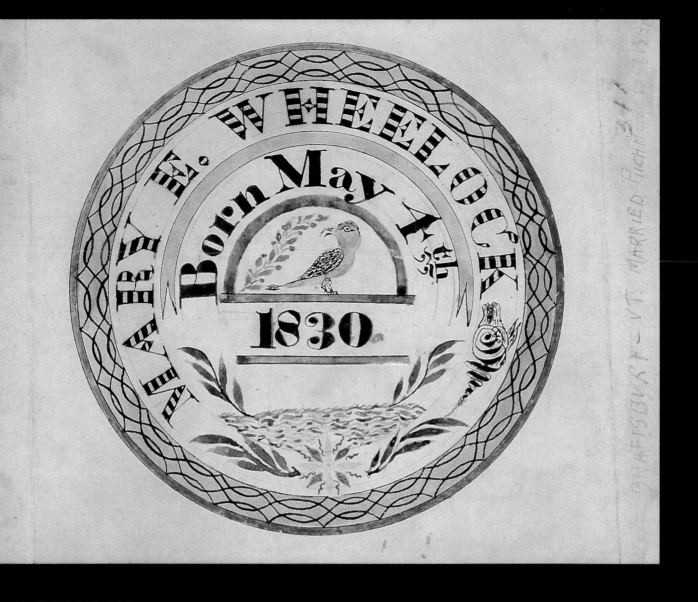

MARY E. WHEELOCK
Born May 4th
1830

or English records of the 1830–1835 period. Interestingly, there is no moralistic, patriotic, or religious verse on this piece. This seems to be the case with English examples because, unlike the German certificates, they rarely served as documents of baptism. Also, many fraktur pieces were produced by ministers and by parochial schoolteachers, while the English records were usually made by talented laymen who, in some cases, produced other artwork for their livelihoods.

Another type of pictorial folk art that is associated with English-speaking Americans of the nineteenth century has been unappreciated until recently: the colorful and meticulously rendered religious drawings of the Shakers. *A Present From Mother Ann to Mary H.* (plate 116) is attributed to Polly Ann ("Jane") Reed (1818–1881) and was made in New Lebanon, New York, in 1848.

In 1774, Ann Lee led a small band of religious dissenters from England to America to found the first of the Shaker communal societies in this country at Watervliet, near Albany, New York. Mother Ann, who considered herself the daughter of God, advocated celibacy, confession, repentance, and withdrawal from the everyday world. Her followers called themselves Believers in Christ's Second Appearance, but outsiders soon dubbed them Shakers, or Shaking Quakers, because their spiritual faith manifested itself in visions, miraculous cures, speaking in tongues, and seizures of whirling and shaking.

A gradual relaxation of Shaker principles followed Mother Ann's death in 1784, but this laxity was arrested in 1837. In a trancelike state, a group of schoolgirls forecast Mother Ann's "Second Coming," and the next ten to fifteen years witnessed a remarkable period of revelation and rededication to Shaker teachings. It was during this revival period that inspirational messages, spiritual presentations, and divine revelations abounded, as illustrated in

part by several types of drawings created by and for members of the Society.

The Center's drawing, featuring a "Tree of Life" at its center, is one of the more complex types of Shaker drawings, which developed toward the end of the revival period, when millennial laws forbidding ornament and display were less strictly applied to interpretive artwork. It is inscribed as if it had been made by Mother Ann herself, in accordance with the artists' conception of themselves as mere instruments of revelation for a divine source of wisdom.

The most celebrated of America's folk painters of religious pictures was Edward Hicks (1780–1849). It seems ironic that the man who called himself "but a poor old worthless insignificant painter" in 1846 was destined to become, by the early twentieth century, one of the most familiar and beloved folk artists. His Peaceable Kingdom paintings, based on the prophecy of Isaiah (Isa. 11:6-9: "The wolf also shall dwell with the lamb . . . and a little child shall lead them "), are the best known of his compositions, though Hicks painted landscapes and historical pictures as well (see plates 62 and 124). Hicks was a converted Quaker, and in his lifetime was more famous as a minister than as an easel artist. During the early 1830s, he developed a format for his Peaceable Kingdoms, featuring a seated lion. His earlier use of motifs borrowed from printed sources for the Kingdom pictures (the one in plate 123, for example, was based on an engraving by Richard Westall, published in an English Bible of 1815) was gradually replaced by the arrangement seen in his fine later versions (plate 125). The concept and design of this picture is thoroughly Hicks's. He rejected the grapevine motif, which indicated the salvation of man through outward sacraments; in later versions, he used elements that symbolized salvation through the "Light Within," which in Quaker belief meant the Holy Spirit. The prominent seated lion shown here has

123
Edward Hicks, THE PEACEABLE KINGDOM OF THE BRANCH, Bucks County, Pennsylvania, 1830–1840, oil on canvas, 32⅛ × 37⅞ inches (67.101.1).

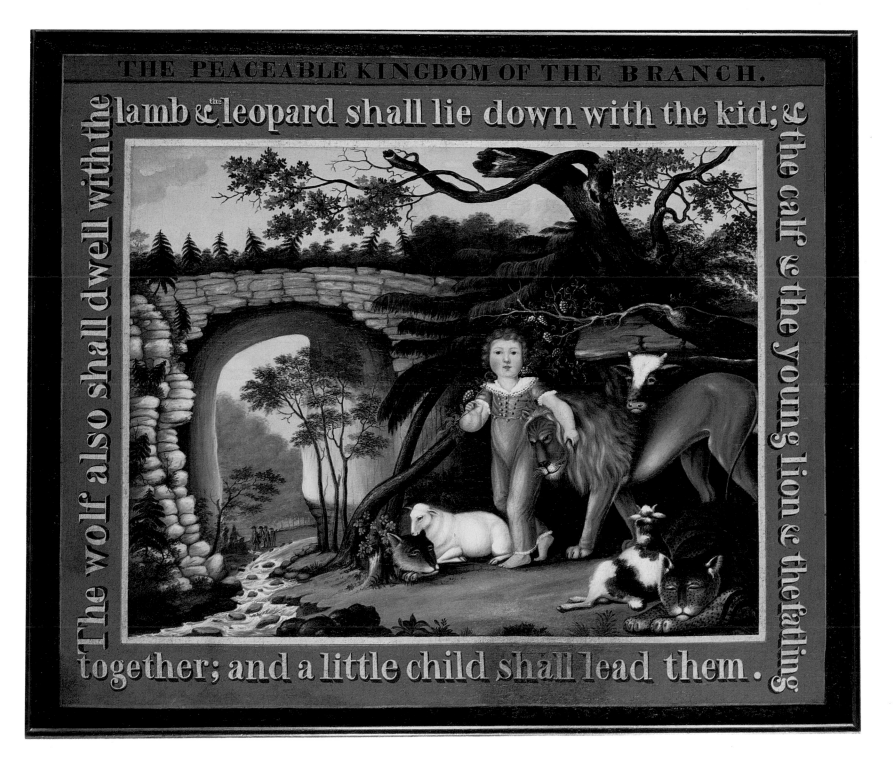

THE PEACEABLE KINGDOM OF THE BRANCH. The wolf also shall dwell with the lamb & the leopard shall lie down with the kid; & the calf & the young lion & the fatling together; and a little child shall lead them.

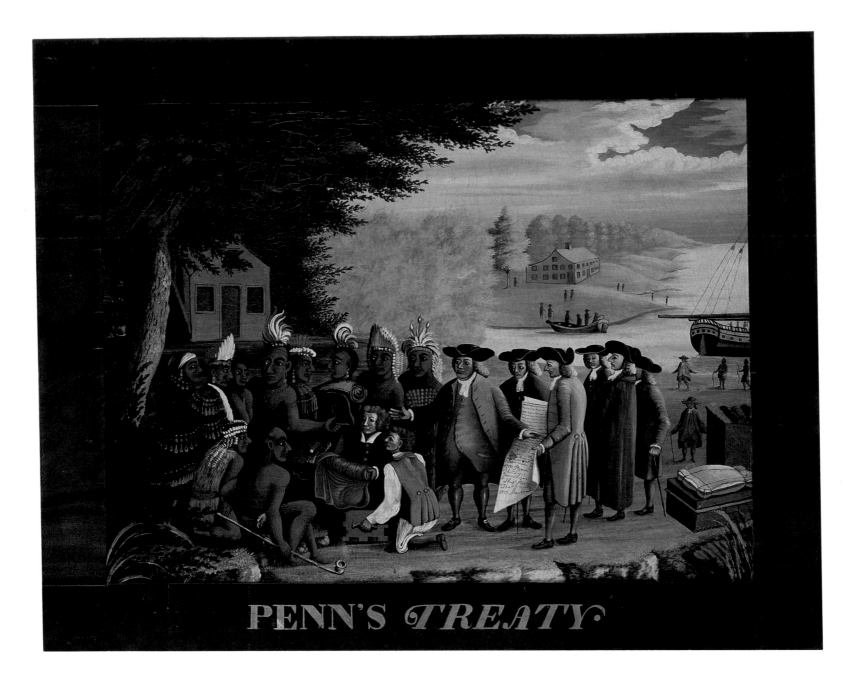

PENN'S *TREATY*

124
Edward Hicks, PENN'S TREATY
WITH THE INDIANS, *Bucks
County, Pennsylvania, 1830–1835,
oil on canvas, 17⅝ × 22¾ inches
(58.101.3).*

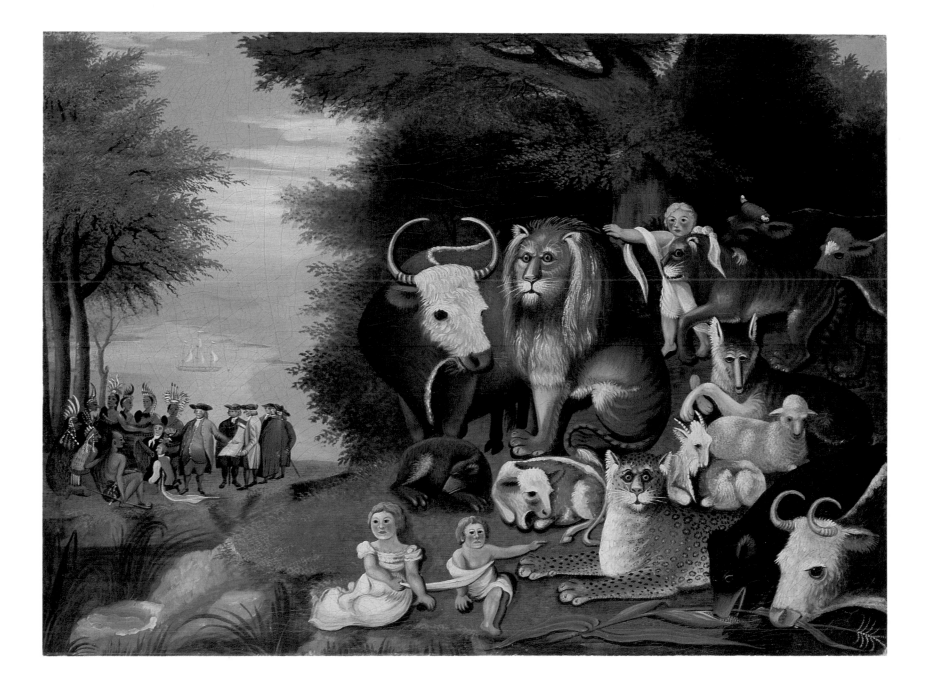

125
Edward Hicks, PEACEABLE
KINGDOM, *Bucks County,*
Pennsylvania, 1832–1834, oil on
canvas, 17¼ × 23¼ inches
*(32.101.1).**

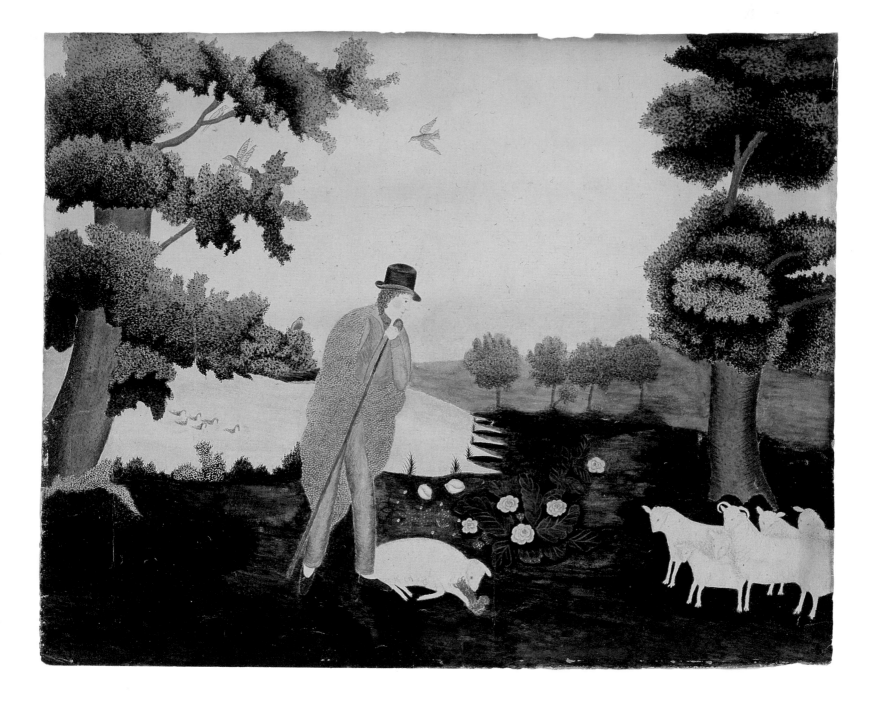

stalks of grain in his mouth, a pictorial representation of Hicks's interpretation of the prophecy in Isaiah that "the lion shall eat straw like the ox." Disobeying nature's law, the lion has chosen to eat grains instead of red meat. Thus he has yielded his self-will to the Divine Will of God, in accordance with the very heart of Quaker theological teaching.

In the background of the 1832–1834 Peaceable Kingdom painting in plate 125, there is a small vignette of Penn signing his treaty with the Indians. Such scenes appear in nearly all of the artist's Kingdom pictures, as well as in thirteen surviving full-size canvases showing only the signing of the treaty (plate 124). The event was significant for Pennsylvania Quakers, particularly those living in Bucks County, Hicks's home area, which Penn had named for his native Buckinghamshire, England, and where he had built his home, Pennsbury. It is also telling that Edward Hicks associated Penn's

∧
126
Unidentified artist, SHEPHERD AND HIS FLOCK, *probably New York or New England, ca. 1820, watercolor and ink with pinpricking, 12 1/8 × 15 3/16 inches (33.301.1).*

127 >
Mary Rees, BARNYARD SCENE, *probably Pennsylvania, 1827, silk and wool threads on linen, 21 1/2 × 23 1/4 inches (57.602.1).*

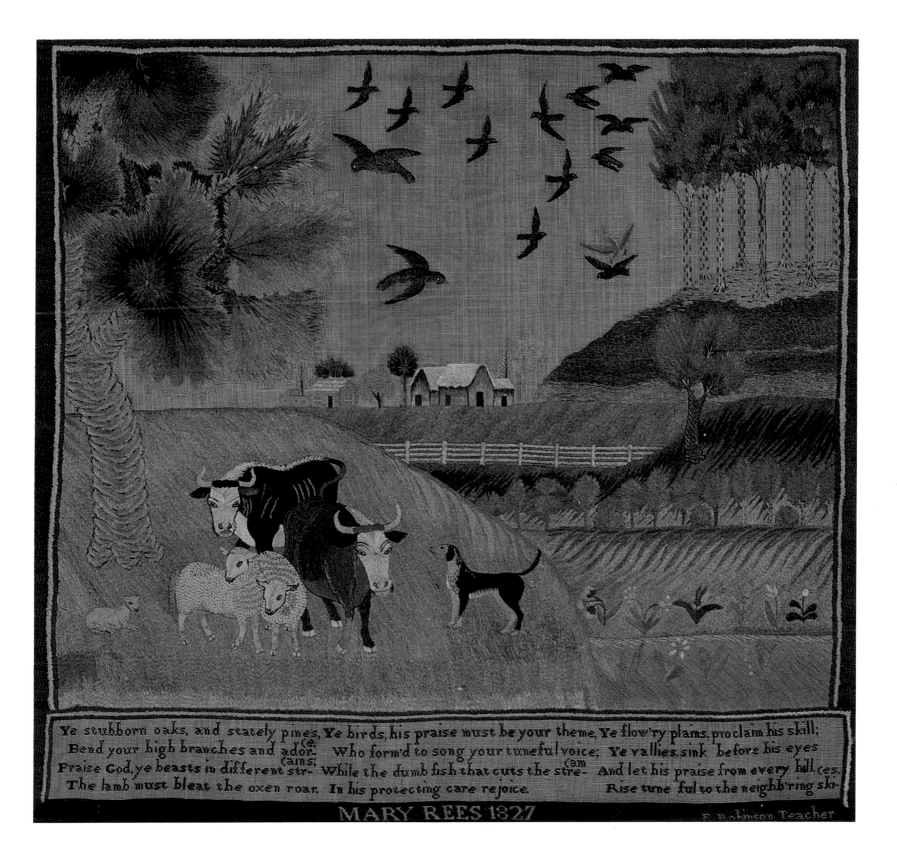

Ye stubborn oaks, and stately pines, Ye birds, his praise must be your theme, Ye flow'ry plains, proclaim his skill;
Bend your high branches and ador- (ce. Who form'd to song your tuneful voice; Ye vallies sink before his eyes
Praise God, ye beasts in different str- (ains; While the dumb fish that cuts the stre- (am And let his praise from every hill (ces.
The lamb must bleat the oxen roar. In his protecting care rejoice. Rise tune ful to the neighb'ring ski-

MARY REES 1827   E. Robinson Teacher

treaty with the fulfillment of God's Peaceable Kingdom on earth, as related in Isaiah.

During the first half of the nineteenth century, a
well-educated girl was expected to master the
basics of drawing, painting, embroidery, and fine
penmanship, in addition to her academic studies.
An enormous amount of amateur artwork was produced by students as part of their school curriculum. That adept pupils could achieve memorable
results is evident in the *Barnyard Scene* (plate 127),
created by Mary Rees in 1827, probably in Pennsylvania, and in the small picture of a shepherd and
his flock (plate 126). Both works reflect some of the
same pastoral ideas contained in Hicks's work,
though neither has specific biblical associations.
Mary's cross-stitched verse admonishes all living
things to praise their Maker, and her pictorial composition shows some of the plants and animals that
were supposed to pay such a tribute. Her careful
selection of thread color, and of the direction and
type of stitching, makes the scene both decorative
and naturalistic.

Nineteenth-century needlework students commonly
used French knots to depict the nubby wool of
sheep, but Mary further emphasized this quality of
their fleece by using silk threads for all but their
bodies, where she employed wool. Her choice of a
linen canvas ground is unusual, for most nineteenth-century silk embroideries were worked on
satin. The picture is nicely executed and represents
a pleasing merger of embroidered picture and sam-
pler formats. Perhaps the design was supplied by
Teacher Robinson, whose name is stitched along
the lower right edge.

Shepherd and His Flock (plate 126) was apparently
derived from a late-eighteenth- or early-nineteenth-
century English print. Such bucolic themes were
also common among young ladies' copywork and
were produced in abundance in school and academy drawing classes in the nineteenth century. The
technique of pinpricking, used for the shepherd's

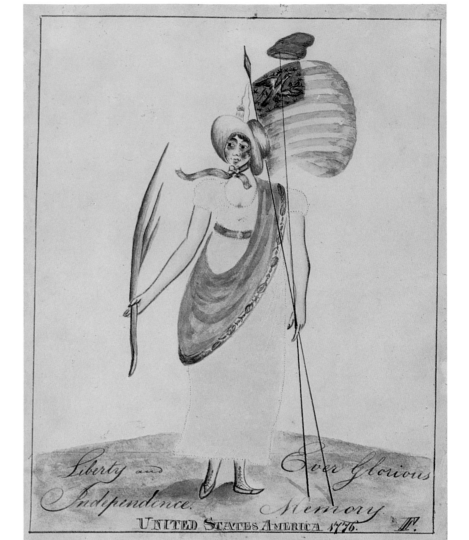

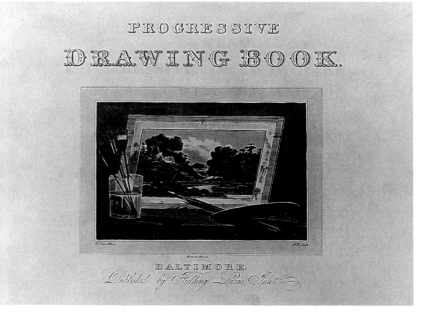

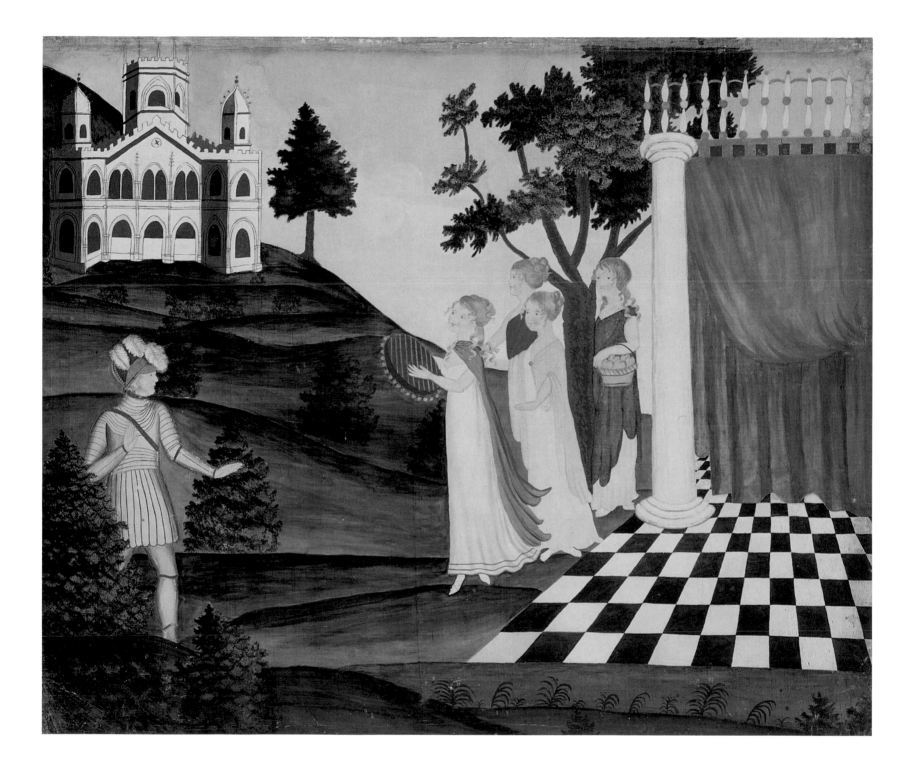

128
Unidentified artist, MISS LIBERTY,
*possibly New Jersey, probably 1810–
1820, watercolor and ink on wove
paper with pinpricking, 10^{1}/$_{16}$ ×
8^{1}/$_{16}$ inches (35.301.4).**

*Figure 12
Fielding Lucas, Jr.'s* PROGRESSIVE
DRAWING BOOK, *published by
Lucas in Baltimore. This drawing
book "in three parts" is typical of the
many examples of print sources used
for copywork by students and others
(57.1003.25).*

129
Betsy B. Lathrop, JEPHTHAH'S
RETURN, *probably New York or
New England, possibly 1812,
watercolor on silk with gold-
painted-paper collage elements, 29^{7}/$_{8}$
× 25^{5}/$_{8}$ inches (39.401.1).**

cloak, some foliage, and the sheep's fleece, supplements the embroidery-like effect of the trees, where the drawing was indeed meant to simulate needlework.

Old and New Testament stories figured prominently in handmade decorative pictures created for many American homes; "Jephthah's Return," based on Judges 11:30–34, is one of these. In this story, the Gileadite Jephthah vows that if the Lord will grant him victory over the Ammonites, he will sacrifice whichever member of his family first emerges from his house to meet him on his return from war. When Jephthah comes home, it is his only child— a daughter— who dances forth to greet him, with timbrels jingling. The story must have been a popular subject with schoolgirls; two versions are owned by the Center (see plate 129 for one example) and three works closely related are known. None of the three related works includes the building seen at upper left in both Williamsburg examples. The structure has been identified as a temple built in the 1730s at Stowe in Buckinghamshire, England; it was illustrated in B. Seeley's 1773 guide to Stowe, indicating once again how pervasive printed sources were in amateur art.

Jephthah's Return reflects the increasing emphasis on education during the nineteenth century. The Bible continued to serve as a principal inspiration for the many rich images produced in the academies and by older women at home. And these literal interpretations often enhanced the instructional value of the images by providing distinctive, easily recognized attributes or clues for identifying the Bible's many characters and events. The same may be said for images of literary and historical subjects.

Again, a burgeoning sense of pride, of self, and of national identity is reflected in numerous commemorative pieces celebrating military triumphs or heroes. Allegorical symbols that reflected Americans' ambitions and their triumphs over life's struggles also were widely used. There were strong tastes for both the classical and the romantic. Subjects from ancient mythology and especially from Homer's epics were favored. On the other hand, there was a passionate preoccupation with romantic literature and such popular authors as Defoe, Goethe, and Scott. Such works influenced and ultimately served as sources of inspiration for many folk pictures.

The small picture of *Miss Liberty* in plate 128, executed in watercolor and pinpricking, is one of the most original and appealing of the countless depictions of the nation's symbolic First Lady. Her stylish costume suggests the contemporaneous dress of a clothes-conscious adolescent of 1815, rather than anything out of the classical tradition. The figure holds a palm of peace in one hand and supports the flag and a liberty pole, topped by its symbolic cap, with the other. The curiously positioned bird that the artist worked into the flag's corner block looks more like a frightened goose than the intended eagle!

Similar symbols of national pride were popular throughout the nineteenth and early twentieth centuries, and the female figure known as Columbia or Liberty eventually assumed the form that is so familiar today, that of the Statue of Liberty. The weather vane in plate 131, made sometime between 1886 and 1910, was inspired by the colossal figure that was dedicated on October 28, 1886, as the "Statue of Liberty Enlightening the World." It is important to understand that the impetus for the French sculptor Frédéric-Auguste Bartholdi's great lady came in 1865, when a French historian proposed that the statue be created to commemorate the alliance of France with the American colonies during the American Revolution. Although the Revolution was but a memory passed down from their parents and grandparents, most Americans were sharply conscious of its importance, and the plethora of patriotic art that survives from through-

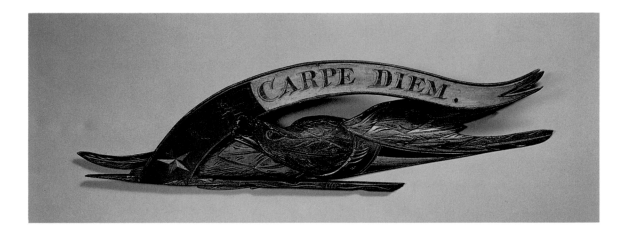

130
Attributed to John H. Bellamy,
"CARPE DIEM" BANNER,
probably Kittery Point, Maine,
probably 1875–1900, carved and
painted wood, 7³/₄ × 25³/₄ × 3
inches (69.701.1).

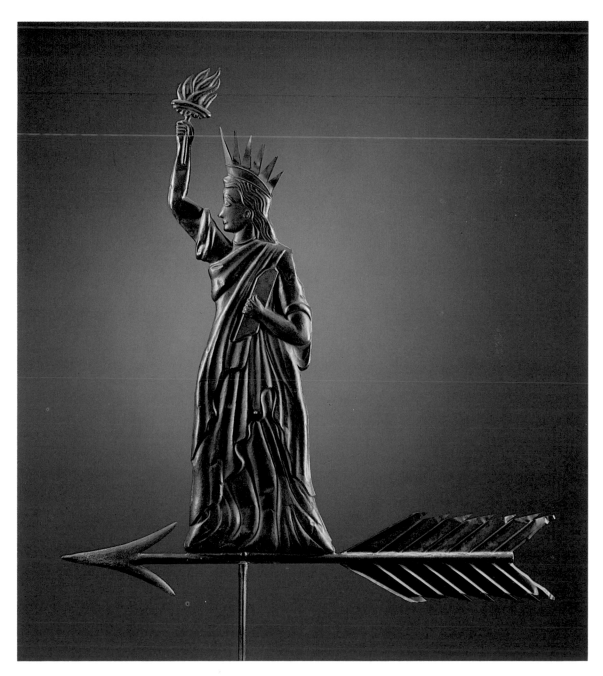

131
Unidentified maker, STATUE OF
LIBERTY, *United States, probably*
1886–1910, copper and zinc, 39¹/₄ ×
36³/₄ × 2¹/₂ inches (32.800.4).*

out the nineteenth century demonstrates a continuing belief in the humanistic principles fought for and won in that historic conflict.

Works such as the eagle with a banner (plate 130), by John Haley Bellamy (1836–1914), and *Washington and Lafayette at the Battle of Yorktown* (plate 132), by Reuben Law Reed (1841–1921), both executed about 1885, are now considered icons of the nonacademic tradition in American art. These pieces were meant to inspire Americans and to remind them of the sound ideals and the accomplishments of their forebears. Reed was descended from men who had fought in the American Revolution, at the battles of Lexington and Bunker Hill; he was a granite worker and later a housepainter, but his interest in history led him to create this imaginary composition, which was based on the factual account of an eyewitness to the Yorktown encounter.

Bellamy, the carver of the eagle with its "Carpe Diem" ("Seize the Day") banner, was employed by the Boston and Portsmouth shipyards as a carver of figureheads, sternboards, gangway panels, and other kinds of decoration, many patriotic in theme, for naval and mercantile vessels. He carved dozens of these smaller eagles, probably as gifts for friends.

Particularly in the work of nineteenth-century students and amateurs, patriotic motifs are often mingled with subjects that had literary, mythological, or ideological associations, which the maker may not have fully comprehended. Thus the seemingly straightforward picture *Colonel C. S. Morgan Addressing His Friends* (plate 135), which was done about 1840 and combines freehand painting with the use of cut stencils on a velvet ground, is actually a rather complex and unusual composition. The subject, Colonel Charles S. Morgan, was born near Morgantown, Virginia (now West Virginia), on June 4, 1799, and died in 1859. As a young man, he was active in politics and became a delegate from the Seventeenth District to the General Convention of the Commonwealth of Virginia in 1829–1830. In

this capacity, he distinguished himself as a brilliant orator, which explains the scene at left in the picture, where he is shown giving one of his famous addresses. In the lower center of the picture there is a representation of Grave Creek Mound, a large Indian burial ground that was explored in 1838. The two figures standing beside the mound are probably Morgan and his wife, with their young daughter, Alcinda, playing nearby. The relationship of the mound, the Morgans, and the liberty pole in this vignette is unclear, though the pole may symbolize some aspect of Morgan's career or the reforms he sought.

Of the pictures utilizing literary themes, Eunice Pinney's *Valencourt and Emily* (plate 136), painted about 1805–1825, ranks among the best. The scene illustrates a sentimental incident from the *Mysteries of Udolpho*, a widely read romantic novel by Anne Radcliffe, first published in London in 1794. Pinney (1770–1849) is of particular interest because her dated drawings all fall within the period from 1809 to 1826, when she was between thirty-nine and fifty-six years of age. Thus her work— all of it created by a mature woman— provides an excellent contrast to early-nineteenth-century schoolgirl art.

The same literary and historical sources that inspired many of the decorative schoolgirl pictures — as well as, in at least a few cases, the work of Eunice Pinney— also influenced the related mourning art of the nineteenth century. Mourning pictures, too, were expressions of the new taste for neoclassical forms as popularized in England by Robert Adam, Josiah Wedgwood, and Angelica Kauffmann. As early as 1782, printed versions of Kauffmann's painting *Fame Decorating the Tomb of Shakespeare* were widely circulated, and eighteen years later, after George Washington died, the engraving inspired a number of memorials honoring him. Other motifs for mourning pictures were gleaned from engraved illustrations in magazines and novels, including Joseph Addison's *Spectator* and translations of Goethe's *Sorrows of Young*

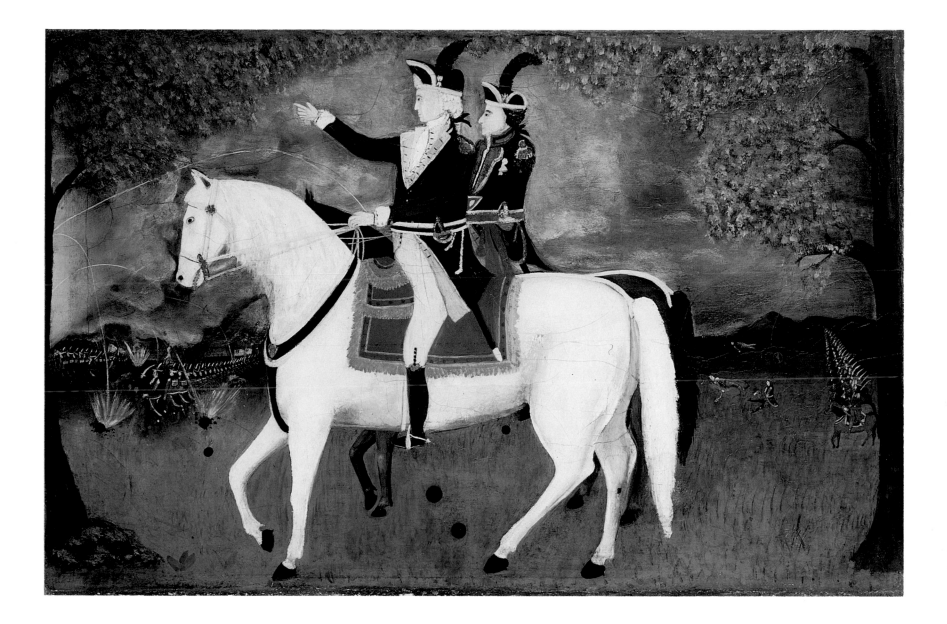

132
Reuben Law Reed, WASHINGTON
AND LAFAYETTE AT THE
BATTLE OF YORKTOWN, *Acton,
Massachusetts, probably 1860–1880,
oil and gold paint on canvas, 22¼
× 33⅞ inches (31.101.1).* *

Werther (see figure 13). Mourning pictures were especially popular in towns and cities, where women had more leisure time and where the techniques of making such pictures were frequently taught in female seminaries.

The enormous popularity of memorial scenes featuring weeping willows, funeral urns, and grieving relatives reflects an aspect of romanticism wherein a preoccupation with the inevitability of death is combined with a confident belief in immortality. The idea of providing such works for oneself, one's friends, and one's loved ones was intricately tied to the widespread interest in patriotic symbols and the virtual apotheosis of the nation's first hero, George Washington.

Within weeks of the sudden death of Washington on December 14, 1799, the nation was flooded with commemorative souvenirs in many media honoring the first President. A number of patriotic prints were published, promptly inspiring countless painted and embroidered pictures, executed with varying degrees of skill by a generation of young people. As the memorial format gained popularity, similar works were produced for departed loved ones, and an amazing amount of individuality emerged, in surprisingly varied combinations of stock elements. Hand-painted and embroidered memorials continued to be made until the 1840s, when the development of lithography made inexpensive, printed mourning pictures readily available.

Memorial to Daniel Ma—— (plate 134), probably made in Massachusetts about 1810, is typical in its use of two mourning figures and a central monument, which in this case has been damaged, so that some of the family name is obscured. Nothing is known about the young man being honored, other than that he died in Suriname. The costumes of the two figures, who probably represent the dead youth's parents, suggest that the watercolor was painted about a decade after 1801, the death date inscribed on the monument. The unidentified artist

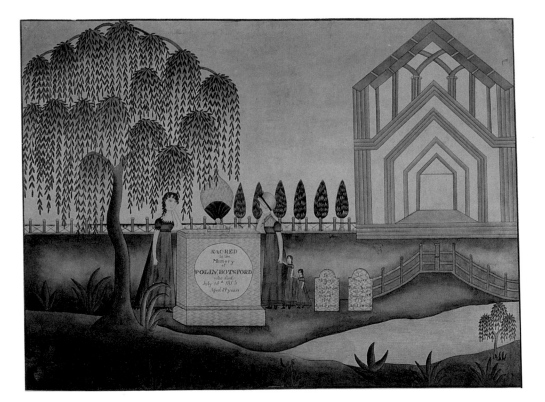

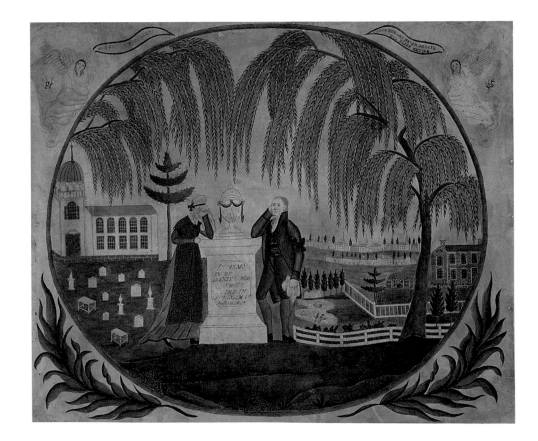

< 133
Unidentified artist, MEMORIAL FOR POLLY BOTSFORD AND HER CHILDREN, *possibly Newtown, Connecticut, ca. 1815, watercolor and ink on wove paper, 18 × 23½ inches (33.304.1).*

134
Unidentified artist, MEMORIAL TO DANIEL MA—, *probably Massachusetts, ca. 1810, watercolor and ink with pinpricking on wove paper, 13⅜ × 16¾ inches (58.304.5).*

135 >
Unidentified artist, COLONEL C. S. MORGAN ADDRESSING HIS FRIENDS, *United States, possibly 1835–1840, paint and ink on velvet, 15 × 21¼ inches (35.401.1).*

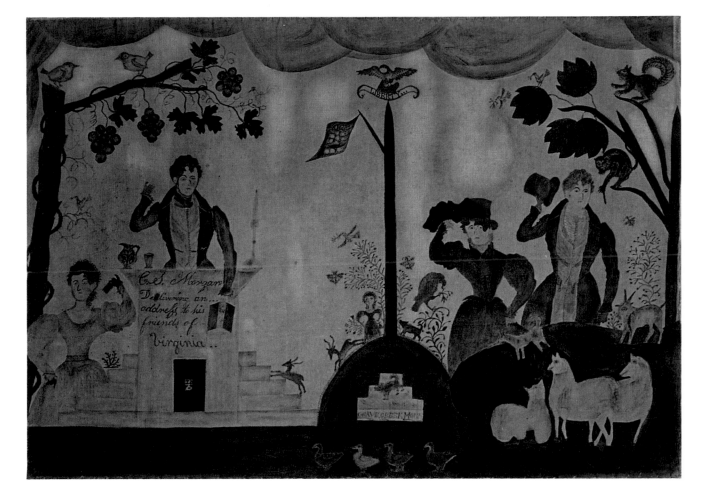

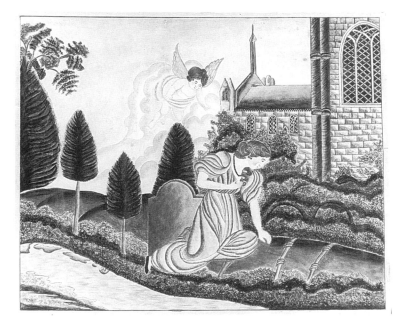

Figure 13
Unidentified artist, CHARLOTTE WEEPING OVER WERTER'S TOMB, *United States, ca. 1815, watercolor and ink on wove paper, 13 × 16¹/₁₆ inches (63.301.1). Driven to distraction by his love for a married woman, Charlotte, Werther kills himself at the end of Goethe's famous story.*

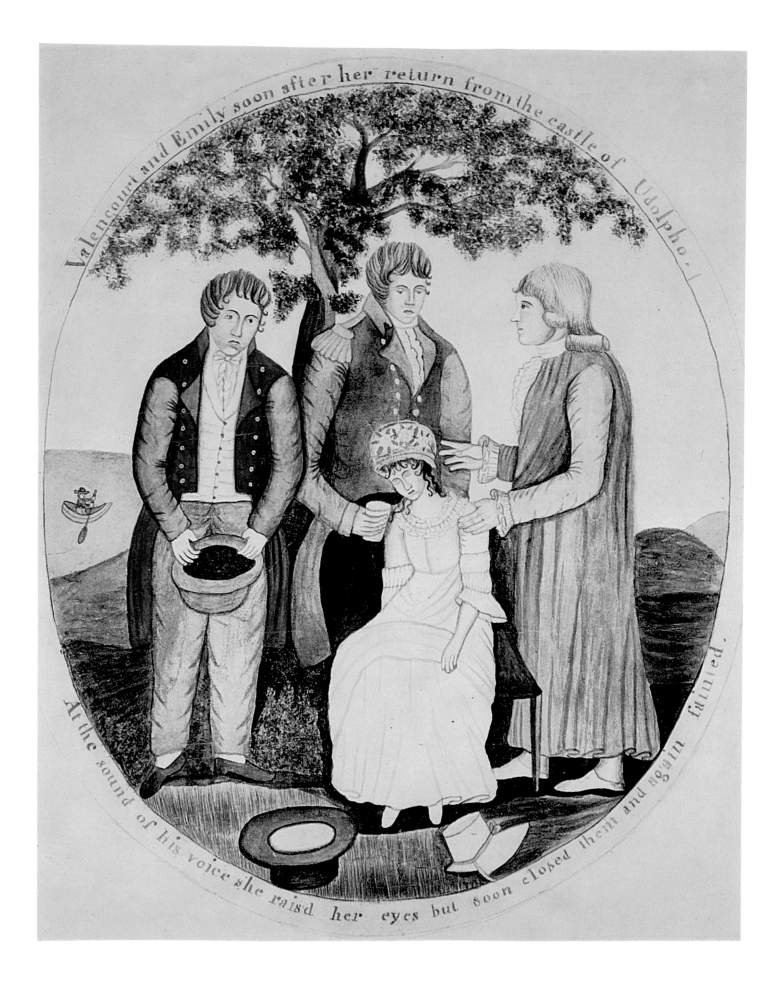

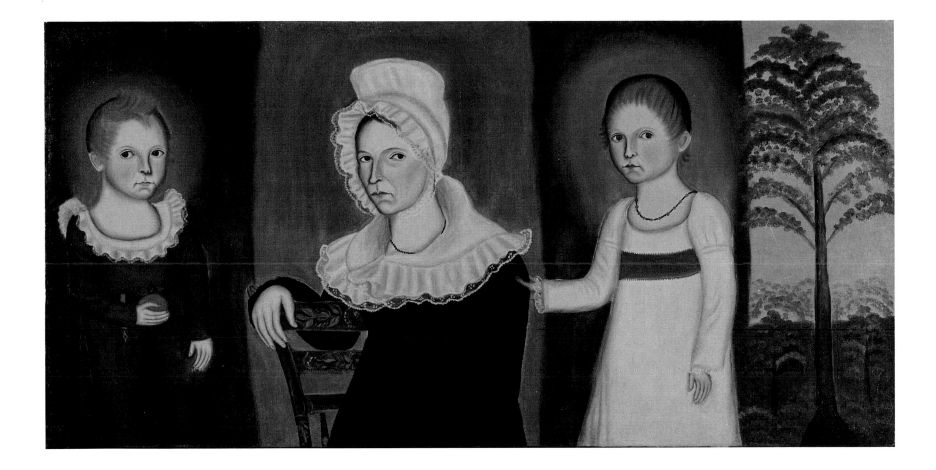

Attributed to Eunice Pinney,
VALENCOURT AND EMILY,
Connecticut, probably 1805–1825,
watercolor, ink, and pencil on wove
paper, 12⁵⁄₁₆ × 10 inches (58.301.4).

∧ 137
Unidentified artist, MARYLAND
FAMILY, *probably Maryland, ca.*
1825, oil on canvas, 29⁵⁄₁₆ × 59¹⁄₄
*inches (34.100.2).***
Neither the identity of the subjects
nor the meaning of the unusual
four-part division of this composition
is known, though certain aspects
suggest that the piece may be a me-
morial. The tall tree flanked by two
smaller ones, on the right, may sym-
bolize a deceased father and two
children, and the woman's black
dress and jet beads could be con-
strued as mourning attire. The halo
effect around the children's heads
might have indicated their recent
deaths.

meticulously detailed a variety of architectural motifs, fences, and grave markers, and several of the
design elements, including the woman's cap, the
man's stock, their handkerchiefs, and the covering
festooned over the urn, have been pinpricked to
suggest embroidery stitches. Oval compositions of
this type were usually framed with glass that had
been reverse-painted black and embellished with
gold-leaf decorations.

Memorial for Polly Botsford and Her Children (plate
133), possibly made in Newtown, Connecticut, is
extraordinary in both its composition and its finely
rendered, stylized forms. The interplay of the curvi-
linear and linear elements that create the interesting geometric shapes in the church contributes to
the picture's appeal and immediately brings to
mind the relationship between folk art and modern
art. The picture memorializes Polly Botsford, who

died in 1813, and two of her children, a little girl
named Polly and an infant son named Gideon,
both of whom predeceased her.

This preoccupation with commemorating the passing of loved ones (to heaven, it was hoped) took
many forms during these and later years, and
mourning jewelry of all sorts, armbands, cards, coffin furniture of various kinds, embroidered hanker-
chiefs, and other items became standard emblems
and mementos of the departed. Tombstone art also
flourished, and professionally designed burial parks
were introduced. Many cemeteries throughout the
United States still contain stones cut by folk carvers,
with an occasional funerary figural piece made by a
folk potter.

Will Edmondson's *Crucifixion* (plate 138) is a good
example of the kind of work produced by amateur

stonecutters, who also provided grave markers. In 1943, when he was probably in his fifties, Edmondson (1882?–1951), a lifetime resident of Nashville, Tennessee, had a vision in which God appeared to him with a special message. "I knowed it was God tellin' me what to do. God was tellin' me to cut figures. He gave me them two things." He may have meant a simple mallet and a steel point that he fashioned from a railroad spike, his only tools. With these, in the years that followed, Edmondson produced hundreds of sculptures while continuing his work as a tombstone carver. His limestone *Crucifixion* is an outstanding example of folk art, though it is typical in its reliance upon strong form and stylized, minimally worked details for its aesthetic success. Today Edmondson is considered one of the outstanding folk carvers of the twentieth century.

The crucifixion form, celebrating Christ's death on the cross and his resurrection, has been and continues to be used by twentieth-century folk artists, many of whom attribute their artistic creativity to God's calling. Their resulting art is often perceived as God's message, worked through and made visible by their hands. Howard Finister's folk art falls into this category, as does that of Elijah Pierce and of Sister Gertrude Morgan. In many other cases, even from the twentieth century, pieces of folk art

with overt religious associations cannot be linked to specific makers, whose background and training might help explain their purpose or intent. The creator of the exquisitely carved *Catholic Funeral Procession* in plate 107 is one such mystery, despite an exhaustive search for his name. It is not known whether this group of figures had some personal significance for the carver or whether it merely depicts a scene familiar to most people— a visual representation of a culture's collective memory.

Catholic Funeral Procession was fashioned by caring hands, even down to the wizened corpse, which can be suspended from the coffin by a cleverly devised wire attachment. The harness and the sled furniture is made of real leather, again well crafted in miniature.

Much of America's surviving folk art shares the anonymity and the unknown provenance of the *Catholic Funeral Procession*. This does not make them lesser works, nor does it mean they are any the less valuable as cultural documents. Their messages can be read and felt— in this case, deeply. The altar boy holding the age-old symbol of the cross, the second clerical figure, the priest with his biretta, and the driver, plainly clad in secular dress, all participate in this last ceremony on earth of one human who was born and is now gone.

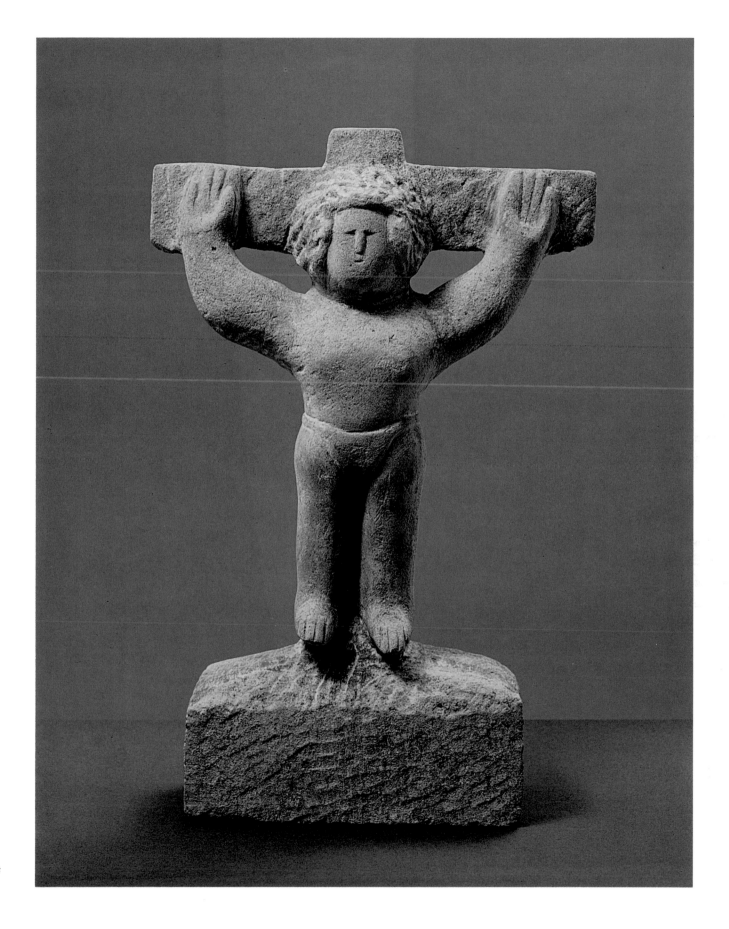

138
William Edmondson,
CRUCIFIXION, *Nashville,*
Tennessee, ca. 1935, carved
limestone, 24³/₈ × 17 × 4⁵/₈ inches
(71.907.1).

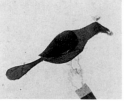

CHAPTER SIX
For Friends and Family

A number of the objects illustrated in this volume were made as presentation pieces for special friends or family members. Some of the occasions for giving gifts were ones that are still celebrated today, including Christmas, Easter, Saint Valentine's day, birthdays, and weddings. Other presents were gestures of personal affection or appreciation; some instructors, for instance, gave handmade rewards of merit to students on their successful completion of a project or a group of assignments.

The lively little *Easter Rabbit* by John Conrad Gilbert, illustrated in plate 143, was undoubtedly a gift to a child in the fraktur artist's family or from his neighborhood, though nothing is known of the first owner, not even his or her age. The piece dates from about 1795–1800, and it is believed to be the earliest American representation of the mythical rabbit bearing his basket of colored eggs. The 1769 dower chest in plate 86 was also a gift, probably from parents to a young daughter in anticipation of her marriage and the start of a new household. Many album quilts, too, including those discussed on pages 132–136, were really gifts in kind, since they were lovingly and meticulously worked by many hands for the benefit of one woman's household.

Similarly, the numerous works executed by nineteenth-century schoolchildren, including mourning pictures (plate 133, for example) and theorem still lifes (plates 153, 154, and 156), were rarely produced for income, and many were no doubt given to proud parents by offspring who may or may not have enjoyed completing these classroom exercises.

Student art was often inspired by prints in magazines and illustrated Bibles or in popular novels of the day. Girls cleverly utilized elements from these sources in their fancy pieces and mourning pictures, while schoolboys appropriated some of the same motifs and combined them with others from penmanship sample books, using them as the basis for the calligraphic drawings they were required to execute with steel pens. In the artwork of both girls and boys, the schoolmistress or schoolmaster, respectively, exerted considerable influence on the type of work created and its final look.

If a specific piece of excellent quality has no documentation, it is difficult to ascertain whether it was prepared for students to copy or whether it was itself a copy of the teacher's prepared example, executed by a talented student. Such is the case with J. W. Hamlen's *Horse with Trappings* (plate 140), an unusually pleasing calligraphic drawing that successfully combines very intricate penwork motifs with a simple outline of the animal and hatching for its mane and tail. Hamlen's name is prominently placed, decorated with surrounding flourishes and ornate letters. The verse inscribed by the artist at the bottom of the drawing was composed by Jonathan Mitchell Sewall in his "Prologue to Addison's *Cato*," which served as a preface to that play when it was performed at the Bower Street Theatre in Portsmouth, New Hampshire, in 1800.

Leaping Deer (plate 141), by an unidentified hand, exhibits the rhythmic designs typical of the best calligraphic drawings. The technique of drawing with a steel pen was popular during the last half of the

139
Anny Mohler, ANNY'S GIFT, *Stark County, Ohio, possibly ca. 1830, watercolor, pencil, and ink on wove paper, 12⅝ × 15¹¹⁄₁₆ inches (58.305.15).*

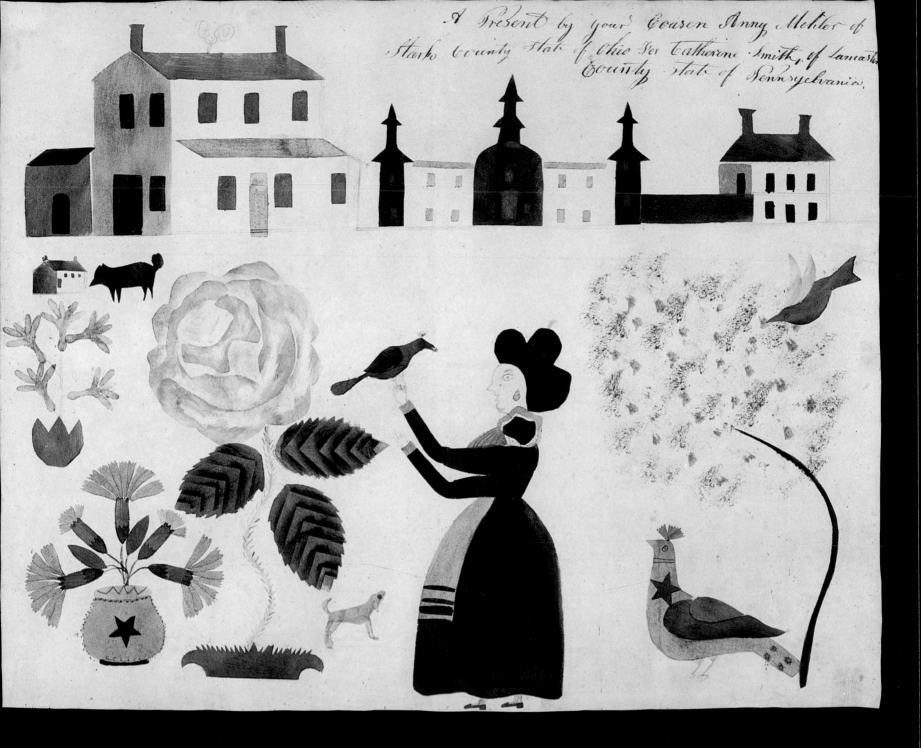

A Present by your Cousen Anny Mohler of Stark County State of Ohio for Catherine Smith, of Lancaster County State of Pennsylvania.

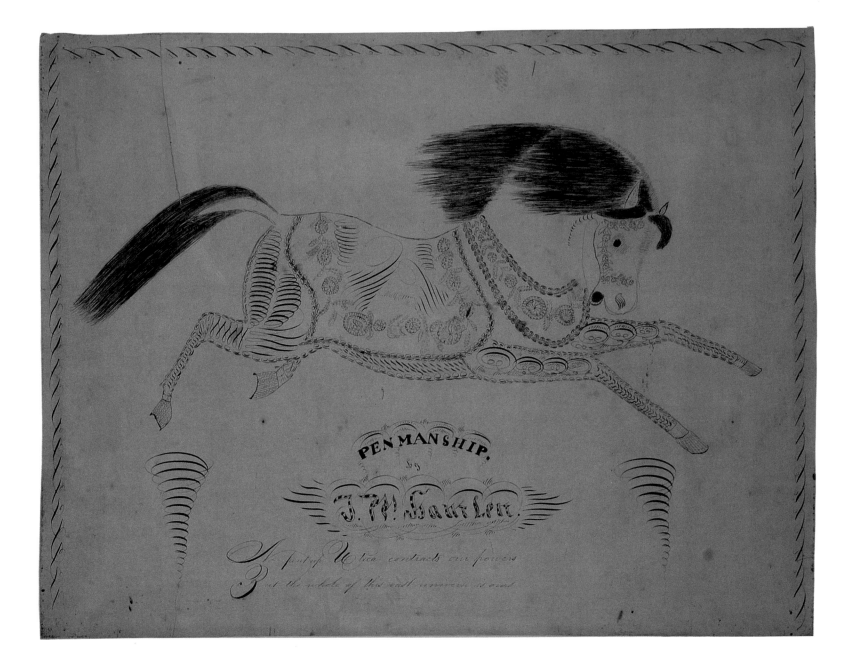

PENMANSHIP.
by

J. W. Hamlen

nineteenth century. Originally used as an exercise to train students to perfect their handwriting, this art form was later professionalized by penmanship masters (see Arnold's *Self-Portrait*, plate 73) and practiced with varying degrees of proficiency by a vast number of amateurs. Steadiness of hand and accuracy of eye were required to produce the countless free-flowing pen strokes that created this graceful deer.

Anny's Gift (plate 139) derives its name from its inscription, which begins, "A present by your cousin Anny Mohler of Stark County stat[e] of Ohio. . . ." We know little about the amateur artist, Anny Mohler, except that she made this highly original and decorative picture for her cousin Catherine Smith, who was then living in Lancaster County, Pennsylvania. The piece appears to date from about 1830. The rose in full bloom may have been cre-

140
J. W. Hamlen, HORSE WITH TRAPPINGS, *possibly New England, ca. 1850, ink on wove paper, 15¾ × 20¼ inches (57.312.3).*

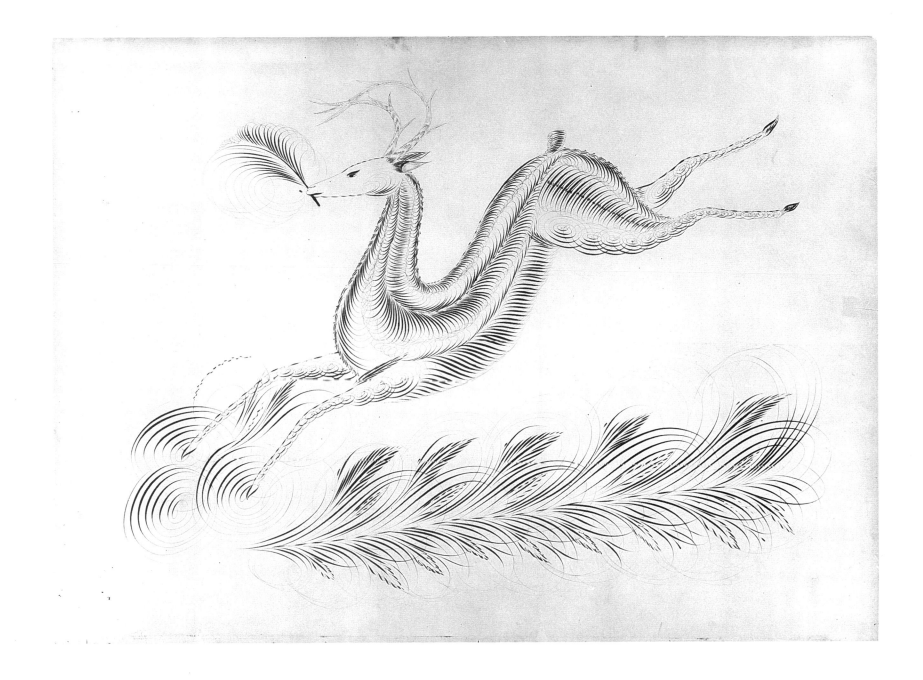

141
Unidentified artist, LEAPING
DEER, *United States, ca. 1860, ink
on wove paper, 29¹/₈ × 21⁷/₈ inches
(31.312.2).*

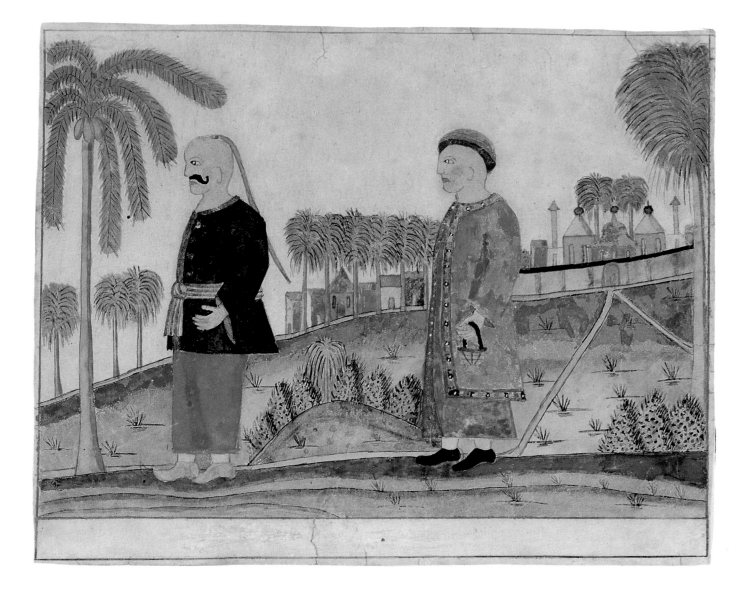

ated with a stencil from a set intended to be used for a conventional nineteenth-century still life, but the other elements in the picture are less commonly found in theorem painting of the period. This fact, combined with the unusual scale and random arrangement of the various motifs, suggests that Anny designed and cut her own patterns for the token. The methods she employed, including stippling (for the tree at right) and stenciling, were among the most common techniques taught in schools of the period.

The inspiration for the delightful and unusual early-nineteenth-century watercolor titled (in the twentieth century) *Pennsylvania Chinoiserie* (plate 142) is unknown. Some scholars suspect that the artist responsible for this work also produced fraktur. Nine other watercolors stylistically related to this example all feature exotic birds. Scattered tufts of grasslike vegetation and low, bushy shrubs dot the landscapes and serve to break up space. These watercolors were probably intended as presentation pieces, but the histories of their original ownership

∧
142
Unidentified artist, PENNSYLVANIA CHINOISERIE, *possibly Montgomery County, Pennsylvania, possibly 1810–1815, watercolor, gouache, ink, and gold and silver paint on wove paper, 7⁷/₈ × 10 inches (32.301.6).*

143 >
Attributed to John Conrad Gilbert, EASTER RABBIT, *Berks (now Schuylkill) County, Pennsylvania, probably 1795–1800, watercolor and ink on laid paper, 3³/₁₆ × 3³/₁₆ inches (59.305.3).*

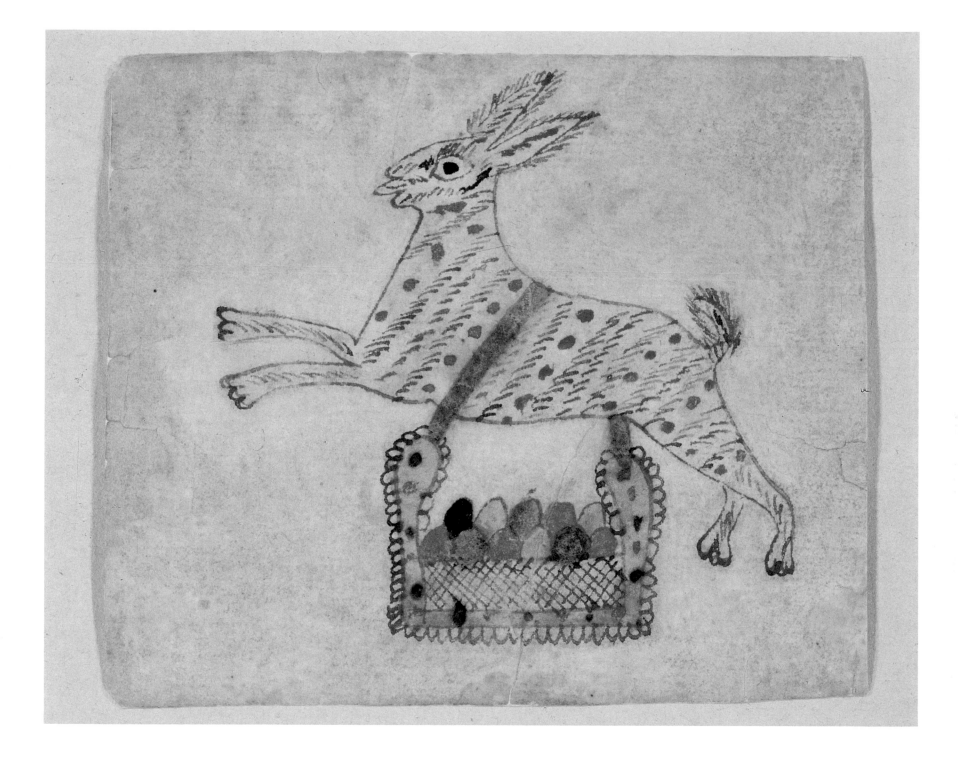

are unknown. We can only speculate as to what prompted their creation— it may have been illustrated accounts or prints of the Orient, imported wallpapers, fabrics, or porcelains, or other objects with figurative scenes.

A particularly poignant story about a piece that was probably a gift involves the terrier *Prince* (plate 152). The maker, Irvin Weil, loved working with wood, and his leisure hours frequently were devoted to carving and whittling figures for his own amusement and as gifts for friends. *Prince*, however, represents a real, flesh-and-blood terrier that belonged to Weil's three young sons in the 1930s. At the age of seven, this beloved family pet was killed by a butcher's truck, and shortly thereafter Weil carved and painted this wooden likeness of him.

Perhaps *Prince* was created as a consolation for the boys, or as a remembrance of the lost animal; surviving family members are not clear on this point. One of Weil's sons does, however, recall a practical, amusing, and probably unanticipated use for the carving: in summertime, his father traditionally placed *Prince* on the porch by the front door, and traveling salesmen subsequently gave the Weil household a wide berth!

Irvin Weil, born in 1887, was originally from Allentown, Pennsylvania, but moved to Coopersburg, where *Prince* was made, about 1910. Weil worked as a casket maker until 1945, when the company that employed him was destroyed by fire. He died in 1979.

Lewis Miller (1796–1882), the carpenter-artist from York, Pennsylvania, made and gave innumerable gifts during his lifetime. Typically these were in the form of watercolor-and-ink drawings, sometimes grouped thematically, as if taken from a journal; one drawing was a valentine for his great-niece (plate 144). Miller drew for his own and others' enjoyment. Near the end of his life, he sent a group of sketches, now known as the *Sketch Book of Land-* *scapes in the State of Virginia* (see plates 145, 146, and 147), to John Hays, an old friend from York, in appreciation of the occasional gifts of cash that Hays had sent him during those last, rather lean years. Many of the 147 drawings in the book depict Virginia towns and everyday life in the 1850s and 1860s; several extremely rare and important sketches describe the condition and role of black Americans prior to the Civil War. Other annotated scenes illustrate the progress of the railroad through western Virginia, the residences of successful farmers, and the places of natural beauty and the popular spas that Miller and the other members of his family living in Christiansburg, Virginia, often visited. The *Sketch Book* also includes a group of botanical studies and a series of European views, the latter drawn in sepia ink and possibly copied from prints purchased by the artist during his European sojourn in 1840–1841.

The Virginia sketchbook was made over a number of years, probably from 1853 to 1867. The many verses and descriptions it contains indicate that Miller made the drawings much the way one would write entries in a diary; it is a highly personal work, in which the artist chronicled much about his and his family's travels and activities.

John Hays was also the recipient of a larger work by Miller, *Orbis Pictus, A Picturesque Album to the Ladies of York, 1849* (see plates 148, 149, and 150). Apparently Miller presented this volume to him at the same time as the Virginia sketchbook.

Orbis Pictus ("The World Depicted") was a major work for Miller, and it ranks among the most important of his known journals both for its extraordinary variety of topics and because of its overall excellent condition, which accounts for the brilliant, crisp colors seen in many of the drawings. Since it is the most personal of Miller's known works, it also provides information that is significant for the understanding and interpretation of his art and his character. The book is dominated by two major

144
Lewis Miller, VALENTINE, probably Montgomery County, Virginia, watercolor and ink on wove paper, 4¹³/₁₆ × 8³/₄ inches (81.301.1).

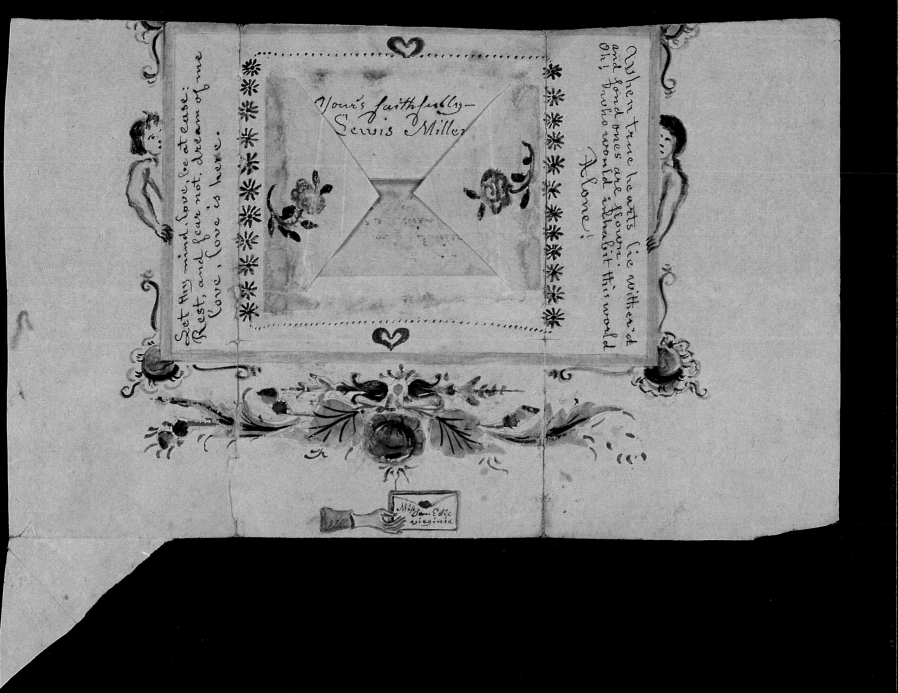

Your's faithfully —
Lewis Miller

Set thy mind, love, be at ease;
Rest, and fear not, dream of me
Love, love is here.

When true hearts lie wither'd
and fond ones are flown;
Oh! who would inhabit this world
Alone!

Miss Jane Edie
virginia

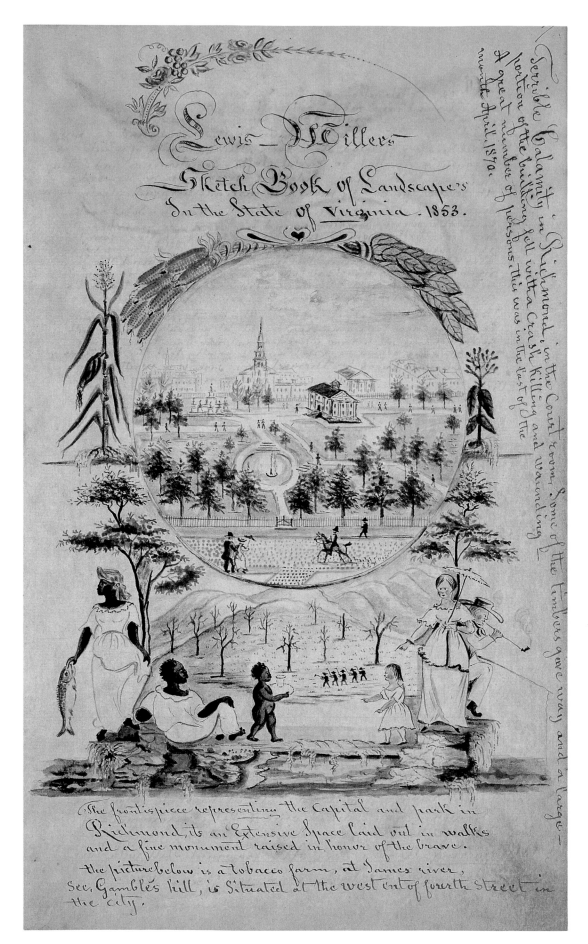

145
Lewis Miller, TITLE PAGE *from*
SKETCH BOOK OF LANDSCAPES
IN THE STATE OF VIRGINIA,
Virginia, 1853, watercolor, ink, and
pencil on wove paper, 12⁹/₁₆ × 7⁹/₁₆
inches, Gift of Dr. and Mrs. Richard
M. Kain in memory of George Hay
Kain (78.301.1).

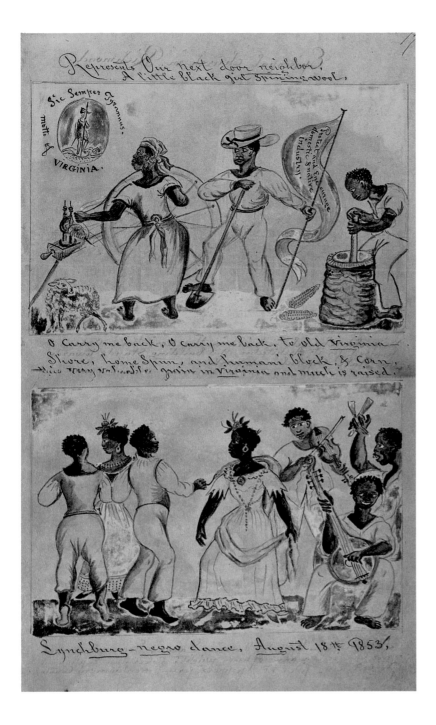

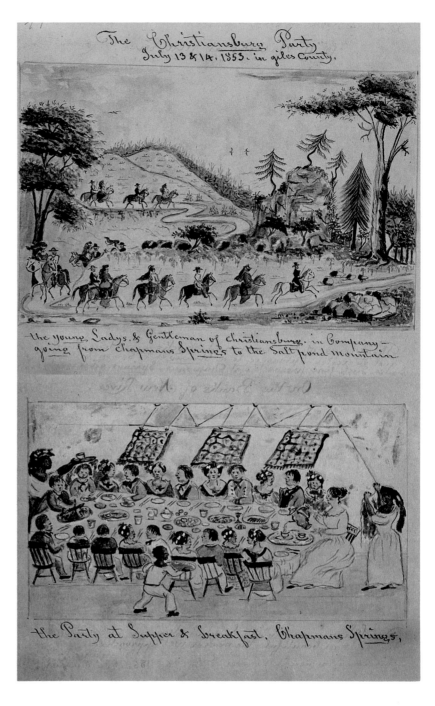

146
Lewis Miller, DOMESTIC
INDUSTRY *and* LYNCHBURG
NEGRO DANCE, *from SKETCH
BOOK OF LANDSCAPES IN THE
STATE OF VIRGINIA, Virginia,
1853, watercolor, ink, and pencil on
wove paper, 12⁷/16 × 7¹/2 inches
(78.301.1).*

147
Lewis Miller, THE
CHRISTIANSBURG PARTY *and*
THE PARTY AT SUPPER AND
BREAKFAST, CHAPMANS
SPRINGS, *from SKETCH BOOK OF
LANDSCAPES IN THE STATE OF
VIRGINIA, Virginia, 1853,
watercolor, ink, and pencil on wove
paper, 12¹/2 × 7¹/2 inches, Gift of Dr.
and Mrs. Richard M. Kain in
memory of George Hay Kain
(78.301.1).*

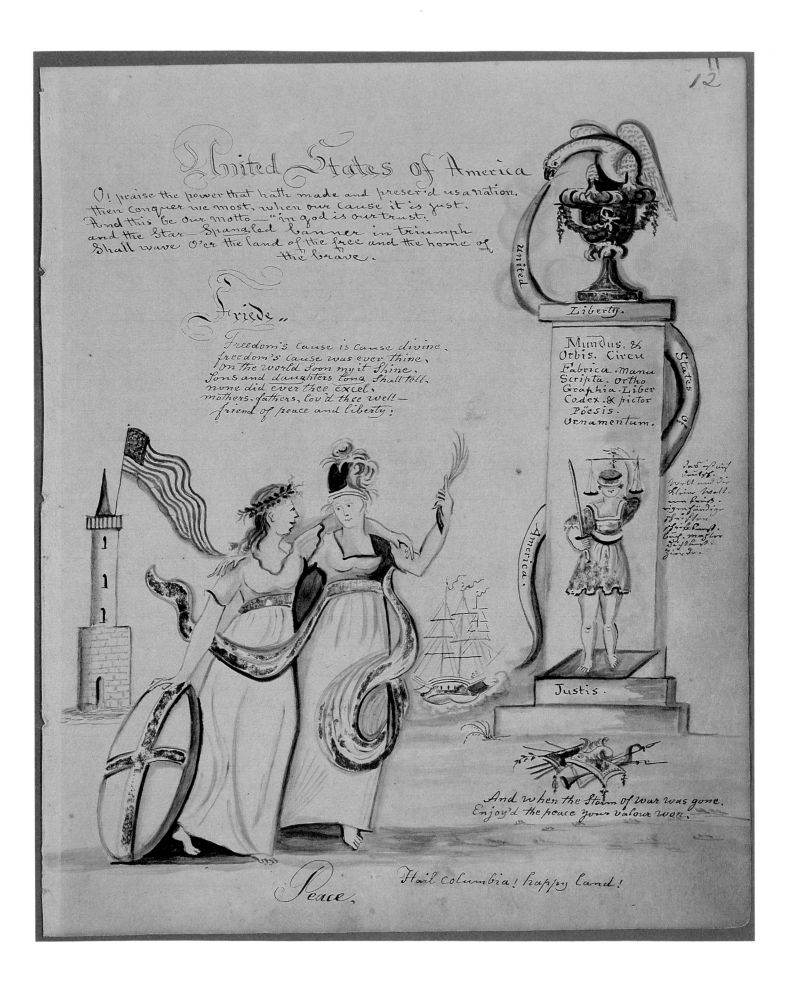

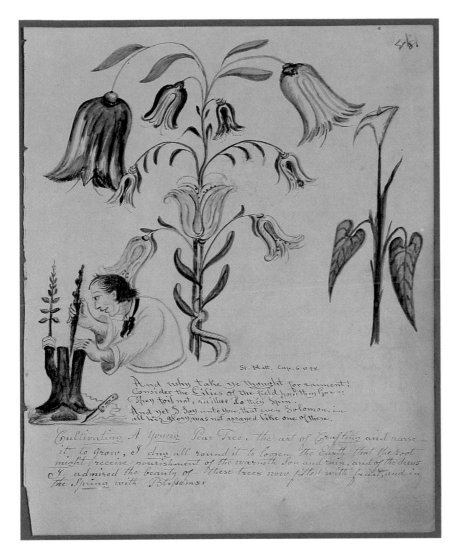

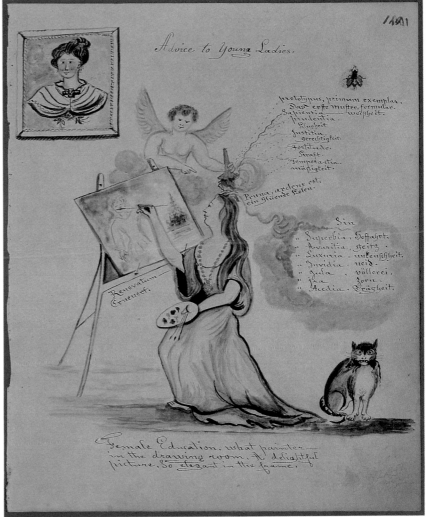

< 148
Lewis Miller, UNITED STATES OF
AMERICA, *from* ORBIS PICTUS,
*Pennsylvania or Virginia, ca. 1849,
watercolor and ink on wove paper,
9¹¹/₁₆ × 7⅞ inches, Gift of Mr. and
Mrs. William H. Kain in memory of
George Hay Kain (78.301.2).*

∧ 149
Lewis Miller, CULTIVATING A
YOUNG PEAR TREE, *from* ORBIS
PICTUS, *Pennsylvania or Virginia,
ca. 1849, watercolor and ink on
wove paper, 9¹¹/₁₆ × 7⅞ inches, Gift
of Mr. and Mrs. William H. Kain in
memory of George Hay Kain
(78.301.2).*

150
Lewis Miller, ADVICE TO YOUNG
LADIES, *from* ORBIS PICTUS,
*Pennsylvania or Virginia, ca. 1849,
watercolor and ink on wove paper,
9¾ × 7⅞ inches, Gift of Mr. and
Mrs. William H. Kain in memory of
George Hay Kain (78.301.2).*

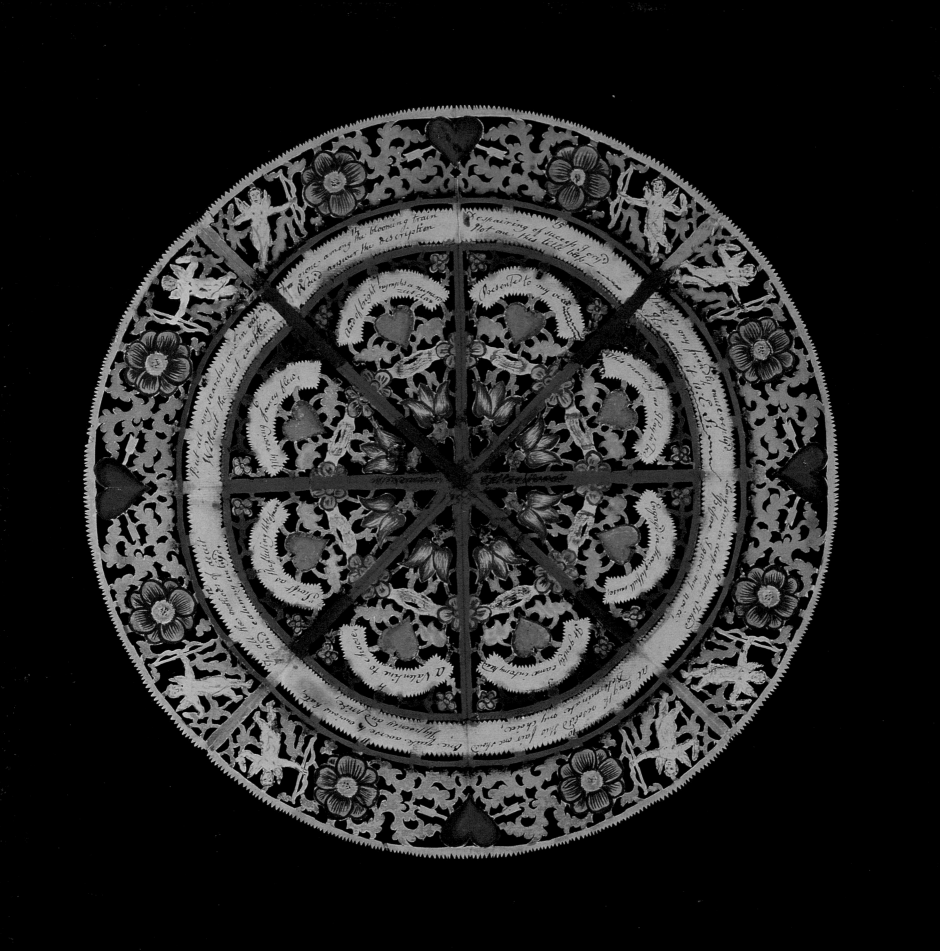

themes— lost love and dying— and filled with scenes seldom found in Miller's other works, notably illustrations of women with children in idyllic settings, accompanied by sentimental Victorian poetry. Many of the text selections indicate that Miller had a serious and morbid side, and evidently he was a prodigious reader, as the inscriptions demonstrate that he was very familiar with contemporary prose and poetry. The selections illustrated here include *United States of America; Cultivating a Young Pear Tree;* and the charming, if not humorous, *Advice to Young Ladies.*

Lewis Miller's valentine to his great-niece Jane Edic (plate 144) was executed in the same neat style as his drawings; it boasts the same kind of calligraphic flourishes, small flowers, and neatly penned script seen in the sketchbooks, though here the messages about love were carefully composed by the artist for the adored recipient, who was probably then in her early twenties. In one of these, Miller wrote, "Let thy mind, love, be at ease:/Rest, and fear not. dream of me/love, love is here."

The use of specific love tokens, known as valentines, is first documented in the mid–eighteenth century in America, and the delicate cutwork example made for Elizabeth Sandwith surely ranks among the earliest of these surviving (plate 151). The sixteen numbered verses inscribed on the pinked arcs of the valentine's face are a tribute to Elizabeth, who is rather secretively identified as "E. S."

On January 13, 1761, Elizabeth Sandwith married a Philadelphia Quaker, Henry Drinker (1734–1809). According to family tradition, Drinker was the artist responsible for the valentine, but inscriptions recently discovered on the back of the piece suggest that another, earlier suitor of Elizabeth's probably fashioned the love token. There, a partially obliterated name appears, followed by, ". . . to E. S.: February 14, 1753." The intentionally ink-covered name is now largely illegible, but it may have been "W. Chandler" or some variant thereof. One wonders whether Henry Drinker tried to mark over the earlier beau's name or whether Elizabeth intentionally obscured the lettering to keep the identity of her former suitor secret from Henry!

< *151*
Possibly W. Chandler, CUTWORK VALENTINE, *probably Philadelphia, Pennsylvania, 1753, watercolor and ink on laid paper, 13 inches in diameter (57.306.1).*

152 >
Irvin Weil, PRINCE, *Coopersburg, Pennsylvania, 1935–1940, carved and painted wood, 15³/₄ × 17¹/₂ inches (81.701.1).*

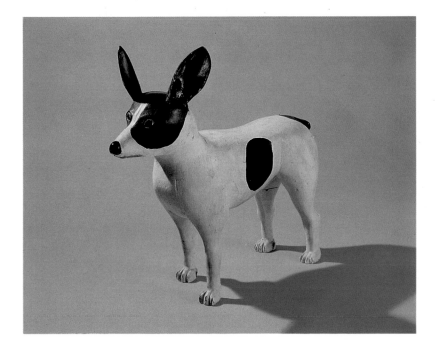

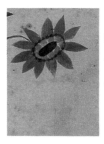

CHAPTER SEVEN

Nature's Bounty

Still-life painting, which is intricately tied to design considerations and fashions in household furnishings, was first recognized as an independent genre in the seventeenth century, though related pictorial work had been done in previous centuries. Painters from the Low Countries of Europe perfected this type of painting by carefully rendering the textures, colors, and shading of motionless objects, with an emphasis on the beauty of familiar forms. Popular groupings included fruits and flowers, vegetables, game and fish, meals on tables, and precious or natural articles such as pearls, stones, or shells. By the eighteenth century, the still-life genre was considered so inferior to the ennobling and enlightening depiction of literary and historical subjects that it declined in popularity. During this period, still lifes became vignettes in larger works or assumed purely ornamental functions, as in the decoration of furniture or other household objects. It was mainly in these uses that the still life survived through much of the eighteenth century.

In nineteenth-century America, the circulation of European prints of flowers and foliage and the exhibition of still-life subjects by noted American artists stimulated a renewed interest in the genre. At the popular level, among middle-class Americans, the still life's appeal was boosted enormously by the appropriateness of the form to theorem, or stencil, painting, a fad that peaked in America about 1820–1840 and resulted in a temporary decline of embroidery as the primary aesthetic diversion for women.

Pictures of the sort illustrated in this chapter were executed both by amateurs— usually as leisure work by women or as part of their school curriculum by young girls— and occasionally by semi-skilled professional folk painters, who worked in both watercolors and oils. Most theorem still lifes involved the use of hollow-cut paper patterns or stencils on velvet or paper supports; arrangements of fruit and flowers were especially popular, and different stencils were artfully combined to create pleasing compositions. Each element of a design was first traced on oiled paper and then cut out with a knife, leaving a stencil or theorem. The stencils were held carefully in place on the velvet or paper background while watercolors or oils mixed with gum arabic were applied with various brushes through the openings or perforations. The technique required some manual skill and a great deal of patience; directions were provided in the art-instruction books that appeared in increasing numbers throughout the nineteenth century. Sometimes the stencils were obtained ready-made from art teachers or drawing schools, and to judge from the multiple versions of several subjects represented in the Center collection, designs were widely distributed.

Few examples, however, approach the exquisite quality of Mary Bradley's *Basket of Fruit* (plate 159), executed about 1825 in Lee, Massachusetts. The expert shading of leaves and fruit gives this composition a strong three-dimensional quality often lacking in theorems. The colors remain ex-

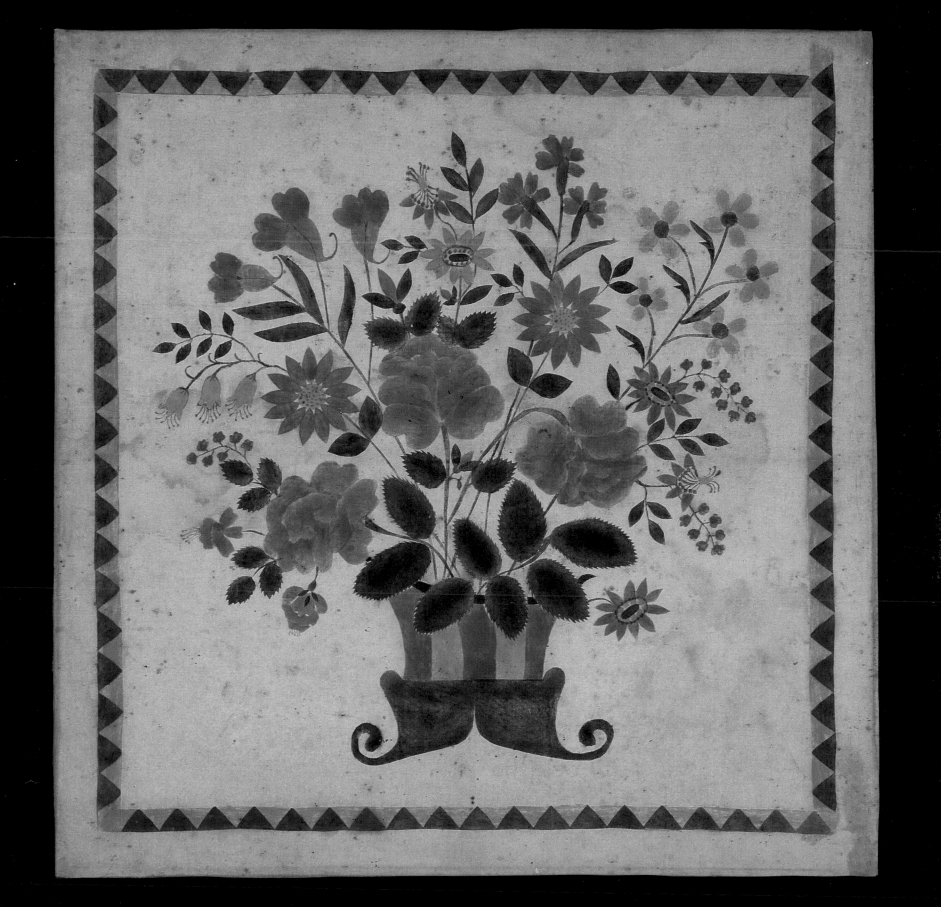

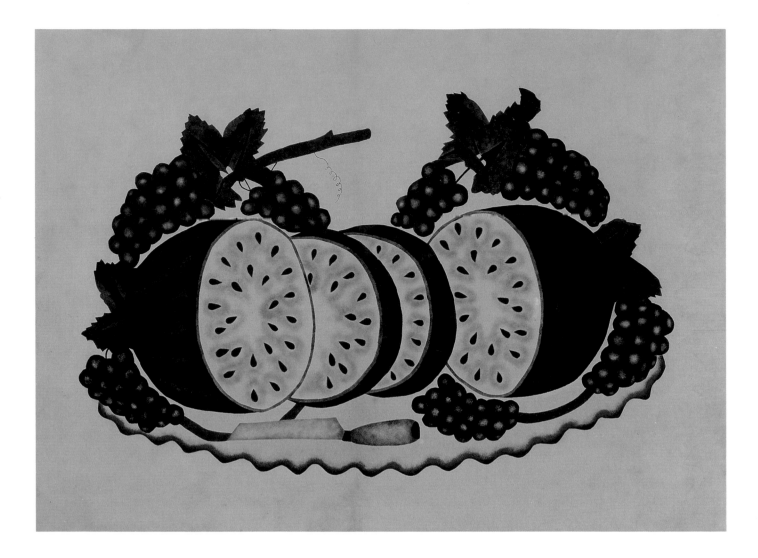

ceptionally fresh and vibrant, particularly the reds and greens. Mary Bradley had mastered the use of her stencils, as is indicated by the crisp edges of the leaves and the well-defined forms of the cherries and their stems. Bradley's proficiency with a pen is exhibited not only by the abundant grapevine tendrils but also by her accomplished calligraphic signature.

Most American theorems from the nineteenth century make use of rather conventional designs showing fruit or flowers mounded in baskets, in bowls, and on tabletops, but the unidentified and talented amateur responsible for the *Grapevine* in plate 156 dispensed with the more common arrangements

and suspended clusters of grapes and currants from curving, unsupported vines. The grapevines cross over a currant branch that slopes to the lower left, creating an airy, free, and imaginative composition that is expertly shaded and balanced.

Bright Flowers (plate 153) is another still life created with theorems, though the support in this instance is linen rather than the more popular velvet used for most stenciled pictures. Linen was more commonly stenciled to make domestic items such as bed covers, tablecloths, and an occasional article of clothing. The stenciled nature of this picture can best be seen in the uniform petals of the flowers, though some details do seem to have been drawn

154
Unidentified artist, SLICED MELON AND GRAPES, *United States, ca. 1840, watercolor on wove paper, 17⅝ × 27⅞ inches (57.303.5).*

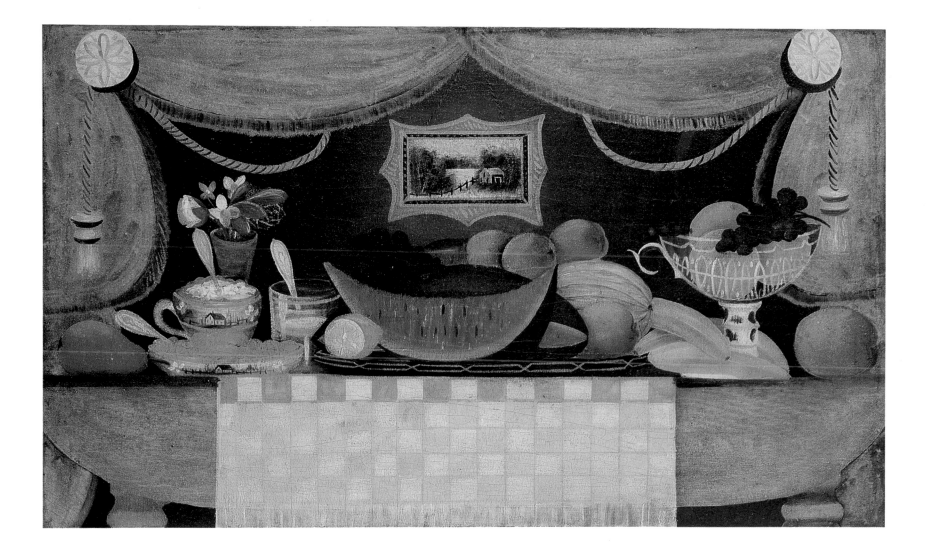

freehand, which is often the case in such paintings. An unusual feature, the yellow and green sawtooth border, is seen on only one other theorem in the Center's collection. Because the border did not meet evenly in the upper right-hand corner, the artist extended the yellow segment to complete it.

Watercolor still lifes executed without stencils and with various types of pencils and brushes were also produced by American amateur artists during the nineteenth century. Countless instruction books were published both here and abroad, making available to students and laymen much basic information on mixing colors, using pencils, and achieving a three-dimensional effect through shading.

Exercises in still-life painting were assigned not only in art classes but also as part of the study of botany, in which students were required to copy both pictures of flowers and actual specimens. The designs for these watercolor still lifes varied little from the ones employed in theorem painting; no doubt many young women became well-versed in both art forms.

The simplicity of its design, combined with the linear quality of the upright melon slices and the encircling grape clusters, makes the small painting in plate 154 one of the most visually pleasing watercolors in the Center's collection. Stencils and freehand work are combined in this piece, but the

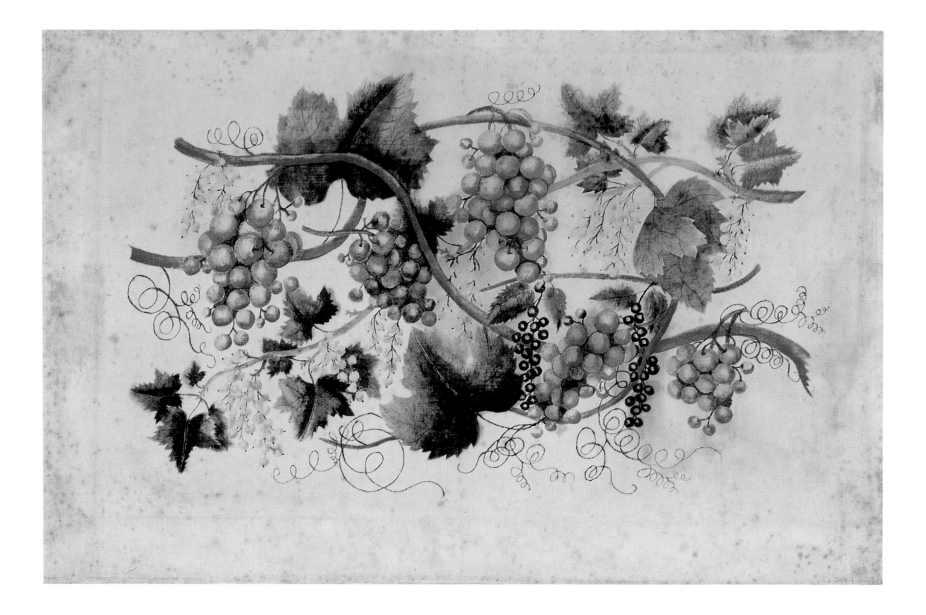

artist's lack of familiarity with the former is suggested by the thick, stylized stems and flat, unmodeled leaves, as well as by the incomplete bunch of grapes found on the back of the painting, abandoned after a faulty start. The paring knife was a conventional element in both academic and folk still-life paintings, but here it rests precariously on the plate, its blade pointing up. No doubt this work was derived from a print source, since a slightly smaller but very similar composition is known.

Still-life pictures, often called pieces during the period, displayed the homey symbols of abundance and the good life— cornucopias or baskets laden with fruit or vegetables— in much the same way that the fashionable decorations seen on other household items did. The table device seen in many of these pictures, sometimes indicated by a mere marble slab, may have symbolized a groaning board; usually the baskets in these pictures are overflowing with fruit, indicating an abundance of fresh food. And, too, the many bright flowers, depicted in a variety of containers, functioned then as flowers still do today— as emblems of cheerfulness and good will.

156
Unidentified artist, GRAPEVINE, *United States, ca. 1825, paint on velvet, 14⅞ × 22⅞ inches (32.403.9).**

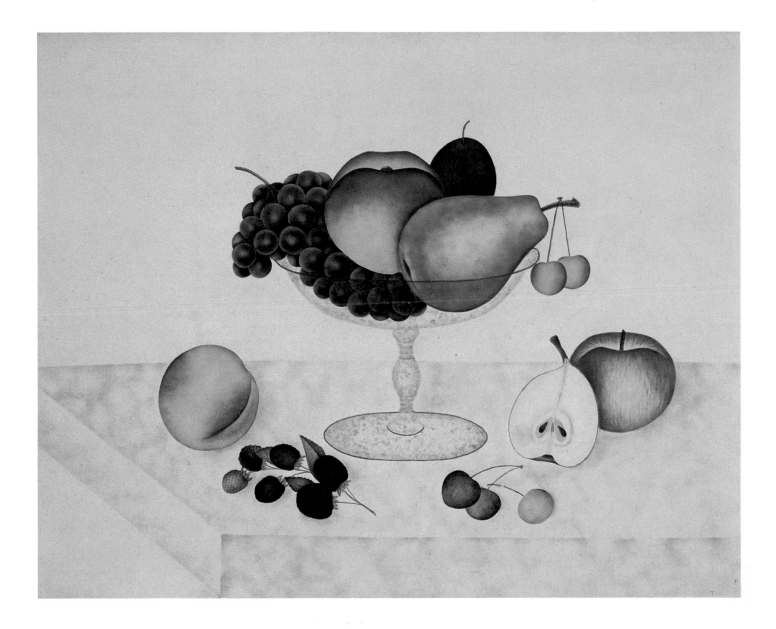

In *Bountiful Board* (plate 155), the unidentified
artist conceived a most dramatic way to prepare the
stage for the food and dishes spread across the table
— the generally symmetrical composition, framed
by heavy, tasseled draperies, is viewed from an intriguing eye-level perspective. The china cup and
saucer, decorated with a "house pattern" popular
during the second quarter of the nineteenth century, are unusual elements in an otherwise conventional arrangement. We will probably never know
whether the artist included these detailed objects
and the picture in the background expressly to per-
sonalize this piece or to balance the composition,

though the rarity of such elements in other works
certainly suggests that the former is the case.

Fruit in Wicker Basket (plate 158) reflects the theme
of plenty and abundance better than most still lifes
of the period. The basket is so heavily laden with
food, in fact, that one has to marvel at its ability to
contain it all. This is an unusually vivid painting,
and the apples are especially notable, segregated
from the rest of the composition by narrow rims of
an intense red that quickly shades to an acid green.
Only the grapes appear dull and lackluster— the
effect, it is thought, of chemical changes in their

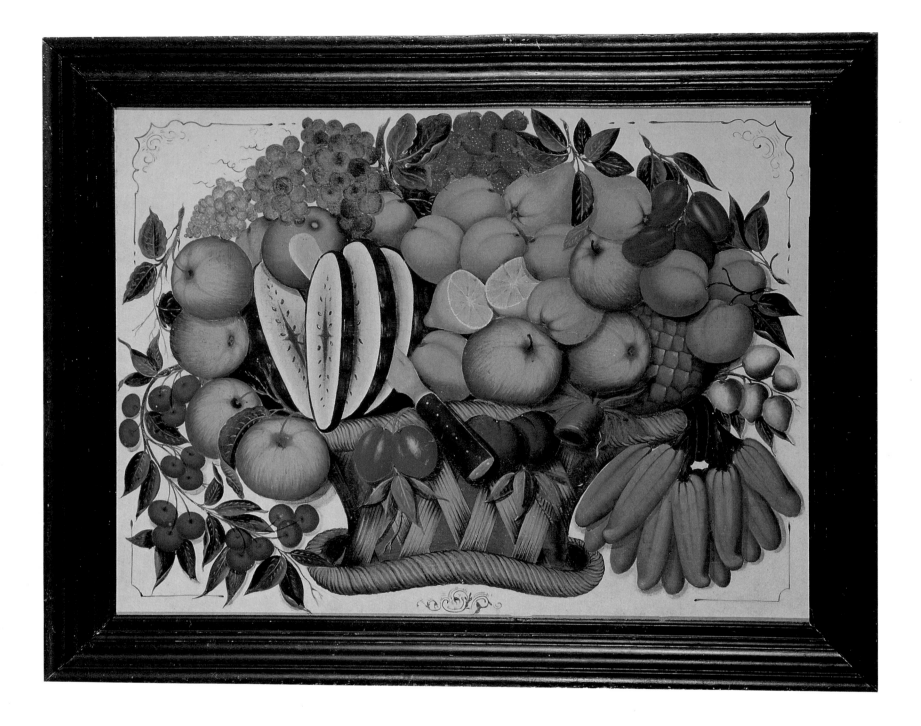

paint structure over time; originally they probably rivaled the wealth of other fruits in their rich, deep color. One can imagine this picture hanging in a best room of some household in about 1850, reminding its viewers of the bounty reaped through honest work and of the simple enjoyment of good food.

Perhaps the most spectacular of the still-life pieces surviving from the late nineteenth century is Emma

Jane Cady's *Fruit in Glass Compote* (plate 157). Since the 1930s, about the time of the artist's death and the picture's discovery, this work has been acclaimed as a premier example of theorem painting. Cady (1854–1933) was the eldest of three children of Norman J. and Mary E. Bradley Cady. The few details known about her life indicate that she enjoyed farm work and the outdoors and never married. Cady lived in East Chatham, New York, until the deaths of her parents in 1908 and 1911 allowed

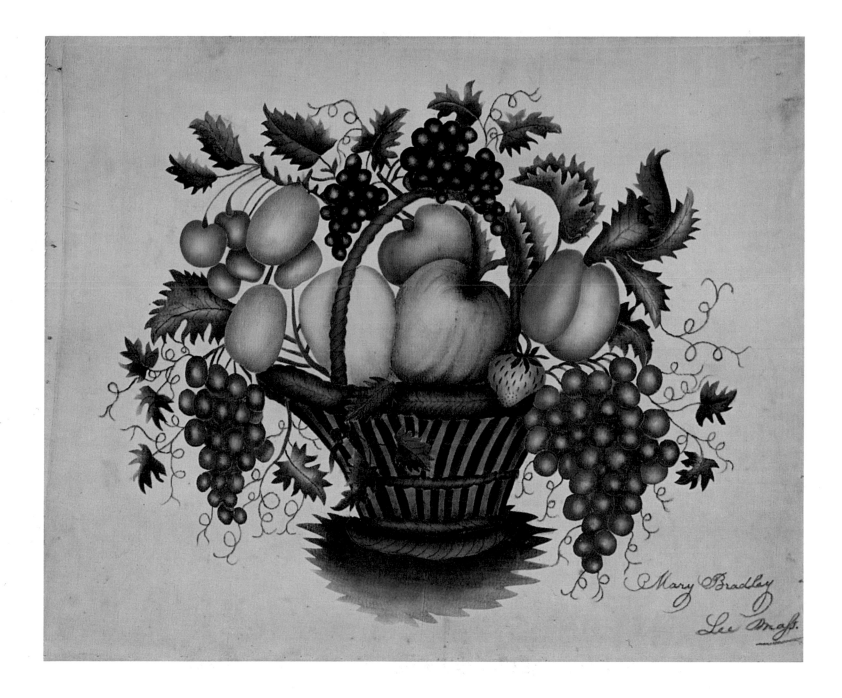

her to move to Grass Lake, Michigan, where she remained until her death.

Cady's rich colors and crisply stenciled renderings seem especially suited to capturing the beauty of these common inanimate objects. She capably created a three-dimensional effect that is particularly noticeable in the blackberries and in the apple at the far right. But it is the stark white background, the highly reflective surface of the delicate glass compote, and the soft-gray marbleized tabletop that intensify the contrasting jewel-like tones of the grapes, the berries, and the plum and the yellow-orange color of the peaches. Such a simple, clear, and remarkably compelling work as this helps us understand the intuitive response modern artists have had to folk art over the years. This naive, ethereal picture captures the essence of common things made noble.

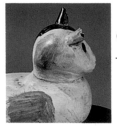

CHAPTER EIGHT
Whimsies and Toys

A proper understanding of American folk art requires that we recognize and respond to the generous amount of humor found in a variety of objects. This is *not* to say that one should view a portrait of a flesh-and-blood ancestor, note the wooden stance or the distortion, and chuckle knowingly over the naïve skills of the maker, thinking all along that his conception is outrageously humorous; indeed, our modern perception of what is amusing (generally conditioned by a learned notion of the correct way for things to look) often blinds us to the folk artist's true intentions. The folk artist's humor, and consequently his whimsy— whether it is realistically or abstractly fashioned, reflected in the whole or in part of an object— is usually intentional, and not the result of a lack of skills or any ignorance of formal art practices.

Humor and whimsy exist in both blatant and subtle ways in many folk art objects that once had utilitarian functions. The punched-tin lantern in plate 104 is a classic example, with its comical little faces placed around the conical top. The patterns of light cast by these piercings when the lantern is lit are amusing, and when the lantern is handled, the faces move about and change shape in a most entertaining way. Less obvious but equally humorous vignettes appear in other folk art objects, such as Edward Hicks's *Residence of David Twining 1787* (plate 62), where a thoroughly annoyed cat confronts a yapping dog in the yard just in front of the family house. There is a similarly amusing canine-feline meeting at the lower left of *The Quilting Party* (plate 84). There are many other small passages of whimsy in folk paintings, but it is the carved and

sculptured, nonutilitarian objects that best demonstrate the innate good will and humor of their makers. Our tendency is to view some of these, such as the calico cat in plate 161, made between 1900 and 1925 by an untrained, unidentified carver, with a questioning eye, invariably asking either "What is it?" or "What does it do?"; the answer, of course, is that the cat does nothing other than sit quietly, existing as a bit of perky whimsy that surely delighted every member of its original household as much as it does us today. The piece shows minimal wear and thus probably never functioned as a doorstop, as has been suggested. It may have been a toy or a plaything, but if so, it was carefully handled over the years. The little skunk in plate 161 is beautifully carved and is painted in a very sleek, smooth style. Like the alert calico cat, he shows minimal wear and apparently also existed only to please and amuse his owner.

The many creatures whittled by Wilhelm Schimmel were also intended to amuse, and in that sense they provide a stark contrast to the peculiar and sad circumstances of their maker. Wilhelm Schimmel (1817–1900) may have had a middle name and was probably the "Heinrich" Schimmel listed in the 1870 United States census as having been born in Hesse-Darmstadt, Germany. If so, he was then about fifty-three years old and living in the Cumberland Valley near Carlisle, Pennsylvania. Oral traditions of families from that region state that Schimmel was a vagrant, moving from one household to another among the German residents of the area. He slept in their outbuildings, did occasional chores for them, and cared for their children. He

160
Unidentified maker, ELEPHANT TOY, *Pennsylvania, possibly ca. 1850, carved and painted wood, 6¹⁵/₁₆ × 8¹/₈ × 1⁷/₈ inches (79.1200.4).*

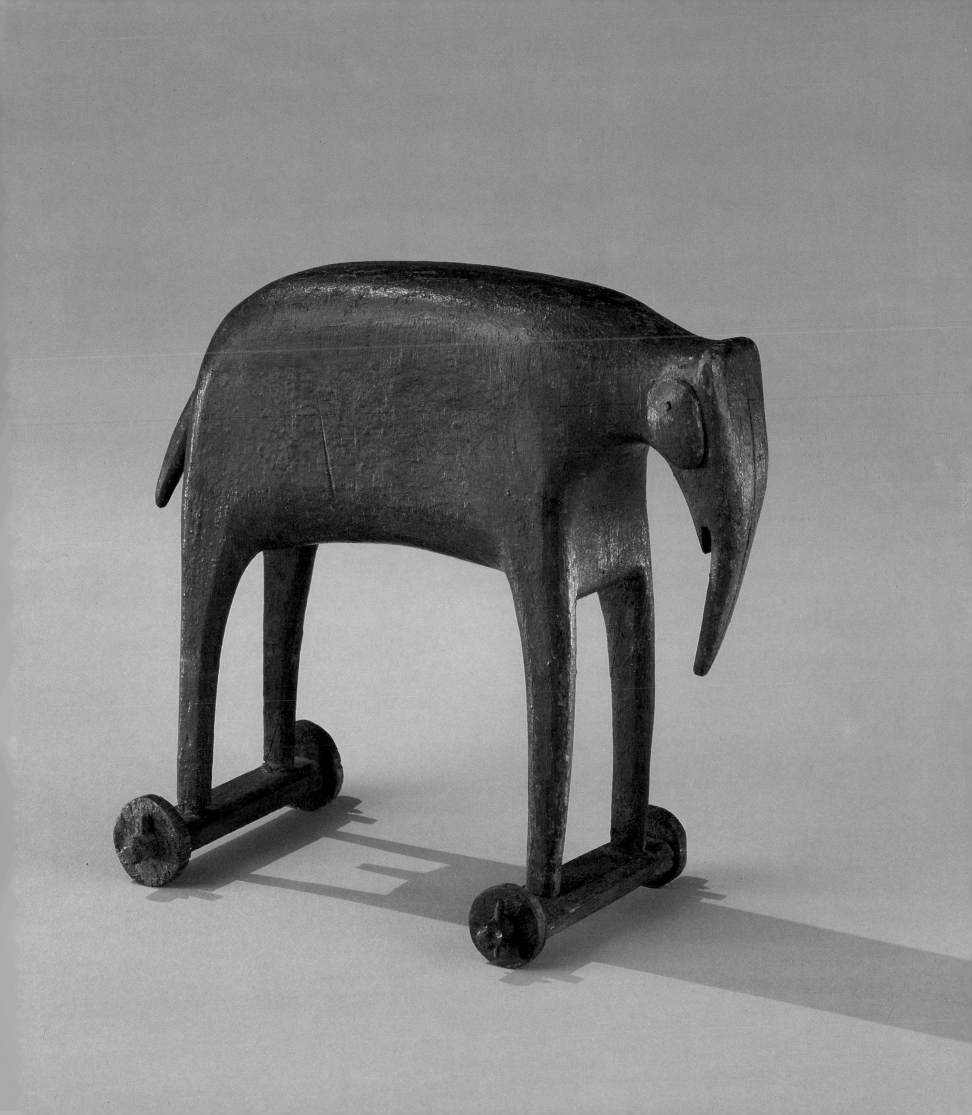

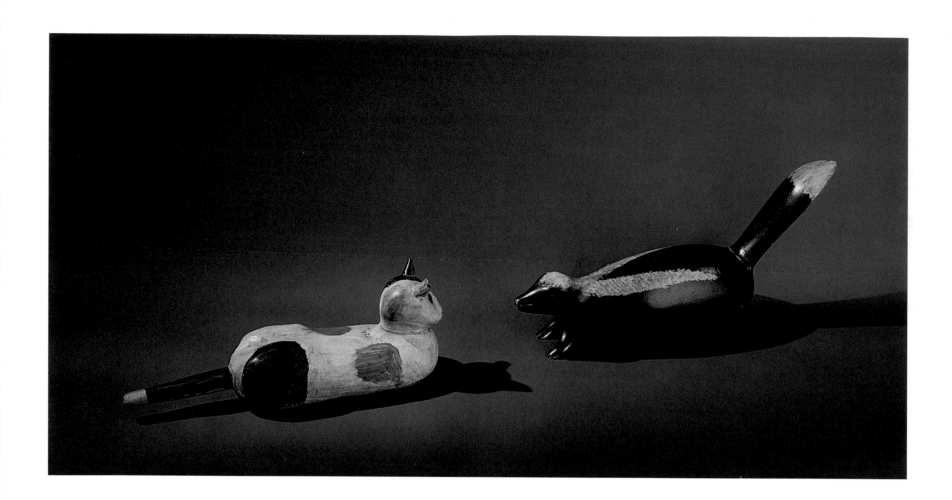

gathered small pieces of wood from sawmills and carpentry shops near Carlisle to carve into birds and animals, sometimes selling them but more often presenting them as tokens in exchange for the food, drink, and shelter that he received from local citizens. It is said that shelves in the area's barrooms and saloons were lined with his woodcarvings.

Most of Schimmel's pieces were sculpted from soft pine, covered with a white sealant (perhaps a type of gesso), and then painted. He fashioned hundreds of figures, principally animals and birds, and all display a style that is very spontaneous and unmistakably his. Many of his works are chip-carved in a crosshatched pattern to simulate fur or feathers, as seen on the eagle in plate 162. Schimmel carved so

many eagles that the form virtually became his trademark. These haughty birds, created in a range of sizes, are vaguely reminiscent of the Hapsburg eagles of the artist's native Germany. The diamond-shaped chip-carving on their bodies, their brown and black painted plumage, and widespread wings (usually carved separately and doweled or mortised into the bodies) are all distinctive of Schimmel's work. The smaller birds may have been used as table ornaments, while the larger ones decorated houses and fenceposts. The one in plate 162 is the largest of those in the Center's collection. Tradition indicates that similar eagles were placed atop poles in gardens or carried around Carlisle on victory poles at election time.

∧
161a
Unidentified maker, CALICO CAT, *United States, possibly 1900–1925, painted wood and metal, 8 × 21 × 5 inches (58.701.1).*

161b
Unidentified maker, SKUNK, *United States, probably 1925–1940, carved and painted wood, 11 × 22¼ × 5½ inches (67.701.13).*

162 >
Attributed to Wilhelm Schimmel, EAGLE, *probably Cumberland Valley, Pennsylvania, probably 1875–1890, carved and painted wood, 15¾ × 32¼ × 15½ inches (32.701.3).**

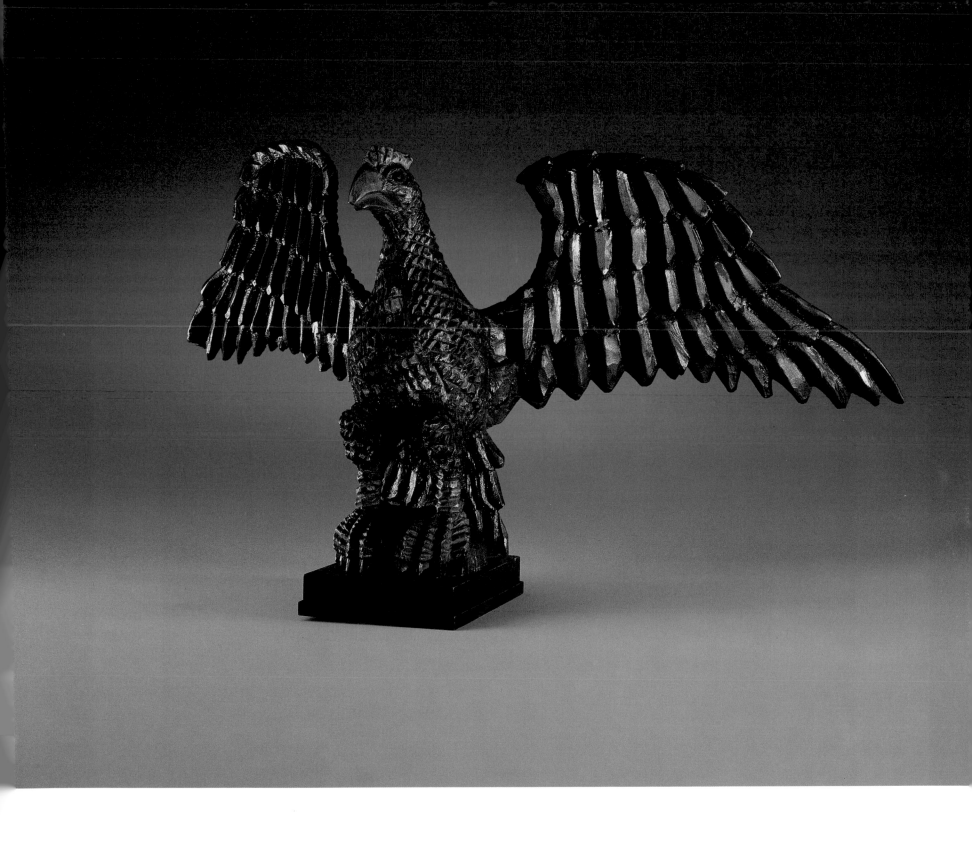

Although Schimmel favored carving dogs, eagles, roosters, and parrots, he sometimes fashioned more exotic animals, such as the tiger and the lion in plate 163, both of which are boldly painted. The spaces gouged out between the little tiger's white teeth are painted a dramatic red, giving him a fierce expression. Sometimes the artist had to piece wood together to obtain the desired block size for his animals. Such is the case with the lion, whose body is in two halves, joined down the center, with the tail added separately. Small parrots, boldly carved and colored, were typical of Schimmel's production; most are the same size as the one in plate 163d. Of interest are the small round protrusions that surround the bird at the base, which represent flowers or flower buds.

Schimmel was a well-known figure and was probably considered quite a character by those living in the Cumberland Valley. In spite of the fact that he was poor and suffered from alcoholism, he seems to have made many friends during his twenty years of wandering. He was admitted to the Cumberland County Almshouse in the summer of 1890 and died about two months later, in early August. His obituary from the *Carlisle Evening Sentinel*, published on August 7, noted that " 'Old Schimmel,' the German who for many years tramped through this and adjoining counties, died at the Almshouse on Sunday. His only occupation was carving heads of animals out of soft pine wood. . . ."

Schimmel's work greatly impressed at least one lad in the area, Aaron Mountz (1873–1949), who probably played with the old man's carvings as a child. Schimmel taught Mountz to carve, and Mountz gradually formed his own meticulous style, but his stylistic debt to his teacher is obvious. Aaron was only seventeen years old when Schimmel died, but his skill in wood carving was already evident. Although his output was relatively small, perhaps a few dozen figures to Schimmel's hundreds, Mountz's work displays considerable originality; the owl in plate 163b is among his most distinctive

pieces. Preferring the look of natural carved wood, he painted few of his carvings. His figures, like Schimmel's, consist primarily of small animals and birds, eagles of various sizes, and other whimsies.

Mountz lived a quiet life, never married, and worked alternately as a farmer and well driller. After failing in business in his later years, he lived out his last days in the Cumberland County Home and eventually died in the same almshouse where his mentor, Schimmel, had died fifty-nine years earlier.

There were a number of talented carvers at work in Pennsylvania throughout the nineteenth century; most of them were, like Schimmel and Mountz, of German origin. Few of these folk artists are known by name today, but they have left us a rich assortment of comical carvings, some made as playthings for small children. It is not known whether these toys were sold or bartered in great quantity, but they functioned as delightful and colorful objects in many homes. The group of animals in plate 164 was acquired by the Center in January 1979. These pieces were among the folk art collected in the 1920s by Juliana Force, director of the Whitney Museum of American Art from 1930 to 1948. In terms of their form, painted surface, and condition, they rank among the best of the surviving American folk toys with Pennsylvania origins. Center staff members are uncertain as to whether they were all made by the same hand; the elephant (plate 160) and giraffe are similar in design and construction, while the cow, bull, antelope, and snake constitute another stylistically related group.

American-made toys that can be classified as both folk and art do not survive in large numbers. Among the rarest examples are pieces incorporating perishable materials such as textiles, leather, and dried natural substances. The two dolls in plate 169, made sometime between 1880 and 1910, are dressed in various fabrics and have metal and ceramic buttons, leather boots, and bead eyes. The

Clockwise from upper left:

163a
Attributed to Wilhelm Schimmel, LION, *probably Cumberland Valley, Pennsylvania, probably 1875–1890, carved and painted wood, 7 3/4 × 8 1/4 × 4 inches (63.701.3).*

163b
Attributed to Aaron Mountz, OWL, *probably Carlisle area, Pennsylvania, probably 1885–1900. carved pine, 12 7/8 × 5 1/4 × 6 15/16 inches (80.701.1).*

163c
Attributed to Wilhelm Schimmel, TIGER, *probably Cumberland Valley, Pennsylvania, probably 1875–1890, carved and painted wood, 2 3/8 × 4 1/2 × 1 1/2 inches (60.701.3).*

163d
Attributed to Wilhelm Schimmel, PARROT, *probably Cumberland Valley, Pennsylvania, probably 1875–1890, carved and painted pine, 6 1/2 × 3 × 3 1/2 inches (59.701.4).*

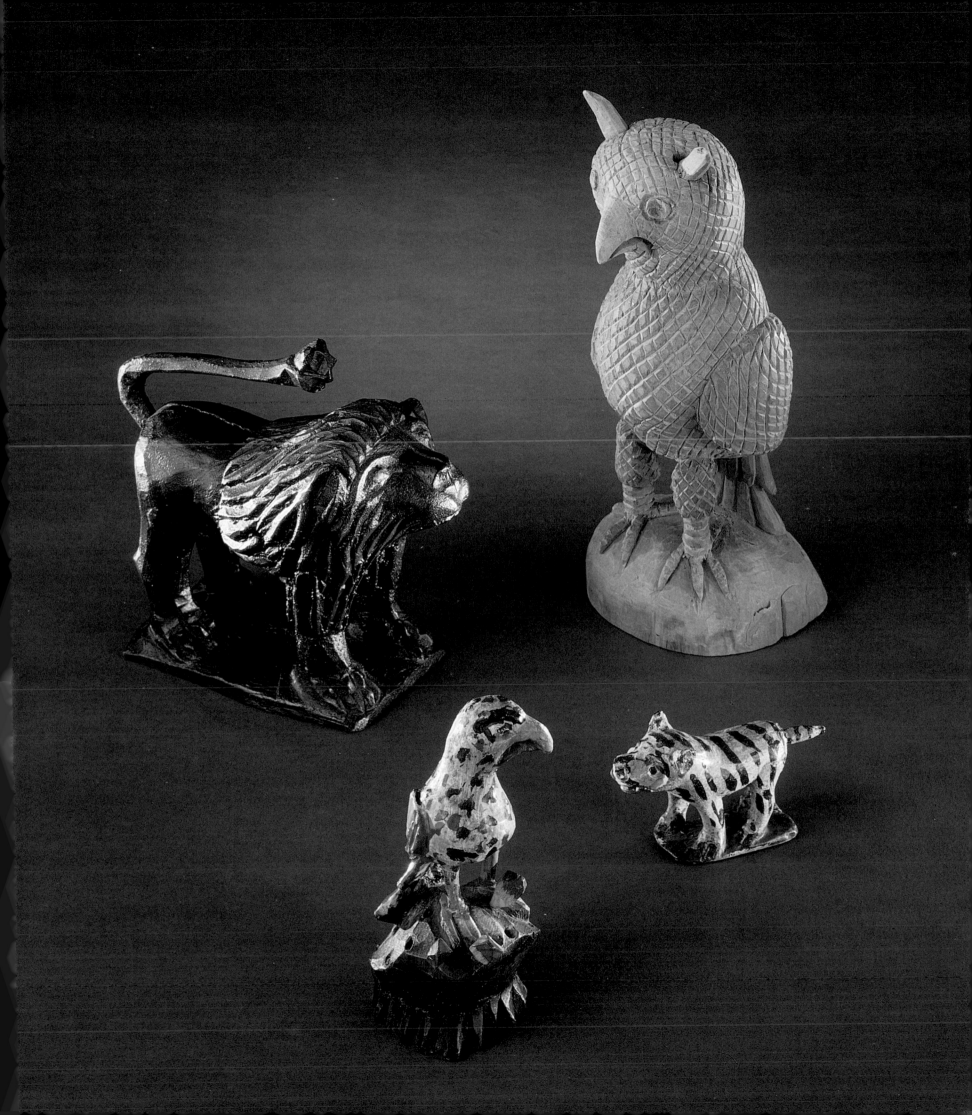

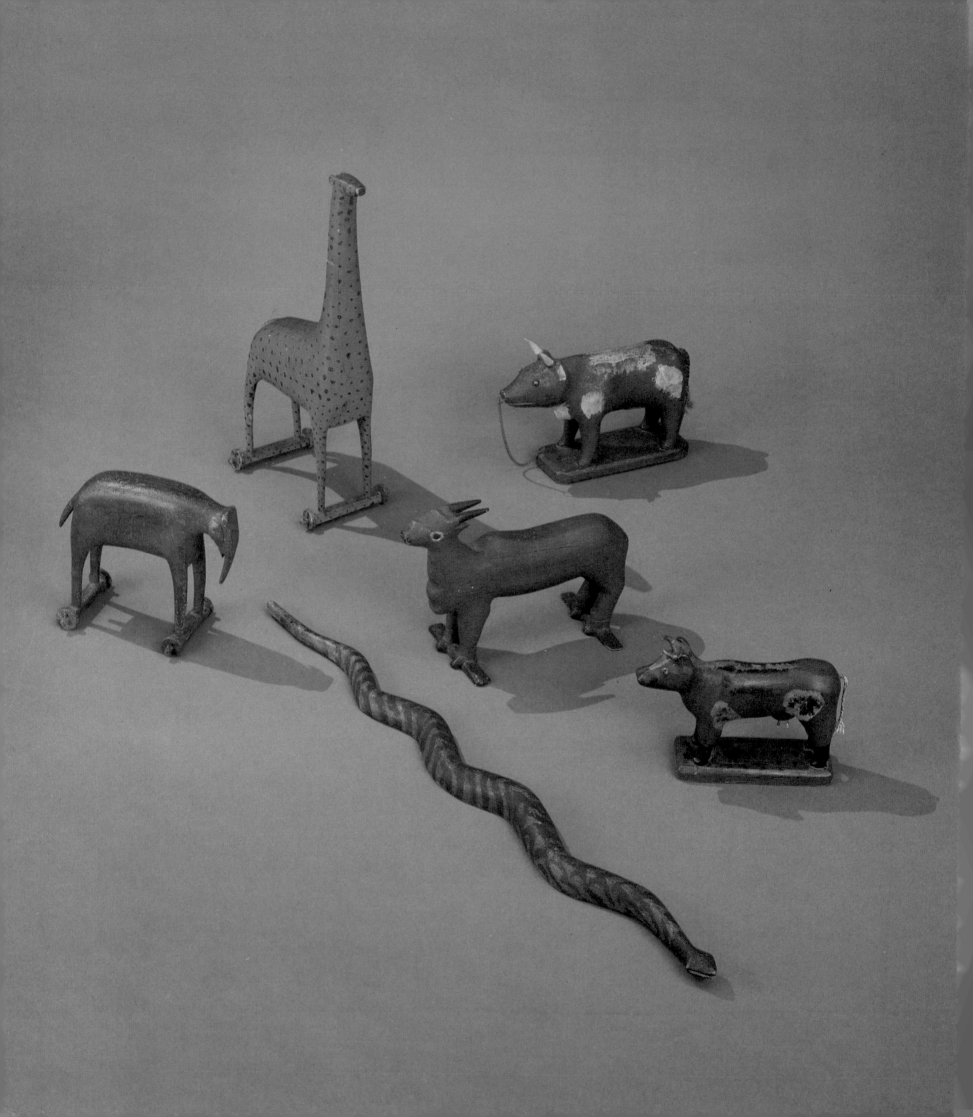

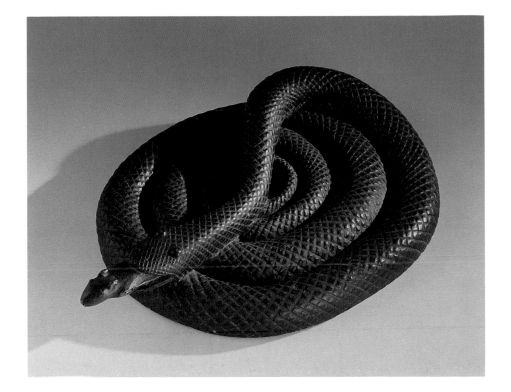

165
Unidentified maker, SNAKE
SWALLOWING A MOUSE, *United
States, possibly 1890–1910, painted
wood, 3 1/2 × 18 × 12 inches
(66.701.1)*

164
Unidentified makers, ANIMAL
TOYS, *Pennsylvania, possibly ca.
1850, carved and painted wood;
elephant (see plate 160); giraffe, 16 1/4
× 7 11/16 × 2 13/16 inches (79.1200.8);
bull, 6 3/4 × 10 3/16 × 2 13/16 inches
(79.1200.6); snake, 1 1/8 × 1 1/4 × 28
inches (79.1200.3); antelope, 7 × 2 1/2
× 10 1/2 inches (79.1200.7); cow, 5 5/8
× 8 1/2 × 2 1/4 inches (79.1200.5).*

unidentified maker took exceptional care with their
fine detailing. The fingers, for instance, are individ-
ually rendered; the facial details include not only
stuffed applied noses but also teeth and smiling
lips; the eyebrows were created by split stitches in
white cotton thread. The costumes are equally intricate: the man's shirt shows top-stitching in a contrasting color on the placket and collar; his cap and
matching blue suit have red piping, and his jacket
even includes a back vent for ease of movement!
His female companion's apparel includes two petti-
coats, a gingham apron, and a plaid cap. Both figures wear finely sewn leather boots over striped
stockings. The fine quality and the excellent condition of these two dolls raise questions about
whether they were ever in fact played with as toys.

The seated woman in plate 168, by an unidentified
maker who was probably working in the Ephrata,
Pennsylvania, area between 1850 and 1875, may
have been made either as a toy or as a decorative piece. The figure was skillfully carved and
still retains much of its colorful painted surface.
The most unusual feature is the woman's white-

stockinged legs, with their red garters, which may
be seen beneath her skirt from the back. To date,
no other carvings resembling this figure, which was
collected by Mrs. Rockefeller in 1931, have been
identified or recorded by the Center's staff.

An unusual example of a humorous piece— actually, one of two similar creatures owned by the
Center, both with possible Pennsylvania provenances— is the rather sinister coiled snake in the
act of swallowing a mouse (plate 165).

Of the many kinds of action whimsies fashioned by
American folk artists, whirligigs, or windtoys, are
probably the best known and most eagerly sought
by collectors. Designed for the fascination of adults
as well as children, they were generally set up on a
fence or a post, where their broad paddles acted as
baffles, twirling amusingly on a single axle when
caught by the breeze. Authority figures such as the
policeman shown in plate 167 were popular subjects among whirligig makers. Special delight was
taken in spoofing military officers and lawmen;
their serious expressions and upright poses are

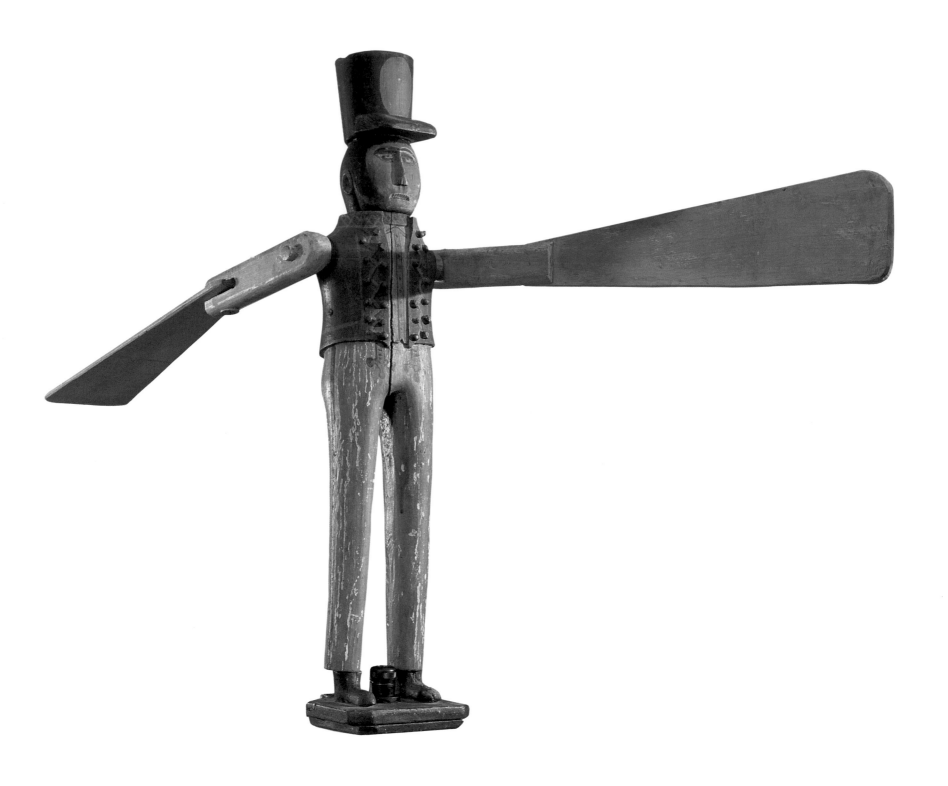

166
Unidentified maker, MILITARY
MAN, *United States, possibly 1860–
1880, carved and painted wood, 55
× 15¹/₂ × 5¹/₂ inches, Bequest of
Effie Thixton Arthur (79.700.2).*

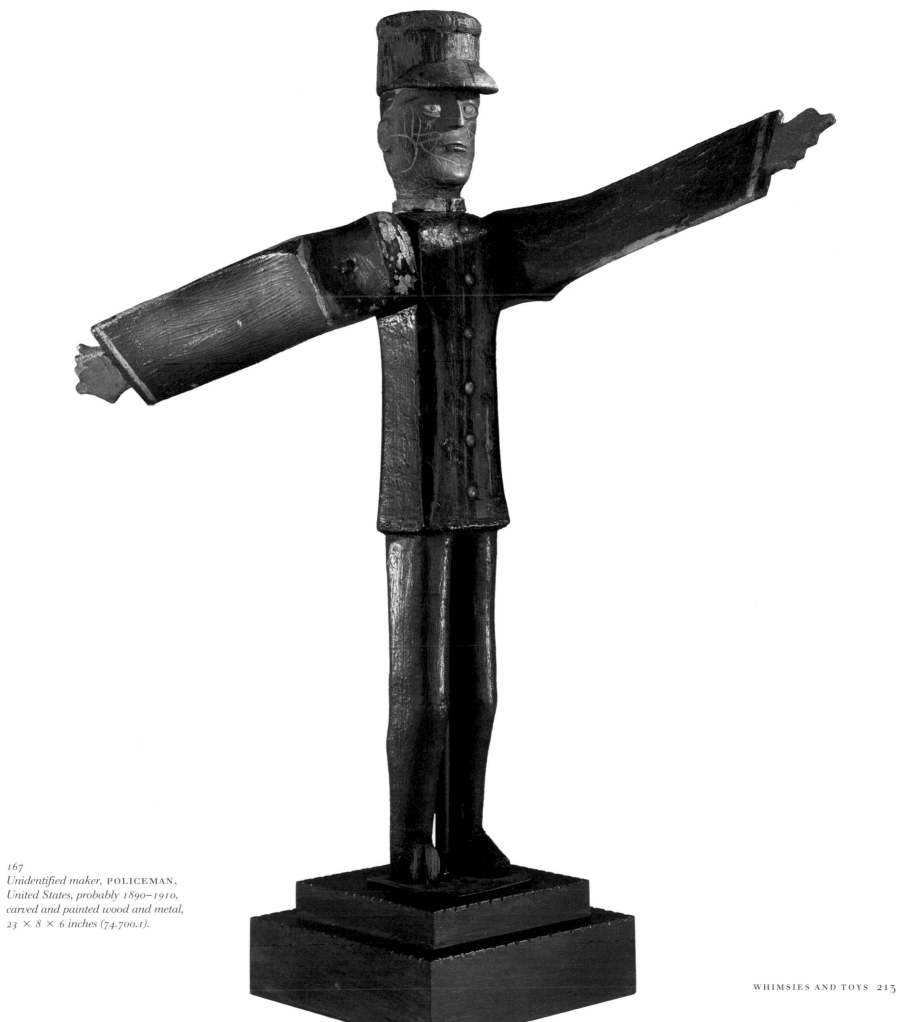

167
Unidentified maker, POLICEMAN,
United States, probably 1890–1910,
carved and painted wood and metal,
23 × 8 × 6 inches (74.700.1).

comically undermined by arms that flail uncontrollably in the wind. The Center's *Policeman* is distinguished by his large size, his bug-eyed expression, and his propeller-like arms, which terminate in cleverly stylized hands. The whirligig man in plate 166 is also large and is remarkable for his separately carved buttons, his hollowed-out ears, and his grim facial expression.

A good percentage of the American folk art pieces that display humor and whimsy were created by potters as end-of-the-workday pieces or as gifts for friends or family members. German-Americans led the production of such pieces for many years, and it is not suprising to find design and subject parallels between their carvings, their fraktur and other representational art, and their pottery. *Fiddler with Dog* (plate 170), attributed to Samuel Bell (1811–?), illustrates the level of skill such potters had achieved by the mid–nineteenth century.

Bell was the second-oldest of three brothers who established potteries in the Shenandoah Valley of Virginia. Their father, Peter Bell, had moved his pottery business from Hagerstown, Maryland, to Winchester, Virginia, in 1824. Samuel worked there with his father until 1833, when he moved south to Strasburg and purchased the old Beyers pottery. Although his production consisted primarily of utilitarian wares, Samuel also made a number of small animals and other whimsical pieces for his friends and family. *Fiddler with Dog* is one of a very few complex figural pieces attributed to this well-known potter. The tooling on the dog's body, the treatment of the man's eyes, and the oval-and-circle pattern stamped on the base are all similar to motifs found on single figures associated with Bell.

The *Fiddler* in plate 171, carved from black walnut by Edgar Alexander McKillop (1878–1950) about 1930, makes use of a similar theme, though in this case the figure has no canine partner. The *Fiddler,* one of the few human forms carved by McKillop, embodies an important aspect of the art-

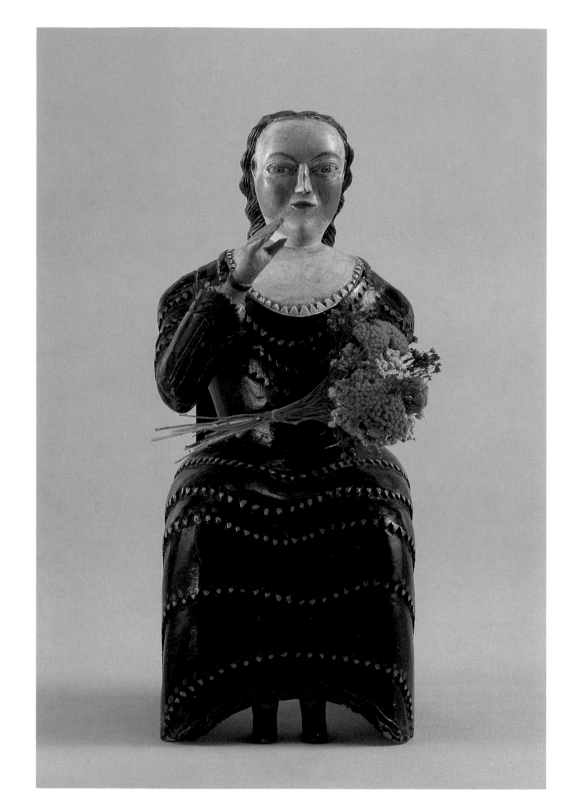

168
Unidentified maker, SEATED WOMAN, *probably Pennsylvania, ca. 1875, carved and painted wood, 12 × 5 × 6 inches (31.701.3).*

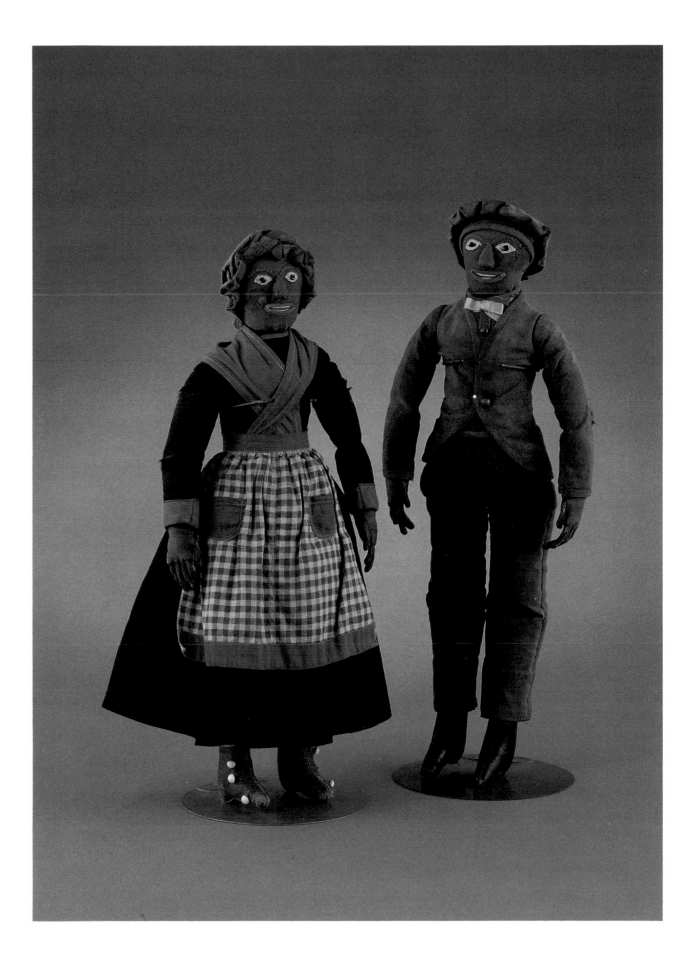

169
Unidentified maker, DOLLS, *United States, probably 1880–1900, various fabrics, leather, ceramics, and metals on stuffed body; male, 19 × 7¼ × 3 inches (85.1200.1); female, 18¼ × 10 × 4 inches (85.1200.2).*

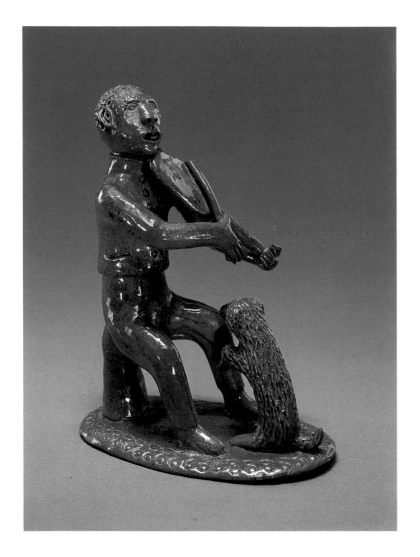

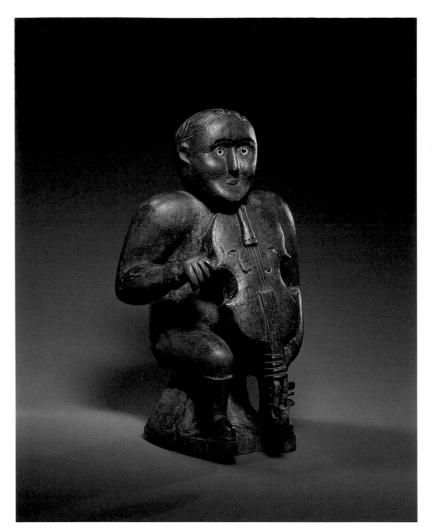

ist's life and of the community in which he lived. McKillop is known to have made instruments, and he knew local players, but his biographer notes that he was not a musician himself.

McKillop was an extraordinary artist. What is known of his life has recently been published by Charles G. Zug III, who cites a story of a young boy visiting the McKillop household and seeing the carver's works for the first time. The sheer wonder and delight the boy experienced probably sums up the effect such decorative whimsies had in their own time as well as now; among the pieces he remembered was the Center's large *Hippoceros*, apparently a cross between a hippopotamus and a rhinoceros. This fanciful creature (plate 172) has a

Victrola set into his back, and when the machine is activated, his leather tongue wags back and forth.

Like many folk carvers, McKillop had no training in his craft. About 1926, the artist was given the wood from several black walnut trees, a gift that prompted him to begin carving decorative sculptures and other items. He subsequently enjoyed a certain reputation as a carver, and family tradition indicates that visitors came from nearby towns to see his work. Zug recounts a story passed on by family members about McKillop's response to one visitor's question about how the artist came up with ideas for his carvings. McKillop reportedly said, "You just eat a big mess of fatback and go to bed and go to sleep and dream how to do it."

170
Attributed to Samuel Bell, FIDDLER WITH DOG, *Strasburg, Virginia, ca. 1850, glazed earthenware, 6½ × 5 × 2¾ inches, Gift of William E. Wiltshire III (79.900.6).*

171
Edgar A. McKillop, FIDDLER, *Balfour, North Carolina, 1926–1937, carved and varnished walnut, 25 × 13¾ × 11 inches (61.701.14).*

McKillop's folk sculpture, his comments on the source of his ideas for the pieces, and the circumstances of his life resemble those of a number of American folk artists known to us. Few had any pretensions of sophistication about the creative origins or the styles of their art, or overestimated its intrinsic worth in comparison with the formal art of their periods. Through continuing research and study of individual objects, we can learn about these artists' approach to their work, and in the process make certain assumptions and draw certain conclusions about their folk art. Many of these concepts have been discussed in this volume, but they do not tell the complete story, nor will they be accurate forever.

For most of us, American folk art seems straightforward in terms of its visual simplicity and its interpretation of common forms and everyday activities. The meanings and associations inherent in these works are usually quickly understood and appreciated by modern viewers— or so we tend to think. This is not always the case, however; in fact, it would be wrong for us to believe we knew or could discover all the important nuances these

works had for their original makers and owners. Edgar McKillop's pithy remark on the source of his sculpture ideas, for instance, was undoubtedly tongue-in-cheek, but it probably reflects his earnest attempt to provide some logical answer to a question posed by an inquisitive and perhaps more urbane admirer. McKillop, like most folk artists of any period, rarely used lofty terms to articulate his rationale for producing art, but this does not mean that form, color, surface and texture, balance, rhythm, and pattern had no meaning for him or for other untutored artists. These were intuitive, felt and "dreamed" rather than spoken or analyzed in a conscious or contrived way.

The inability to speak in eloquent or sophisticated terms about their artistic aspirations and, ultimately, their fulfillment— that is, the works themselves— does not imply naïveté on the part of folk artists; rather, it underscores the depth of their humanity. If the artists could have written down or spoken the ideas behind *The Preacher*, the *Peaceable Kingdom*, or almost any other object in this volume, then there would have been no reason for them to fashion such wonderful objects.

172
Edgar A. McKillop, HIPPOCEROS, Balfour, North Carolina, 1926– 1937, carved walnut, 29½ × 16 × 58¼ inches (61.701.15).

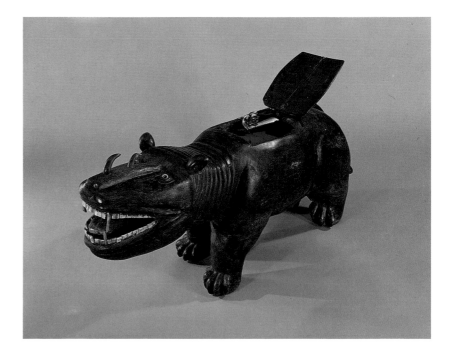

Acknowledgments

Numerous scholars have contributed to the study of American folk artists and their products since the subject first received public acclaim in the 1920s and 1930s. Previous curators and directors of the Abby Aldrich Rockefeller Folk Art Center are counted among these researchers and authors of major monographic works on individual artists. This book contains information based on research gathered by former Folk Art Center staff and also draws heavily on the published and unpublished material shared with us over the years by a host of colleagues. While the selected bibliography on pages 220–221 lists the principal works consulted during the preparation of this book, it does not acknowledge the many individuals whose family histories of objects and artists and personal research notes are recorded in the Folk Art Center archives. Often it is the observations and memories of these people that provide the most revealing insights about makers and about many of the objects included in this book.

Treasures of American Folk Art from the Abby Aldrich Rockefeller Folk Art Center and the exhibition by the same title are the result of many hours of work by staff at the Colonial Williamsburg Foundation whose names do not appear on the title page. Editorial assistance and the overall coordination of numerous exhibition needs and requirements were skillfully handled by Barbara Luck, Curator, Richard Miller, Associate Curator, and Anne Watkins, Registrar at the Abby Aldrich Rockefeller Folk Art Center. They were ably assisted by Exhibit Preparators Douglas Canady and Osborne Taylor, and by Karen Laws, Museum Secretary. Patricia Hurdle, Deputy Director of Museums, coordinated many logistical details and thereby greatly facilitated this project. Special thanks go to Wallace Gusler, Director of the Department of Conservation, and his staff for the countless hours of consultation and treatment they competently provided to insure the safety of the objects in transit. To Betty Childs, Senior Editor at Bulfinch Press, Dorothy Straight, Senior Copyeditor, Greer Allen, the designer of the book, and Amanda Freymann, Production Manager, we express our gratitude for their enthusiasm and many contributions to this shared endeavor.

Where to See American Folk Art

There are a number of museums in the United States whose collections include examples of American folk art. These include the New York State Historical Association in Cooperstown, New York; the Shelburne Museum in Shelburne, Vermont; the National Museum of American Art, a part of the Smithsonian Institution in Washington, D.C.; and the Museum of American Folk Art in New York City.

Other institutions in the United States that have strong holdings in particular aspects of American folk art include the Museum of Fine Arts, Boston (paintings); Old Sturbridge Village in Massachusetts (New England furniture and pottery); and the Henry Ford Museum and Greenfield Village in Deerborn, Michigan (pottery, furniture, and some paintings). The Museum of Art and the Free Library in Philadelphia and the Henry Francis du Pont Winterthur Museum in Delaware have strong holdings in Pennsylvania-German materials. Additionally, the collections at the Bucks County Historical Society in Doylestown, Pennsylvania; the Landis Valley Farm Museum in Lancaster, Pennsylvania; Old Salem, Incorporated, and its Museum of Early Southern Decorative Arts in Winston-Salem, North Carolina; and the Schwenkfelder Museum in Pennsburg, Pennsylvania, also have excellent regional collections of folk art. Fine examples of southwestern folk art in the Spanish tradition may be seen at the Museum of International Folk Art in Santa Fe, New Mexico.

BIBLIOGRAPHY

Andrews, Edward Deming, and Faith Andrews. *Visions of the Heavenly Sphere: A Study in Shaker Religious Art.* Virginia: University of Virginia Press, 1969.

Art in Our Time: An Exhibition to Celebrate the Tenth Anniversary of the Museum of Modern Art and the Opening of Its New Building. New York: Museum of Modern Art, 1939.

Bacon, Lenice Ingram. *American Patchwork Quilts.* New York: William Morrow, 1973.

Barber, Edwin Atlee, A.M., Ph.D. *Tulip Ware of the Pennsylvania-German Potters.* Philadelphia: The Pennsylvania Museum and School of Industrial Art, 1903.

Barber, Joel. *Wild Fowl Decoys.* New York: Dover, 1954.

Bishop, Robert. *American Folk Sculpture.* New York: E. P. Dutton, 1974.

———. *Folk Painters of America.* New York: E. P. Dutton, 1979.

Black, Mary. "Rediscovery: Erastus Salisbury Field." *Art in America* 54 (January–February 1966).

———. *Erastus Salisbury Field: 1805–1900.* Springfield, Mass.: Museum of Fine Arts, 1984.

Black, Mary Childs, and Stuart P. Feld. "Drawn by I. Bradley from Great Britton." *Antiques* 90 (October 1966).

Cahill, Holger. *American Folk Art: The Art of the Common Man in America, 1750–1900.* New York: Museum of Modern Art, 1932.

Carpenter, Miles B. "Art for Folks." *VCU Magazine,* May 1974.

———. *Cutting the Mustard.* Tappahannock, Va.: American Folk Art Company, 1982.

Christensen, Erwin O. *Early American Wood Carving.* New York: World Publishing Company, 1952.

Coffin, Margaret. *American Country Tinware, 1700–1900.* Camden, N.J.: Thomas Nelson & Sons, 1968.

Davison, Mildred, and Christa C. Mayer-Thurman. *Coverlets.* Chicago: Art Institute of Chicago, 1973.

The Decoy as Folk Sculpture. Bloomfield Hills, Mich.: Cranbrook Academy of Art, 1986.

Deutsch, Davida Tenenbaum, and Betty Ring. "Homage to Washington in Needlework and Prints." *Antiques* 119 (February 1981): 402–419.

DeVoe, Shirley Spaulding. *The Tinsmiths of Connecticut.* Middletown, Conn.: Wesleyan University Press, 1968.

Dewhurst, C. Kurt, Betty MacDowell, and Marsha MacDowell. *Religious Folk Art in America: Reflections of Faith.* New York: E. P. Dutton, 1983.

Dillenberger, Jane, and Joshua C. Taylor. *The Hand and the Spirit: Religious Art in America, 1700–1900.* Berkeley, Calif.: University Art Museum, 1972.

Dinger, Charlotte. *Art of the Carousel.* Green Village, N.J.: Carousel Art, 1983.

Early Decorated Stoneware of the Edgefield District, South Carolina. Greenville, S.C.: Greenville County Museum of Art, 1976.

Edward Hicks: A Gentle Spirit. New York: Andrew Crispo Gallery, 1975.

Elder, William Voss, III. *Baltimore Painted Furniture, 1800–1840.* Baltimore: The Baltimore Museum of Art, 1972.

Fabian, Monroe H. *The Pennsylvania-German Decorated Chest.* New York: Universe Books, 1978.

Fales, Dean A., Jr. *American Painted Furniture, 1660–1880.* New York: E. P. Dutton, 1972.

Fleckenstein, Henry A., Jr. *Decoys of the Mid-Atlantic Region.* Exton, Pa.: Schiffer, 1979.

Flower, Milton E. *Wilhelm Schimmel and Aaron Mountz: Wood Carvers.* Williamsburg, Va.: Abby Aldrich Rockefeller Folk Art Collection, 1965.

———. *Three Cumberland County Wood Carvers: Schimmel, Mountz, Barrett.* Carlisle, Pa.: Cumberland County Historical Society, 1986.

Folk Art in America, a Living Tradition: Selections from the Abby Aldrich Rockefeller Folk Art Collection, Williamsburg, Virginia. Atlanta: High Museum of Art and Abby Aldrich Rockefeller Folk Art Center, 1974.

Ford, Alice. *Edward Hicks: Painter of the Peaceable Kingdom.* Philadelphia: Philadelphia Museum of Art, 1982.

———. *Edward Hicks: His Life and Art.* New York: Abbeville, 1985.

Fraley, Tobin. *The Carousel Animal.* Berkeley, Calif.: Zephyr Press, 1983.

Fried, Frederick. *A Pictorial History of the Carousel.* New York: A. S. Barnes, 1964.

———. *Artists in Wood: American Carvers of Cigar Store Indians, Show Figures, and Circus Wagons.* New York: Crown, 1970.

Fuller, Edmund L. *Visions in Stone: The Sculpture of William Edmondson.* Pittsburgh: University of Pittsburgh Press, 1973.

Garvan, Beatrice B. *The Pennsylvania German Collection.* Philadelphia: Philadelphia Museum of Art, 1982.

Gould, Mary Earle. *Antique Tinware and Tole Ware: Its History and Romance.* Rutland, Vt.: Charles E. Tuttle, 1958.

Greer, Georgeanna H. *American Stonewares: The Art and Craft of Utilitarian Potters.* Exton, Pa.: Schiffer, 1981.

Guilland, Harold F. *Early American Folk Pottery.* Chilton Book Company, 1971.

Gusler, Wallace B. "The Arts of Shenandoah County, Virginia, 1770–1825." *Journal of Early Southern Decorative Arts* 5 (November 1979): 6–35.

Heisey, John W. *A Checklist of American Coverlet Weavers.* Williamsburg, Va.: Colonial Williamsburg Foundation, 1978.

Hemphill, Herbert Waide, Jr. *Folk Sculpture USA.* Brooklyn and Los Angeles: Brooklyn Musem and Los Angeles Museum of Art, 1976.

———. *Folk Art USA since 1900 from the Collection of Herbert Waide Hemphill, Jr.* New York: Publishing Center for Cultural Resources, 1980.

Hemphill, Herbert W., Jr., and Julia Weissman. *Twentieth-Century American Folk Art and Artists.* New York: E. P. Dutton, 1974.

Holdridge, Barbara C., and Lawrence B. Holdridge. "Ammi Phillips 1788–1865." *Connecticut Historical Society Bulletin* 30 (October 1965).

———. *Ammi Phillips: Portrait Painter, 1788–1865.* New York: Clarkson N. Potter, 1969.

Holstein, Jonathan. *The Pieced Quilt: An American Design Tradition.* Greenwich, Conn.: New York Graphic Society, 1973.

Hornung, Clarence P. *Treasury of American Design.* New York: Harry N. Abrams, 1976.

Janis, Sidney. *They Taught Themselves: American Primitive Painters of the Twentieth Century.* New York: Dial Press, 1942.

Johnson, Jay, and William C. Ketchum, Jr. *American Folk Art of the Twentieth Century.* New York: Cynthia Parzell, 1983.

Johnston, Pat H. "E. R. McKillop and His Fabulous Woodcarvings." *Antiques Journal* 33, no. 11 (November 1978).

Kangas, Gene, and Linda Kangas. *Decoys: A North American Survey.* Spanish Fork, Utah: Hillcrest, 1983.

Katz, Martha B. "J. O. J. Frost: Marblehead Artist." M.A. thesis, State University of New York College at Oneonta, 1971.

Katzenberg, Dena S. *Baltimore Album Quilts.* Baltimore: Baltimore Museum of Art, 1981.

Ketchum, William C., Jr. *Potters and Potteries of New York State, 1650–1900.* New York: Syracuse University Press, 1987.

Klamkin, Marian, and Charles Klamkin. *Woodcarvings: North American Folk Sculptures.* New York: Hawthorn Books, 1974.

Kline, Robert M., and Frederick S. Weiser. "A Fraktur-Fest." *Der Reggeboge* 4 (September–December, 1970).

Lasansky, Jeanette. *To Cut, Piece, and Solder: The Work of the Rural Pennsylvania Tinsmith, 1778–1908.* University Park, Penn.: Pennsylvania State University Press, 1982.

Lea, Zilla Rider. *The Ornamented Chair: Its Development in America (1700–1890).* Rutland, Vt.: Charles E. Tuttle, 1971.

Lipman, Jean. "Eunice Pinney— An Early Connecticut Watercolorist." *Art Quarterly* 6 (Summer 1943): 213–221.

———. "I. J. H. Bradley, Portrait Painter." *Art in America* 33 (July 1945).

Lipman, Jean, and Alice Winchester. *The Flowering of American Folk Art, 1776–1876.* New York: Viking, 1974.

Lipman, Jean, and Tom Armstrong, eds. *American Folk Painters of Three Centuries.* New York: Hudson Hills, 1980.

Little, Nina Fletcher. "Doctor Rufus Hathaway, Physician and Painter of Duxbury, Massachusetts, 1770–1822." *Art in America* 41 (Summer 1953).

———. *The Abby Aldrich Rockefeller Folk Art Collection.* Williamsburg, Va.: Colonial Williamsburg, 1957.

———. "Little-Known Connecticut Artists, 1790–1810." *Connecticut Historical Society Bulletin* 22 (October 1957).

———. "John Brewster, Jr., 1766–1854: Deaf-Mute Portrait Painter of Connecticut and Maine." *Connecticut Historical Society Bulletin* 25 (October 1960).

———. *Land and Seascape as Observed by the Folk Artist.* Williamsburg, Va.: Colonial Williamsburg, 1969.

Livingston, Jane, and John Beardsley. *Black Folk Art in America, 1930–1980.* Jackson, Miss.: University Press of Mississippi, Jackson, and the Center for the Study of Southern Culture, 1982.

Lowry, Robert. "Steve Harley and the Lost Frontier." *Flair* 1 (June 1950): 12–17.

Luck, Barbara R., and Alexander Sackton. *Eddie Arning: Selected Drawings, 1964–1973.* Williamsburg, Va.: Colonial Williamsburg Foundation, 1985.

Mackey, William J., Jr. *American Bird Decoys.* New York: E. P. Dutton, 1965.

Mankin, Elizabeth. "Zedekiah Belknap." *Antiques* 110 (November 1976).

Mather, Eleanor Price, and Dorothy Canning Miller. *Edward Hicks: His Peaceable Kingdoms and Other Paintings.* Newark, Del.: University of Delaware Press, 1983.

Montgomery, Pauline. *Indiana Coverlet Weavers and Their Coverlets.* Indianapolis: Hoosier Heritage Press, 1974.

Muller, Nancy C., and Jacquelyn Oak. "Noah North (1809–1880)." *Antiques* 112 (November 1977).

O'Neil, Isabel. *The Art of the Painted Finish for Furniture and Decoration.* New York: William Morrow, 1971.

Orlofsky, Patsy, and Myron Orlofsky. *Quilts in America.* McGraw-Hill, 1974.

Parmalee, Paul W., and Forrest D. Loomis. *Decoys and Decoy Carvers of Illinois.* DeKalb, Ill.: Northern Illinois University Press, 1969.

Paulsen, Barbara. "Eddie Arning: The Unsettling World of a Texas Folk Artist," *Texas Journal* 8, no. 1 (Fall–Winter, 1985–1986).

Peluso, A. J., Jr. *J. & J. Bard, Picture Painters.* New York: Hudson River Press, 1977.

Pennsylvania German Folklore Society. *The Pennsylvania German Folklore Society, Volume Thirteen.* Allentown, Pa.: Schlechter's, 1949.

Peto, Florence. *Historic Quilts.* New York: American Historical Company, 1939.

Pinckney, Pauline A. *American Figureheads and Their Carvers.* New York: W. W. Norton, 1940.

Piwonka, Ruth, and Roderic H. Blackburn. *A Remnant in the Wilderness: New York Dutch Scripture History Paintings of the Early Eighteenth Century.* Albany, N.Y.: Albany Institute of History and Art, 1980.

Ring, Betty. *Let Virtue Be a Guide to Thee: Needlework in the Education of Rhode Island Women, 1730–1830.* Providence, R.I.: Rhode Island Historical Society, 1983.

Rumford, Beatrix T. "The Abby Aldrich Rockefeller Folk Art Collection." Gallery guide. Williamsburg, Va.: Colonial Williamsburg Foundation, 1975.

———. "Memorial Watercolors." *Antiques* 104 (October 1973): 688–695.

———. "Mrs. Rockefeller's Folk Art at Bassett Hall." Catalog for *The Twenty-sixth Annual Washington Antiques Show* (Washington, D.C., 1981), 57–59.

Safford, Carleton L., and Robert Bishop. *America's Quilts and Coverlets.* New York: E. P. Dutton, 1972.

Safford, Victor. "John Haley Bellamy." *Antiques,* March 1935.

Schorsch, Anita. *Mourning Becomes America: Mourning Art in the New Nation.* Clinton, N.J.: Main Street Press, 1976.

Shaffer, Sandra C. "Deborah Goldsmith, 1808–1836: A Naive Artist in Upstate New York." M.A. thesis, State University of New York College at Oneonta, 1968.

Shelley, Donald A. *The Fraktur-Writings or Illuminated Manuscripts of the Pennsylvania Germans.* Allentown, Pa.: Pennsylvania German Folklore Society, 1961.

———. *Lewis Miller: Sketches and Chronicles.* York, Pa.: Historical Society of York County, 1966.

Smith, Yvonne Brault, *John Haley Bellamy: Carver of Eagles.* Portsmouth, N.H.: Portsmouth Marine Society, 1982.

Spinney, Frank O. "Joseph H. Davis: New Hampshire Artist of the 1830s," *Antiques* 44 (October 1943).

Swygert, Mrs. Luther M., ed. *Heirlooms from Old Looms: A Catalogue of Coverlets Owned by the Colonial Coverlet Guild of America and Its Members.* Chicago: R. R. Donnelley & Sons, 1955.

Tomlinson, Juliette, ed. *The Paintings and the Journal of Joseph Whiting Stock.* Middletown, Conn.: Wesleyan University Press, 1976.

Walters, Donald R. "Out of Anonymity: Ruby Devol Finch (1804–1866)." *Maine Antique Digest* 6 (June 1978): 1C–4C.

Webster, Donald Blake. *Decorated Stoneware Pottery of North America.* Rutland, Vt.: Charles E. Tuttle, 1972.

Weiser, Frederick S. "His Deeds Followed Him: The Fraktur of John Conrad Gilbert." *Der Reggeboge* 16, no. 2 (1982).

Weiser, Frederick S., and Howell J. Heaney. *The Pennsylvania German Fraktur of the Free Library of Philadelphia.* Vol. 1. Philadelphia: Pennsylvania German Society and the Free Library of Philadelphia, 1976.

Whitney Museum of Art. *Two Hundred Years of American Sculpture.* Boston: David R. Godine, 1976.

Wust, Klaus. *Virginia Fraktur: Penmanship as Folk Art.* Edinburg, Va.: Shenandoah History, 1975.

INDEX

COPYEDITED BY DOROTHY STRAIGHT

DESIGNED BY GREER ALLEN

PRODUCTION COORDINATED BY AMANDA WICKS FREYMANN

COMPOSITION IN LINO WALBAUM BY DIX TYPE, INC.

LUSTRO OFFSET ENAMEL DULL BY S. D. WARREN CO.

COLOR SEPARATIONS AND PRINTING BY VILLAGE CRAFTSMEN/

PRINCETON POLYCHROME PRESS

BOUND BY HOROWITZ/RAE